The Salzburger Saga

Hanns Klammer aus Bischoffshofen.

The Salzburger Saga

Religious Exiles and Other Germans Along the Savannah

GEORGE FENWICK JONES

A Brown Thrasher Original
The University of Georgia Press   Athens

Printed in the United States of America

Designed by Sandra Strother Hudson
Set in Linotron 202 Baskerville
The paper in this book meets the guidelines for
permanence and durability of the Committee on
Production Guidelines for Book Longevity of the
Council on Library Resources.

Library of Congress Cataloging in Publication Data

Jones, George Fenwick, 1916–
The Salzburger saga.

"A Brown thrasher original."
Bibliography: p.
Includes index.
1. Salzburgers—Georgia—History.
2. Salzburgers—Georgia—Ebenezer—History.
3. Ebenezer (Ga.)—History. 4. German
Americans—Georgia—History. 5. German
Americans—Georgia—Ebenezer—History.
6. Georgia—History—Colonial period, ca.
1600–1775. I. Title.
F295.S1J66 1984   975.8'00431   83-10384
ISBN 0-8203-0689-4

Contents

✑ Acknowledgments ✑

Research for this book, including study in Halle and London, was supported by the American Philosophical Society and the National Endowment for the Humanities, to which I am duly grateful. I am also indebted to Pastor Hermann Winde of Magdeburg, who, while a graduate student at the Martin Luther University of Halle, first sifted through the voluminous pertinent material in the archives of the Francke Foundation for his splendid dissertation on the Lutheran church in Georgia.

✑ Introduction ✑

The story of the Georgia Salzburgers was first told more than a century ago by the Reverend P. A. Strobel in his delightful *Salzburgers and Their Descendants* (Baltimore, 1855), which was reprinted in 1953 and again in 1980. Although highly meritorious for its day, this account has meanwhile become woefully obsolete in view of the mass of source material now available but unknown to Strobel. Unaware of the colonial records of Georgia and the missionary archives of the Francke Foundation in Halle, East Germany,[1] Strobel had to rely mostly on popular knowledge, previous historians, and whatever bits and pieces of information and misinformation he could find. As a result, many factual errors crept into his text. He was acquainted with Samuel Urlsperger's *Ausführliche Nachrichten*,[2] yet he cites them very seldom; and his command of German would appear inadequate for such reference purposes if it were judged by his rendition of proper names.[3]

Besides lacking sources, Strobel also belonged to a generation of historians like Ernst Louis Hazelius, Hugh McCall, and William Bacon Stevens, who thought the goal of history to be inspiration and edification and who dutifully suppressed or deleted any documentary evidence running counter to their moral, patriotic, or religious message. For most historians of the period, rhetoric outweighed research, and their side was invariably good and godly while the other side was wicked and perfidious. The following narrative aims at objectivity, with the pious wish that honesty will not offend those Salzburger descendants reared on Strobel and eulogistic orators at festive occasions. Once, while lecturing at Ebenezer, I mentioned that Andreas Lorentz Arnsdorff had drowned while drunk; afterward a lineal descendant thanked me for disabusing him of his misconception that all his ancestors had been saints, for he found them much more lovable with a few human failings. I hope other descendants share his view.

All personal names, even of children born in this country, are rendered in their standard German form for two reasons: first, this will facilitate genealogical research in German archives; second, it would be impossible to handle the myriad of English derivatives, some of which are included in appendix 1. Because Christian names in the *Ebenezer Record Book* have been anglicized, the reader forgets that throughout the colonial period the people in Ebenezer spoke, prayed, sang, and thought in German, a fact hardly suggested when John Henry and William Lewis replace Johann Heinrich and Wilhelm Ludwig.

The translator of these records, A. G. Voigt, deserves hearty thanks for undertaking such a difficult task. Unfortunately, he has confused not only the names Kiefer and Rieser (which look *very* similar in the Old German script), but also the names Ochs and Oechsele and Lastinger and Seckinger. Besides that, misreadings have engendered some twenty-four otherwise unrecorded family names in Ebenezer, namely Asperger (Eischberger), Bandfelder (Landfelder), Behrmann (Bohrmann), Eichelberger (Eischberger), Flukenfuss (Mukenfuss), Glauer (Glaner), Grein (Greve), Haut (Zant), Havkel (Heckel), Heked (Hekel), Kaehli (Stähli), Keiter (Reiter), Kienigus (Kirurgus, surgeon), Koegter (Kögler), Landfreder (Landfelder), Oepl (Oechsele), Paulmueller (Paul Müller), Reidlinger (Neidlinger), Sauftleb (Sanftleben), Scheinlaender (Rheinländer), Schwinthofer (Schwinkhofer), Stand (Staud), and Tubly (Zubly). There are similar misreadings of many Christian names. On two occasions names are confused with professions: Johann Friedrich Ernst Kirigus (surgeon) is rendered as John Frederick Ernest Kienigus, and Johann Martin Burgemeister von Purysburg is rendered as John Martin, mayor of Purysburg.

Except for the opening remarks about Salzburg and the expulsion, the present volume is based almost entirely on original sources, both manuscript and published, which are listed in the Bibliography. Time did not allow scrutiny of all the voluminous material stockpiled in London and Halle, but the amount investigated should give a generally clear and accurate picture of the Salzburgers and other German-speaking settlers in Georgia. Had all the historical evidence collected been documented with footnotes, the resulting work would have become a dissertation rather than a saga, as it aims to be. However, for the benefit of those readers who wish to investigate the Salzburgers' life in more detail, a small number of pertinent secondary works are included in the Bibliography. These go back only to the year 1934; the brief articles by Newton and Hofer, based respectively on the colonial records of Georgia and the *Ausführliche Nachrichten,* adequately supersede all earlier studies. My advice to my graduate students in their research has always been: "The last shall be first." They should read the most recent publications first. Then, armed with accurate and up-to-date information, they can risk reading the earlier works, usually charmingly written but often inaccurate, without risk of absorbing generally accepted but antiquated and incorrect ideas.

For the benefit of those who wish to follow up subjects, parenthetical numbers indicate the bibliographical items in which they are treated in more detail.

Introduction

This little book has been written as a modest contribution to the commemoration of the two-hundred-fiftieth anniversary of the Salzburgers' arrival in Georgia.

1. See items 1, 2, 3, and 4 in the Bibliography.
2. See item 3 in the Bibliography.
3. His spellings of Dreisler, Kieffer, Speilbiegler, Zeigenhagen, and Zeigler indicate that he was unaware that *ei* and *ie* represent different sounds in German. Likewise, his spellings of Wurtemburg and Muhlenburg indicate that he did not distinguish between *berg* and *burg*. Because of their consistency, these errors cannot have been typographical. Cf. also Bolleinger, Chiemre, Hortzog, Landseller, and Salza.

1

The Expulsion

ituated in the heart of Europe, the lovely land of Salzburg is drained mainly by the Salzach River, which, like the city of Salzburg, received its name from the salt produced there. From Salzburg the Salzach flows north into the Inn, which empties into the Danube and flows with it into the Black Sea. The people of Salzburg have much in common with those of England, both culturally and racially. Both areas were overrun four centuries before the Christian era by Celtic tribes, which mixed with the native population and dominated it sufficiently to impose their own language and customs upon it. In turn, both of these Celtic regions were occupied by the Romans early in the Christian era and became important provinces of the Roman Empire, namely, Britannia and Noricum. The city of Salzburg was then called Juvavum.

When the Romans withdrew their troops from Britannia and Noricum in the fifth century, both provinces were exposed to invasions by Germanic tribes that displaced the romanized inhabitants or imposed their own languages and customs upon them. Just as the Britons succumbed to Angles, Saxons, and Jutes, the people of Noricum suffered a series of invasions, the final and most important of which was by the Bavarians, a number of related tribes that had previously lived along the Elbe River and were therefore the kinsmen and neighbors of the invaders of Britannia.

Although still barbarians, the new settlers of Noricum admired the higher civilization of the Romans and were eager to learn their superior methods of agriculture, building, and other arts. This cultural adaptation greatly accelerated when Christianity was introduced in the seventh and eighth centuries, about a century after St. Augustine had carried the gospel to England. To be sure, Christianity had already reached Rome's northern frontiers before the empire's fall, but it seems to have all but disappeared from Noricum during the turmoil of the invasions. When it returned, it did so from a most unexpected direction, to wit, from Ireland, a land not conquered by the Germanic barbarians. In 610 the Irish monk Saint Columbanus was preaching to the heathen Alemanni in Switzerland, where, two years later, his disciple Saint Gallus founded an abbey which still bears his name and from which Irish missionaries carried the good word to the Bavarians in Salzburg and elsewhere.

The Roman city Juvavum regained its importance in 696 when the Duke of Bavaria gave it and its environs to the Frankish missionary Ruprecht. In 739 Salzburg was made a bishopric, over which the bishop ruled as secular prince. Perhaps the most prominent of Ruprecht's early successors was the Irishman Virgil, who ruled until his death in 784 despite the efforts of Saint Boniface, an English missionary, to dislodge him. Boniface eventually brought the bishopric under the rule of Rome, and Pope Leo III, obeying an order of Charlemagne, raised it to an archbishopric in 798. Because of the salt, and later because of the silver mines, the princely rulers of Salzburg became wealthier and were able to maintain their political independence until 1803, when Salzburg was secularized as a result of the territorial changes caused by the Napoleonic Wars. In 1816, reduced in size, Salzburg was given to Austria. Before that year, one has to distinguish between "Salzburgers" and "Austrians," as is done in the following account.

Because of Salzburg's salt and mineral resources, the archbishopric appealed most strongly to materially minded candidates, who usually had to pay enormous bribes to be elected. Consequently, many of the archbishops were from wealthy families and were more concerned with worldly wealth than with spiritual duties. Most of them directed their main energies into amassing treasures and building stately buildings to glorify their reigns, which, of course, was the situation in other German ecclesiastical states as well. The worldly ambition and greed of the clergy, even more than theological considerations, prepared the way for the Reformation.

When Martin Luther defied the pope at the Diet of Worms in 1521, Matthäus Lang, the archbishop of Salzburg and the emperor's most trusted advisor, arranged for Luther to be invited to the diet to defend his cause; Lang also presided at the diet. However, when Paulus Speratus and other reformers introduced Luther's teachings into Salzburg, Lang recognized the threat to his wealth and power and opposed them with force. The first martyr of the new Evangelical religion in Salzburg was the priest Georg Scherer of Rastadt, who was beheaded and whose body was burned in 1528, only seven years after the Diet of Worms. Despite Scherer's fate, the people of Rastadt refused to abandon the new faith, which continued to spread until, by 1560, nearly all of Salzburg had accepted Luther's reforms.

During the two centuries following the Diet of Worms, the various archbishops fought against the heretics in their domain with varying degrees of ardor and varying degrees of success (48). Wolf Dietrich, one of the most conspicuous rulers, succeeded in crushing the Reformation in the city of Salzburg, from which the leading burgher families departed rather than change their faith. On the other hand, he allowed the miners in far-off Gastein to practice their faith openly and even to maintain a Protestant cemetery, no doubt judging the produce of their mines to be more important than the salvation of their souls.

Whereas most secular princes and nearly all free cities of Germany quickly embraced the Reformation, most church princes naturally opposed it. Even though most of the Habsburgers' subjects had embraced the new faith, the dynasty had to resist it rather than lose Spain and its wealthy colonies in the New World. Aided by the new Jesuit order as well as by constant bickering between the Protestant princes, the Catholic forces staged a counter-reformation that regained much of southern Germany for the church and enabled Catholic princes to subdue the Protestants in their lands.

For a half century there was a stalemate, a kind of cold war, between the Protestant princes, united in the Protestant Union, and the Catholic princes, allied in the Catholic League. The powder keg was finally ignited in 1618 when the Catholics suppressed Protestantism in Bohemia; and almost all of Germany was devastated before the Thirty Years' War finally ended in 1648 with the Treaty of Westphalia. Among the stipulations of this treaty was the renewal of the law of *cuius regio, eius religio,* which stated that a ruler could determine the religion of his subjects but had to allow dissidents to leave his realm and to give them three years to do so. This law, however, held only for Catholics, Lutherans, and Calvinists, because all of the other sects were unrecognized and liable to drastic punishment.

The archbishops of Salzburg, who miraculously kept their country out of the long war, continued to suppress their nonconformist subjects, sporadically exiling individuals, families, and small groups. The first major expulsions were those of the Defereggers in 1684 and of the Dürrnbergers in 1686, both groups being required to leave their children behind. One of the leaders of the second group, Joseph Schaitberger, furthered the later great emigration by sending letters of comfort and encouragement from his refuge in Nürnberg to his co-religionists back home. He was also the composer of the "Exiles' Song" (*Exulantenlied*), the anthem of all the exiles.

In 1727 Count Leopold Anton Eleutherius von Firmian was elected archbishop of Salzburg. Whereas his predecessors had sometimes overlooked heresy in the outlying districts, Firmian determined to end all such disobedience permanently. Egged on by his ambitious and ruthless chancellor, Cristian Hieronymus von Rall (Christian di Rallo), he resolved upon an immediate suppression of all heresy. With the collusion of the governors (*Pfleger*) of the districts where the Lutherans resided, von Rall submitted reports declaring the Lutherans rebels intent on overthrowing their archbishop and therefore not protected by the Treaty of Westphalia.

When the Protestant princes complained of the archbishop's unlawful actions and threatened reprisals, Firmian argued that his dissident subjects were not Lutherans but were members of a new sect. The persecuted Lutherans in Salzburg had been without ordained ministers for a long time and had been able to learn the articles of their faith only from their parents, visiting merchants, and journeymen, and smuggled Lutheran theological and inspirational texts; yet rigorous examinations of the exiles usually proved them amazingly well acquainted with the tenets of the Augsburg Confession, the official articles of faith of the Lutheran church.

Firmian's pitiless persecution of his Protestant subjects alarmed the envoys of the Protestant princes, who maintained a caucus called the Evangelical Body (*Corpus Evangelicorum*) at Regensburg, the city in which the Imperial Diet was regularly held. While the law of *cuius regio, eius religio* justified Firmian's expelling his nonconformist subjects, the Treaty of Westphalia required him to give them three years grace to settle their affairs before emigrating. This he was unwilling to do, for fear that the delay would encourage even more of his subjects to embrace the illegal faith and would also enable outside powers to intervene to prevent him from carrying out his plans.

Although Emperor Charles VI personally sympathized with Firmian's religious zeal and ultimate purpose, he begged the archbishop to obey the law because he needed the votes of the Protestant princes to ratify the Pragmatic Sanction and thus ensure the succession of his daughter Maria Theresa as duchess of Austria. In theory, Firmian was a subject of the Holy Roman Empire; but imperial authority had so weakened even before the Thirty Years' War that the individual princes were for all practical purposes sovereign rulers. Consequently, Firmian could ignore those of Charles's complaints that von Rall cared to pass on to him. Even though the pope had strongly urged Firmian to cleanse his lands of heresy, he too advised him to honor the Treaty of Westphalia so as to prevent reprisals upon Catholic subjects in Protestant lands.

Remaining mostly in his all-Catholic capital and seldom visiting his outlying parishes where most of the Lutherans lived, the archbishop firmly believed that the heresy was limited to a few troublemakers who could be easily cowed by a show of force. It came therefore as a shock when the agents he sent to ascertain the number of dissidents collected the names of more than nineteen thousand subjects in the Pongau district alone who were ready to acknowledge their faith and to demand the right to practice it or emigrate. This was more than a sixth of the archbishop's subjects, in some areas a large majority of the population. On 13 July 1731 a hundred and fifty deputies of the Lutheran communities met at Schwarzach and swore to stand by their Evangelical faith, sealing this oath by licking salt, according to an ancient local custom. News of this meeting, greatly exaggerated, strengthened Firmian's resolve to complete his expulsion before the outside powers might intervene.

The Expulsion

On 31 October 1731, after arresting the Schwarzach ring-leaders and calling for Imperial troops to suppress the alleged revolt, Firmian issued his nefarious Edict of Expulsion (*Emigrations-patent*), which required all unpropertied Protestants such as tradesmen, servants, and farm laborers to leave the country within eight days, taking only what they could carry on their backs. Property owners were allowed three months, which was of course far too short a time for them to sell their possessions profitably in view of the large number of farms suddenly dumped on the market at a time when few of the extravagant archbishop's subjects had cash for buying property.

The time limit was particularly hard on people without property, who were expelled just as winter was beginning with all its fury and who still had no particular destination. Needless to say, many of these wretches, particularly among the small children, died on the way as they marched poorly clad and badly fed through deep snow and icy blasts. Their propertied employers fared somewhat better the following spring, since the snow had melted and some of them had horses and wagons for carrying what few possessions they could salvage. Also, by the time they reached Protestant lands, steps had been made to provide for them. They too, however, had to pay dearly for permission to emigrate, to say nothing of taxes, tolls, and payment for the soldiers who guarded them.

After August the Strong of Saxony had embraced Catholicism in 1697 in order to gain the Polish crown, Brandenburg became the champion of Protestantism in Germany. During Firmian's persecution of his Evangelical subjects, Frederick William I of Brandenburg-Prussia, the "Soldier King," accepted the responsibility of protecting the Protestants. His many warnings to Firmian having failed their purpose, he resolved to succor as many of the exiles as he could. Some historians attribute his benevolence chiefly to his desire to have colonists for the areas of East Prussia and Lithuania that recently had been depopulated by a plague; yet his concern does seem to have been charitable as well as practical. In any case, by the time the bulk of the exiles reached Protestant areas, he had made careful arrangements to have them led in small parties along parallel routes to new homes in East Prussia, to which nearly twenty thousand migrated (48).

As the columns of homeless wayfarers approached the Protestant cities along their route, they were lovingly received by the townspeople, even by the nobility and royalty of the region, and were given food and shelter. People were most amazed by the exiles' quaint alpine costumes, which were far behind the clothing styles of the lowlands. The men still wore floppy broad-brimmed hats and *Pluderhosen*, or big baggy trousers somewhere between bloomers and plus-four knickerbockers, like those worn by Peter Stuyvesant in New Amsterdam two generations earlier. The women wore full dirndl skirts reaching half way between the knee and the ankle. Despite their stern religious faith, their clothes were brightly colored, often blue, green, yellow, red, or brown (40).

The emigration of the Salzburg martyrs was a triumphal march that thrilled all Prostestant Germany, where the Lutherans had lost much of their initial fervor. This new show of Christian faith appealed to Protestant hearts and purses even beyond Germany. Since promulgating the Law of Protestant Succession, England had joined Brandenburg-Prussia as a champion of Protestantism and had tried to help the Huguenots, Waldensians, and other persecuted Protestants of Europe. Since George II, king of England, was also the duke of Hanover-Brunswick and, in that capacity, a prince of the Holy Roman Empire, he was greatly moved by the plight of the Salzburger exiles.

Foremost among the British charitable organizations of the time was the Society for Promoting Christian Knowledge, or SPCK, a missionary organization founded to bring the gospel to the poor of Britain and her colonies. Among the Society's corresponding members was Samuel Urlsperger, the Senior of the Lutheran ministry in Augsburg, who was himself descended from Protestants exiled from Austria and who was soon to become the first of the Georgia Salzburgers' "Reverend Fathers" (plate 2). As king of England, George II was the official head of the Anglican church; yet in private life he was a Lutheran like his Hanoverian family. Consequently, he had his own Lutheran chapel, the court chaplain at the time being Friedrich Michael Ziegenhagen, the second of the Salzburgers' "Reverend Fathers." It was partly due to Ziegenhagen that the royal family and its subjects contributed so generously to the Salzburger exiles.

The SPCK worked closely and shared some members with the Trustees for Establishing a Colony in Georgia, a body of philanthropic gentlemen occupied in planning a colony south of South Carolina as a haven for the poor of England, a refuge for persecuted Protestants, a source of raw materials, and a bastion against the Spaniards of Florida. Both the Society and the Trustees quickly saw the desirability of winning some of the Salzburger exiles for their new colony.

Whereas the first English donations had been collected for the Salzburger exiles in general, subsequent ones were restricted to those emigrants who would settle in Georgia. In the summer of 1732 the Trustees commissioned Urlsperger to recruit three hundred Salzburgers for the new colony. Although the flow of emigrants had diminished to a mere trickle, by August 1733 an English agent in Memmingen, an Imperial city on the Salzburgers' route to Prussia, was able to persuade twenty-five Salzburgers to change their destination to Georgia. Part of these were from Gastein, a remote region on the headwaters of the Salzach, where Martin Lodinger had established the Evangelical faith already during the reign of

Archbishop Lang, who hestitated to persecute the Gastein miners because he needed the gold from their mines. Unable to receive Communion in both kinds, that is to say, to receive the wine as well as the bread, Lodinger had gone into voluntary exile, thus being the first of the Salzburger exiles. After his departure, the Gastein miners practiced their religion openly and were even allowed to maintain a Protestant cemetery. This tolerance shown to these indispensable miners may explain why this small party at Memmingen had been able to remain in Salzburg nearly two years after the edict had been issued, unless possibly they had been expelled earlier and had been lingering in Memmingen.

From Memmingen this little band was led to the free city of Augsburg, the city in which their faith had been proclaimed at the Diet of Augsburg in 1530 and where most Lutherans had gained legal recognition in 1555. Upon reaching the city, however, they found the gates closed. Being equally divided between Protestants and Catholics, Augsburg had two city governments, which alternated in office; the emigrants happened to arrive on the day the Catholic council was in power. In view of the precarious balance between the religious factions in the city, it is not surprising that the Catholics were unwilling to open their gates to these Protestants, especially after they had been declared dangerous rebels. Nevertheless, the Protestant faction arranged to open the gates and receive the exiles, whom they housed in the Protestant poorhouse. Here the guests were drilled in the Protestant creed and organized into a regular Lutheran congregation.

When the time came to depart for Georgia, the exiles were put under the charge of a commissioner, Philipp Georg Friedrich von Reck, a young Hanoverian nobleman whose uncle Baron Johann von Reck was serving at the Diet of Regensburg (and also in the Protestant Body) as an envoy of George II in his capacities both as king of England and as duke of Hanover-Brunswick. Leaving Augsburg on 31 October, von Reck led his little party, now numbering thirty-seven, to Marksteft on the River Main. He, the traveling chaplain Schumacher, and the Hungarian-German apothecary Andreas Zwiffler rode in a chaise, while the small children and baggage were carried on three wagons and the adult Salzburgers walked. From Augsburg to Marksteft the exiles followed the "Romantic Way" through Dinkelsbühl and Rothenburg ob der Tauber, being received enthusiastically by the Protestant inhabitants of all the Imperial Cities through which they passed. These first exiles are known as the "First Salzburger Transport." (The word *transport* then designated a traveling group, not a vessel, as the word now does.)

At Marksteft the exiles boarded a ship, having been provided with British and Hanoverian passports and with funds collected for them at Augsburg and along the way. Their passage to England was defrayed by the SPCK. Sailing down the Main and into the Rhine, they stopped off at Wertheim, Frankfurt, and other cities, where they were welcomed and entertained most hospitably. On the way their chaplain drilled them in their Evangelical religion, particularly in the article of justification by faith, which was so dear to the Pietists. Pietism was a reform movement within the Lutheran church that emphasized personal faith. Begun near the end of the seventeenth century by Philipp Jakob Spener of Alsace, the movement was taken by him to Berlin. It soon found a firm base at the University of Halle under the leadership of August Hermann Francke, a professor at Halle and the founder of the Francke Foundation, an educational and charitable institution at Glaucha, a village near Halle. Throughout the eighteenth century Halle remained a beacon of light for all Pietists in North America and Russia.

Upon reaching Rotterdam the exiles met the two pastors who were to minister to most of them for the remainder of their lives. These were Johann Martin Boltzius and Israel Christian Gronau, two instructors from the Latin School of the Francke Foundation who had been chosen by Gotthilf August Francke, son and successor of the recently deceased August Hermann Francke. Boltzius, who had been born at Forst in Lower Lusatia in 1703, was older than his much taller and diffident colleague from Kroppenstedt in Sachsen-Anhalt, who had also studied and taught at the celebrated school in Halle (52). Fortunately for the more assertive Boltzius, Gronau was compliant and awed by his more talented partner, with the result that the two lived in perfect harmony and sealed their brotherhood by marrying sisters from their congregation. Receiving their call too late to join their parishioners in Augsburg, the two divines journeyed directly from Halle to Rotterdam, stopping off at Wernigerode to be ordained into the Lutheran ministry.

On 27 November, Boltzius and Gronau reached Rotterdam, where they were joined two days later by their congregation. Awaiting them at Rotterdam was the *Purysburg,* a two-hundred-ton ship commanded by Captain Tobias Fry, a man with a violent anticlerical phobia, who would not let the young pastors dine at his table but made them eat with their parishioners. On board were an old German schoolmaster named Christopher Ortmann and his wife Juliana, who had come from London to serve as interpreters. Because Ortmann had learned English while serving as a British marine, it was not of the best quality and he was of little use to the highly educated Boltzius. Besides that, Ortmann's wife was worldly and fun-loving.

The voyage from Rotterdam was delayed by contrary winds and by running on a sandbar, the Channel was exceptionally rough, and the *Purysburg* completed the short journey to England after three weeks. Despite this, the exiles fared better than some of their countrymen in East Prussia, whose short voyage from Stettin to Königsberg had lasted even longer and caused a mortality, mostly among children, of over five percent. At Dover the Salzburgers were welcomed by Thomas Coram, a former sea captain who was a Georgia Trustee and a member of SPCK, and also by Ziegenhagen's assistant, Court Chaplain Henry Alard Butienter; both of these gentlemen showed much kindness to the exiles during their stay at Dover. While there, the immigrants swore allegiance to King George and thus earned the rights of native-born Englishmen.

After celebrating Christmas and the New Year and partaking of Holy Communion, the Salzburgers reboarded the *Purysburg* and left England on 8 January in a heavy sea, which again caused much seasickness. Like other immigrants of the time, the Salzburgers were tightly packed in their little ship, five persons sharing a single bunk; their food was spoiled, and the water was stagnant and limited in quantity. The favorable reports given in the published version of Boltzius's travelogue are due in part to his own optimistic and grateful nature but even more to the careful bowdlerizing by Urlsperger, who edited the ministers' journals for promotional and inspirational purposes in an irregular series called *Ausführliche Nachrichten,* or "Detailed Reports" (7). The unexpurgated version shows that the passengers had far more immediate concerns than contemplating the wonders of God.

Whereas Boltzius was well pleased by his pious and docile Salzburgers, he was often vexed by his non-Salzburg parishioners. Among these were Georg Bartholomäus Roth and his wife, Maria Barbara, two quarrelsome converts from Würzburg, and the old schoolmaster Ortmann and his wife, and also Baron von Reck's drunken and ill-behaved lackey, Christian Schweikert. The constant squabbling of these unruly people caused Boltzius and Gronau no end of annoyance and embarrassment. On the other hand, Boltzius was pleased with the behavior of the druggist Andreas Zwiffler.

2

Old and New Ebenezer

n 5 March 1734, after a difficult eight-week voyage, the Salzburgers sighted South Carolina; but even then they had to remain aboard while Boltzius, Gronau, and von Reck went ashore at Charleston. There they were received by Robert Johnson, the governor of South Carolina, and by James Edward Oglethorpe, the founder of Georgia (plate 3). Although Oglethorpe was on his return to England, he postponed his trip in order to conduct the Salzburgers to Georgia, where they were festively welcomed on 12 March by all the inhabitants of Savannah. Here a tent was pitched for them, and they were treated to a breakfast of rice soup by Benjamin Sheftal, a Jew from Frankfurt on the Oder who had arrived in Georgia soon after its founding.

Upon reaching Savannah, von Reck, Gronau, and one Salzburger set out to choose a place for the Salzburg settlement, being accompanied by Oglethorpe, Paul Jenys, the Speaker of the South Carolina Assembly, Noble Jones, the surveyor, and a party of Indians. In theory, the Salzburgers were free to select a location to their own liking; but, in reality, Oglethorpe made the choice by leading them to an area about twenty-five miles northwest of Savannah, where he wanted a settlement for military purposes (plate 4). Once there, he gave von Reck complete liberty to pick out any site he wished. The party was delighted with the chosen site and enthralled by the fertile soil, the gently rolling hills, and the flowing river; but time was to prove that appearances can deceive.

Back in Savannah the remainder of the Salzburgers were earning money laboring in the forests and on the ships, thereby showing the English authorities their German willingness to work. On 17 March one of the women bore a child, the first Salzburger born in the new homeland. On 20 March, after taking Holy Communion, Zwiffler and eight Salzburgers set out to build shelters at the site of the new settlement, which had been named Ebenezer, meaning "Stone of Help." This name gave birth to the myth that the Salzburgers raised a stone there in God's honor, but that is obviously impossible because there are no stones on the coastal plain of Georgia. The name Ebenezer Creek was given to the little river that flowed through the new town and eventually into the Savannah River.

While the Salzburgers were toiling at Ebenezer, von Reck and Jones attempted to find a route from the Savannah River up Ebenezer Creek to the settlement. However, after a short distance from the river they found that each creek disappeared in an impenetrable cypress swamp, and the effort had to be abandoned. Rejoining the pioneers, von Reck was impressed by the amount of work accomplished by the working detail, which had been aided by fourteen Negro sawyers lent by Mr. Jenys. Finding no waterway to Ebenezer, the Salzburgers had to cut a road eight miles from there to Abercorn, a Scottish settlement on the Savannah River, over which all their supplies would have to be carried on their backs or dragged on a sledge.

Having placed the Salzburgers where he wanted them, Oglethorpe wrote to the Trustees on 2 April 1734:

I settled the Saltzburghers in the Situation which they desired, though it occasions an additional Expense, we being obliged to buy Horses to carry up their Provision by Land for they are six miles from the great River, and the Ebenezer is so choaked up with old Trees that Boats cannot go till they are removed. I therefore hired a Packhorseman and have ordered him Ten Horses to attend them. I have bought a sow, a Cow, two fowls, Ducks and Geese for each of them, which will be delivered as soon as they can be got up. The Commissary is a good natured Man, the Ministers are very devout and the eldest is a very Wise man; the whole are a religious, industrious, and cheerful People and in all probability will succeed very well.

Although Oglethorpe no doubt exaggerated what he had done and was going to do for the Salzburgers, he nevertheless did describe them well; and in the following years his opinion never changed.

By 2 April enough shelters had been completed to house the remaining Salzburgers, who then followed by boat as far as Abercorn. The trail still being impassable for hauling baggage, Boltzius remained in Abercorn to guard the supplies and the sick, while all able-bodied men worked on the road. This unanticipated roadwork consumed the time that should have been used in clearing land and planting crops. Whereas the Salzburgers had been unusually fortunate in losing no one on the voyage, death soon began to take its toll. Tobias Lackner died at Abercorn of dysentery he had contracted from the sick Scots there; but he died with such Christian resignation that his death was edifying for all the witnesses.

Despite the sickness and confusion reigning at Ebenezer, and even though four of the fourteen Negroes had escaped for some time and one had murdered another, the road was eventually finished, together with seven bridges. Meanwhile, benefactors in South Carolina had donated oxen, cows, and horses and had also taught the Salzburgers to cope better with the wilderness. Already in Savannah, and again in Abercorn, the Salzburgers had made contact with several German Lutheran families from Purysburg, a Swiss settlement a few miles down the Savannah River and on the Carolina side; these earlier settlers, especially the family of Theobald Kieffer, aided with their experience. Boltzius's reports on the flora, fauna, and Indians showed keen observation and intellectual curiosity, since everything in that wilderness was exotic to a Central European.

Dysentery followed the Salzburgers from Abercorn to Ebenezer, and they began succumbing to this painful and repulsive sickness. Much of their valuable time was spent in nursing the sick and burying the dead, thus leaving little time for clearing the fields. Many of the cows strayed into the swamps; and the corn failed to grow, supposedly because it was planted too late but actually because the soil was barren despite the rank vegetation. Because so many people were sick and the road from Abercorn was constantly flooded, it was difficult and time-consuming to haul the supplies from Abercorn, to say nothing of the labor of transporting them on a heavy barge from Savannah to Abercorn, often against a strong current. This barge, designed by Thomas Causton, the keeper of the stores in Savannah, had a blunt bow and was far too heavy for use on the often swift river (plate 12).

Despite these hardships, life went on in Ebenezer. Boltzius and Gronau were punctilious in their pastoral duties, holding regular Divine services, Holy Communion, prayer meetings, marriages, baptisms, and funerals. Four persons married, namely, Anna Hofer to Georg Schweiger and Sibylla Schwab to Andreas Resch, who was soon lost in the forest and never seen again. The Salzburgers were joined by a German glazier-carpenter named Friedrich Rheinländer and his family, who had accompanied them to Savannah from Charleston, where four of the family's six children had just died. Meanwhile, Zwiffler's fiancée had arrived from Germany. While the pious Salzburgers emulated Boltzius in resigning themselves to the inscrutable dispensations of their all-loving God, the three Bavarians did not; and Matthias Braunberger, at the instigation of the wicked Roths, had the audacity to give von Reck, for forwarding, a letter disparaging the settlement. Fortunately, this calumnious letter fell into the hands of Urlsperger, who censored it and thus concealed adverse news from Ebenezer for a little longer. According to current belief in a "Holy" God, it was surely divine justice that caused Braunberger to die of dysentery soon thereafter.

Having brought the Salzburgers safely to Georgia, von Reck, himself afflicted with dysentery, returned to Europe via New England, where his servant Christian Schweikert remained in the service of a German officer until returning to Ebenezer to die after a protracted illness. Having reported to the Trustees, von Reck returned to Germany via Holland to visit the surviving Dürrnberger exiles who had settled in Cadzand at the invitation of the States General of the Netherlands and were having as much difficulty as their co-religionists at Ebenezer. Despite much confusion and hardship at Ebenezer, von Reck praised the fertility and other advantages of Georgia. His conviction was proved by his impatience to return and take out a grant for five hundred acres, since he expected no inheritance. Boltzius too had submitted favorable reports, which Urlsperger carefully edited in his *Ausführliche Nachrichten*. Before these were published, contradictory rumors began to arrive, but, questioning their veracity, Urlsperger went ahead with publication of the earlier and more optimistic reports.

Encouraged by these earlier reports, Urlsperger organized another transport from the Salzburger exiles residing in Augsburg and neighboring Free Cities. In it was Michael Rieser's family, which had dropped out of the first transport when their son broke his leg. This second transport, consisting of fifty-four persons, left Augsburg on 23 September 1734 under the guidance of Jean Vat, a citizen of Biel in Switzerland. They were joined in Frankfurt by Nikolaus and Christian Riedelsperger, brothers from Salzburg who had arrived in Augsburg just after the transport had left. With the transport were Bartholomäus Zant, a Swiss, and Georg Sanftleben, a Silesian. On the day following the departure from Augsburg, von Reck arrived there with enthusiastic descriptions of Georgia and with English passports for any Salzburgers who wished to go there.

The second transport took the same route as the first, sailing from Rotterdam on the *Two Brothers,* a 150-ton ship built in North Carolina and commanded by an Irish captain named William Thomson, who would soon play a major role in the history of the Germans in Georgia. Three days after leaving Holland the emigrants reached Gravesend, from where they were taken to London to be exhibited to the benevolent public. Here they impressed their English hosts with their hymns and their answers to questions concerning their Protestant faith. As in the case of the first transport, they received many benefactions, even being served at table by English gentlemen of quality.

In London the Salzburgers met the Indian chief Tomochichi and his family, the good friends of the English in Georgia (plate 5). On 21 September they and the Indians boarded the *Prince of Wales* and returned to Gravesend. This ship, until then named the *Prince Frederick,* was commanded by a Scottish captain, George Dunbar. On board was Daniel Weisiger, a German from Pennsylvania, who was returning to Philadelphia after collecting funds for the Lutheran church there. Three English boys were also added to the party to serve the Salzburger pastors, they being Henry Bishop, John Robinson, and Nicholas Carpenter. Bishop, who was the son of a London grocer but literally became a

Salzburger, soon wrote home correctly that the other two lads were "sad reprobate boys" who could neither read nor write.

Completing a relatively easy voyage in seven weeks, the second transport reached Georgia on 28 December and arrived at Ebenezer on 13 January 1735. On the way to Ebenezer, Sebastian Glantz died in Purysburg, and the Schoppacher infant who had been born and baptized at Gravesend died shortly after reaching Ebenezer. Having experienced such a well-organized journey from Augsburg to Georgia, the newcomers were appalled by what they found at Ebenezer. Nine of the little colony had died in nine months, including those who had written the most lavish letters praising Ebenezer; and many of the survivors were dangerously ill with dysentery and scurvy. No land had yet been distributed, even though the Salzburgers had been promised immediate possession of a town lot, a two-acre garden on the edge of town, and a forty-eight-acre farm nearby. Already, while they were in Savannah, godless people had warned the newcomers that the soil at Ebenezer was sterile, a fact that they could see for themselves on their way from Abercorn to Ebenezer. Also, wolves and bears had been devouring the cattle and hogs.

Until now the Trustees had had little idea of how bad conditions really were at Ebenezer because Boltzius thought it ungrateful to man and God to question this holy undertaking. Also, like other Pietists of the Halle variety, Boltzius accepted the theodicy of the famous philosopher and fellow Saxon, Gottfried Wilhelm Leibniz, which taught that this is the best of all possible worlds. It being established that God is all-knowing, all-loving, and all-powerful, it is only rational to believe that whatever He does must be for our own good, even if we cannot always comprehend His inscrutable ways. It is a loving father who chastises his son. Should our child recover from a grave illness, we should thank our merciful

Lord for saving his life (not blame Him for having sent the sickness). On the other hand, even if our child should die excruciatingly in a bed of blood and vomit, we should praise our all-loving Father for having taken the little soul to Himself still free of sin. Boltzius reiterated such Pollyanna platitudes until his congregation repeated them to him almost verbatim, thus proving themselves good Christians. Roth, who could not vindicate God's justice so easily and appears to have threatened Boltzius's life, was forcefully removed from Ebenezer by the Savannah authorities even before Vat arrived. When he died soon thereafter, still impenitent, his death served as a dreadful example for the pious Salzburgers, in contrast to the edifying demise of the saintly Hans Madreiter, who had borne his long and painful final illness without complaint.

Early in 1735 the Trustees began receiving unhappy messages. On 15 January, Samuel Quincy, the Anglican minister in Savannah, wrote no doubt at Vat's behest to Henry Newman, the secretary of the SPCK, and stated that Boltzius and Vat were having difficulty in persuading the second transport to settle on such bad land and that they really should be placed elsewhere. Although Boltzius and Gronau made no complaints in their letters of 6 February to Newman and to James Vernon, the secretary of the Trustees, Boltzius did so the next day in a letter to Oglethorpe, in which he stressed the Salzburgers' high mortality and their infertile, often flooded, and inaccessible land (10).

Far more discouraging was Vat's letter of 10 February to Newman, confirming that the soil at Ebenezer would not repay the seed sown, despite the contrary view of Noble Jones and Thomas Causton, both of whom were determined to keep the Salzburgers where Oglethorpe wished them. Causton, formerly a London wigmaker, had been appointed keeper of the stores in Savannah, and this office gave him such power that Boltzius thought him the mayor of the city.

What appeared to be rich soil at Ebenezer was merely white sand covered by a thin layer of humus, which would support rank vegetation, but only as long as it was undisturbed. As is the case today in the luxuriant rain forests of the Amazon, once the trees were felled and the topsoil was scattered, the remaining sand was entirely sterile.

While gathering acorns for their swine, the Salzburgers had found a strip of oak forest along the Savannah River at the mouth of Ebenezer Creek; and, like the Pennsylvania Germans, they knew that lands bearing the largest deciduous trees are the most difficult to clear but the most productive to plant. Convinced that this area, the Red Bluff, was a better location, Vat left his heavy supplies there rather than manhandle them up to Ebenezer. He then returned to Savannah to request the area for his people; but Causton hesitated to make any decision in Oglethorpe's absence, even though he, Jones, and Captain Dunbar again inspected Ebenezer and saw how poor the soil was. On 9 May, Vat even persuaded Captain Thomson to visit Ebenezer so that he, like Dunbar, could report firsthand to the Trustees about conditions there. Captain Dunbar, who had brought the second transport to Georgia, described the Salzburgers as a "pyous Sobir laborious people."

Vat repeated his arguments even more strongly in a letter to Newman dated 30 May, by which time the Salzburgers had planted a second crop, which sprouted well but soon withered away because the sandy soil retained no moisture after the rains. In addition to the unsuitable soil, he again mentioned the unhealthy situation and stated that nearly all pregnancies had ended in stillbirths or the early death of the child and that nine more people had died since the second transport arrived.

In addition to his hygienic and agricultural problems, Boltzius had to cope with the constant squabbling between the Ortmanns and the Rheinländers, all four of whom considered themselves socially superior to the rural Salzburgers. He also had friction with Zwiffler, who insisted upon encroaching on Boltzius's territory by treating his patients' souls as well as their bodies, badly in both cases according to Boltzius, who claimed that Zwiffler was rapidly curing his parishioners to death. In addition, some Salzburgers like Ruprecht Zittrauer would slip away to get drunk at Purysburg, often with the aid of the profligate shoemaker Jacob Reck of that town, whose services were indispensable in Ebenezer even if his behavior did not suit such a celestial city.

Boltzius also had financial worries: his salary was frequently delayed, and at times he had to cash his bills of exchange at a loss because of the currency differences between Georgia and South Carolina. On one occasion he learned that six fifteen-pound notes he had received from Samuel Montaigut, a planter-merchant in Purysburg, had been counterfeited by William Mellichamp in Savannah, and much time elapsed before he could force Montaigut to make them good.

The Indians also plagued Boltzius (plates 6, 7). When he first arrived, he was determined to learn their language in order to convert them to the Triune God; but he soon discovered that they would not remain in one spot long enough for him to learn their language or for them to learn English. The Salzburgers were pleased to have the Indians bring them venison, since they, being the archbishop's obedient subjects, had never learned the art of killing his game. However, they soon realized that the Indians expected much in return, especially when drunk, as they often were when they passed through Ebenezer. Besides that, the Indians had no clear conception of private property and helped themselves generously to anything growing in the fields, even shooting a cow just for its bell or to cut out a single steak, while leaving the remaining carcass to rot, just as they did their deer after removing the skin.

Like Oglethorpe, and partly because of him, Boltzius arrived in Georgia imbued with the myth of the Noble Savage still uncorrupted by civilization; but it was not long before he agreed with the Anglican ministers Samuel Quincy and John Wesley that the Indians of Georgia were indolent, bloodthirsty alcoholics, whose greatest joy was boasting of their misdeeds and wreaking fiendish torture upon their captives. Even the noble Tomochichi, so dignified in the engraving gracing Urlsperger's *Ausführliche Nachrichten,* ended up as a pitiful drunk. Boltzius did make exceptions for the Cherokees far-off in the mountains, whom he had never met.

Because Benjamin Sheftal and his wife Hanna spoke "good German" (*gut Teutsch*) rather than Yiddish and were generous to the Salzburgers, Boltzius had high hopes of winning them for Jesus. These hopes increased when Benjamin visited the Salzburgers' house soon after their arrival in Savannah to return some money because he did not wish any "unrighteous money" in his house. His wife had inadvertently given change for a half crown instead of for a crown, a coin with which she was not familiar. Sure that such a righteous man would convert if only instructed properly, Boltzius sent to Germany for tractates by Johannes Heinrich Callenberg, a missionary to European Jews. When, even after reading such works, Sheftal clung obstinately to his faith, Boltzius gave up the quest and their friendship cooled. Quincy, perhaps a better judge of the situation, said of the Sheftals, "Their kindness shew'd to Mr. Bolzius and the Saltzburghers, was owing to the Good temper and humanity of the people, and not to any inclination to change their Religion."

It was inevitable that Boltzius would collide with Vat, who considered himself commissioner for both transports and resented the pastor's meddling in secular matters, especially since the members of the first transport always took their problems to their adored minister instead of to the newly arrived commissioner. Boltzius had at first defended Vat against the scurrilous denunciations against him submitted by Andreas Gottfried Dietzius, a German passenger aboard the *Prince of Wales* who had charged Vat with treating his Salzburgers tyrannically; but in time he saw that Dietzius had been the better judge. During one of Vat's long absences in Savannah, Boltzius authorized the Salzburgers to break into the Ebenezer storehouse to distribute some rice to the sick. Vat considered this open rebellion and treated the Salzburgers even more harshly. Besides that, Vat was blamed for making the Salzburgers perform guard duty, a service that demanded much time that could have been expended more profitably otherwise. Boltzius was particularly critical of Vat's treatment of Georg Schweiger, who, after his first wife's death, had married the daughter of a Purysburg schoolmaster with Boltzius's permission but without Vat's.

Boltzius's journal entry for 1 January 1736 frankly admitted, and Urlsperger did not conceal, the deaths of seven of the eleven children born to the Salzburgers the previous year, as well as those of fourteen adults. It will be noted, however, that Urlsperger published this mortality report only later, after more favorable reports had begun to arrive. In spite of, or perhaps because of, the imminence of death, Boltzius's parishioners were intent on marrying, just as quail pair off most readily when their covey has been shot up. The widow Schoppacher married Veit Landfelder three months after her husband's death, the widow Ossenecker married Hans Maurer after a similar interval, and the widow Moshammer waited only slightly longer before marrying Peter Gruber. Schweiger had lost little time replacing his late wife with his bride from Purysburg, and the widower Gschwandel asked for the hand of Mrs. Resch even before her husband was legally dead.

On 7 February 1736 von Reck returned to Ebenezer, having brought a third transport as far as Savannah. Upon returning to Europe a year and a half earlier, he had at once set out recruiting a new transport for Georgia, broadcasting utopian descriptions of that most delightful country in the universe. A number of Bohemian Protestants declared themselves willing to emigrate to Georgia provided they be accompanied by a Czech-speaking minister, but this von Reck could not arrange; and von Reck was reprimanded by the Trustees for making more promises than he could fulfill. In Regensburg many religious exiles from Carinthia were also ready to join him, but only if they could first recover the children taken from them by the Catholic authorities. When a plan for recruiting Waldensians also fell through, von Reck had to be content with sixteen Austrians from Regensburg, including exiles from Upper Austria and Carinthia, and twenty Salzburgers whom Urlsperger had meanwhile collected in Augsburg and surrounding cities.

Following the same route as the previous two transports down the Main and Rhine, this third transport sailed from England on the *London Merchant,* Captain John Thomas, and von Reck indicated on a plan of the ship just where the Salzburgers were quartered (plate 8). The *London Merchant* sailed in convoy with the *Symonds,* on which were Oglethorpe, John Wesley, and a party of Moravians, or Herrnhuters as they were then called, led by August Gottlieb Spangenberg. These had originally been religious exiles from Moravia who had found refuge at Herrnhut in Saxony, an estate belonging to Count Nicolaus Ludwig von Zinzendorf, and had been joined by new members from all parts of Germany. The Moravians claimed to be Lutherans in good standing, but the Halle Pietists vehemently denied this claim and considered them dangerous innovators who caused schisms in all of the Lutheran communities they visited.

When von Reck left Augsburg, he had thirty-five in his party, one of them being his seventeen-year-old brother Ernst Ludwig. Determined to augment his transport in any way possible, he tried to enlist some of the Dürrnbergers in Frankfurt who had returned from the debacle in Cadzand; but they were no longer receptive to even the most convincing offers. While in Frankfurt he did recruit a converted Jew, formerly called Solomon Levi but now christened Johann Gottfried Christ, and also the large family of a clockmaker named Friedrich Wilhelm Müller. Here or elsewhere he also engaged a servant by the name of Christian Heinrich (?) Müller, who may or may not have been related to the clockmaker.

In London von Reck picked up a Swiss tanner named Johann Jacob Helfenstein, his wife, and six children and also a Swiss laborer from Basel named Abraham Grüning. In Savannah he even accepted a Palatine by the name of Andreas Lorentz Arnsdorff and his large family, one of whom was still serving out her indenture in South Carolina. Among the twenty Salzburgers from Augsburg were a Bavarian distiller-brewer named Josef Ernst, his wife Anna Maria, and their daughter Susanna and also a Hungarian-German tailor named Franz Sigmund Herrnberger. While the actual Salzburgers were a minority in the transport, the religious exiles, namely the Salzburgers, Upper Austrians, and Carinthians, when taken together, composed a large majority.

During the stay in Frankfurt, Johann Flerl married Anna Maria Höpflinger, Leonhard Kraus married Barbara Einecker, and Thomas Ossenecker married Anna Catherina Meyer; and in Ebenezer, on 4 May, Johann Cornberger married Gertraut Einecker, Ruprecht Zittrauer married Anna Leihofer, and Stephan Riedelsperger married Catherina Valentin. In eighteenth-century Europe, respectable young people without means had to practice Malthusian morality: they had to postpone marriage until reasonably assured they could support a large family, birth control being sinful and unreliable. As a result, many younger sons and many girls without dowries could never marry, thus filling the world with monks, nuns, bachelors, spinsters, mercenaries, and prostitutes. It was not unusual for promised couples to remain engaged for twenty or thirty years until the groom's father or older and childless brother left him the family farm, business, or guild membership. This explains why so many of the Georgia Salzburgers married immediately upon joining the transport: many of them now enjoyed economic security for the first time, being promised a homestead upon their arrival in America.

Boltzius and Gronau also married soon after reaching Georgia, something they probably could not have done had they remained in Halle as poorly paid schoolteachers. Although their journal fails to mention his "change," Gronau married Catherina Kroehr, the daughter of Barbara Rohrmoser, a Salzburg woman who had emigrated with her sister and two older daughters after being forced to leave her younger children with her second husband, who had remained Catholic. Not long after Gronau married Catherina, Boltzius married her sister Gertraut, a girl half his age: thus the two colleagues sealed their friendship by becoming brothers-in-law and also true members of the Salzburg community. Hearing that the brides were impecunious, some English ladies sent linens to spare them the shame of bringing no dowries into the marriage. Mrs. Rohrmoser proved a capable and devoted housekeeper for both couples and was greatly missed and lamented when she suddenly died not long after. She must have died happy, seeing her two daughters so well provided for as wives of ordained and salaried ministers.

Without asking the third transport's consent, Oglethorpe had decided to take them with him to St. Simons Island off the southern coast of Georgia, where he was establishing the town of Frederica as a bulwark against the Spaniards in Florida. When the Salzburgers refused to go there and instead insisted he keep the Trustees' pledge to settle them with their friends at Ebenezer, he had to accede; but he did so ungraciously. Somehow, all the provisions and tools consigned to the third transport were misdirected to Frederica, while its members arrived in Ebenezer emptyhanded. Besides that, most of them were afflicted with scurvy, which kept many of them bedridden for months or until finally released by death. Some of this transport, including the sickest, were taken via Purysburg directly to the Red Bluff; the remainder went via Abercorn to Ebenezer, where they were met on the way by the older inhabitants and escorted to town with a festive torchlight procession. On the next day, 17 February, von Reck took the old and the new Salzburgers to the Red Bluff and began building a new city (Plate 9).

On the day that von Reck returned to Ebenezer, Boltzius began keeping a secret diary (*Diarium extraordinarium*) in which he could express himself more freely than in his less private journal (30). It tells how he finally realized that his people had been correct with regard to the soil at Ebenezer and how he then took their side and confronted Oglethorpe with the choice of having them move or perish. Oglethorpe offered all sorts of vain excuses and suggested many half-remedies; but Boltzius insisted until Oglethorpe finally acquiesced, saving face by transferring the name Ebenezer to the new location on the Red Bluff to give a semblance of continuity.

The secret diary also reveals the full extent of Boltzius's friction with Vat, whom he blamed for the third transport's hardships and accused of threatening and intimidating the Salzburgers. Meanwhile, surveyor Jones was laying out the new town on the Red Bluff. Among the drawings von Reck brought back to Europe is a bird's-eye view of New Ebenezer soon after its founding (plate 10). This picture has much in common with the famous etching of Savannah commonly attributed to Peter Gordon: both represent oblique aerial views as if taken from an airplane flying low just across the river and showing a narrow strip of the left bank, the river with boats, the high bluff before the town, and the lots and the houses in exact perspective. Since Peter Gordon was no longer in Georgia, the only explanation of the similarities is that both drawings were based on sketches done by Jones himself. Incidentally, Gordon, who took the Savannah sketch to London and put his name on it, was neither a surveyor nor a draftsman.

Notwithstanding the continued sickness and the infighting of the leaders, a good start was being made with the shelters, and crops were being planted communally in the town squares. The good land around New Ebenezer being of limited quantity, Boltzius and von Reck tried to persuade Oglethorpe to let the Salzburgers settle across Ebenezer Creek, where good land was abundant; but this was not permitted until thirteen years later because it belonged to the Uchee Indians. When surveying the garden plots, Jones preferred to situate them in the pine barrens, where surveying was easy, rather than in thickets and canebrakes, where the soil was fertile but the surveying difficult.

Boltzius's secret diary and the unexpurgated version of his journal reveal the skill with which he played one commissioner against the other, the hotheaded and impractical young Hanoverian nobleman against the older and more experienced Swiss burgher. Von Reck enjoyed the love and confidence of the Salzburgers, except for some members of the third transport who complained that he had made too many false promises. On the other hand, Vat enjoyed the support of Causton, who relied on him to carry out Oglethorpe's unpopular orders such as maintaining a twenty-four-hour six-man guard and reserving twenty building lots on each side of the town for English latecomers. Gradually deprived of all authority by the clever clergyman, Vat left in disgust, receiving from von Reck a noisy, and no doubt malicious, send-off. Boltzius's complaints against the excitable young baron must have impressed the Trustees, for their secretary, Benjamin Martyn, wrote on 10 June 1736, "And lest the Restlessness of Mr. van Reck's temper should have any influence on the Saltzburghers, the Trustees desire that his Lot of 500 acres may be laid out at as great a distance from them as possible."

In May von Reck had traveled to Frederica to see Oglethorpe in hopes of winning supplies and concessions, but he succeeded only in annoying and alienating him. He did, however, keep an interesting journal describing his journey and the plants, animals, and Indians he encountered. Leaving Frederica, the von Recks visited the Uchee Indians at Palachocolas on the Savannah River above Ebenezer to attend their busk, or ceremonial dance (plate 11). From there they returned sick to Ebenezer, where they would have died had they not been taken down to Savannah and put into the loving care of the minister John Wesley and the schoolmaster Charles Delamotte.

Partially restored to health, the von Recks returned to Europe, bringing with them a collection of drawings, some of them colored, of the flora, fauna, and Indians in Georgia, which included a scene of the building of the first shelters on the Red Bluff (plate 9) and of the clumsy barge on which the Salzburgers had to haul their heavy loads up the river from Savannah (plate 12). These illustrations, never mentioned in von Reck's correspondence, were discovered in the Royal Library in Copenhagen in 1976 by Dr. Kristian Hvidt and were published by him (32). All these pictures have been attributed to von Reck himself, but their varied styles suggest different hands. Besides that, if he had had such talent, he would certainly have made some drawings on his earlier journey. The pictures of plants and animals would appear to have been the work of a botanically and zoologically trained illustrator, whereas those directly concerning the Salzburgers could have been by von Reck's servant Christian

Müller, who was with him all the time and is known to have painted a portrait of Oglethorpe (probably the one now hanging in the Chatham Club in Savannah [plate 13]). Having arrived home from his fiasco in Georgia, von Reck studied law, held various civil posts in several little German states, married a somewhat older heiress of the higher nobility, and finally moved to Ranzau in Holstein, where he entered the Danish civil service and reached a very ripe old age. His Danish service explains why the drawings became the property of the Danish king.

Oglethorpe could not understand the Salzburgers' desire to abandon Old Ebenezer after expending so much work on the buildings there, nor could he fathom Boltzius's and Gronau's readiness to renounce their relatively comfortable parsonages without any assurance of receiving substitutes in the new town. Vexed at the Salzburgers' recalcitrance, Oglethorpe made them leave all buildings, lumber, and fences behind them in Old Ebenezer, which was to serve henceforth as a cowpen, or cattle ranch, for the Trustees' cattle. Much of this lumber had, to be sure, been sawn by Jeny's slaves and by Salzburger sawyers paid by Oglethorpe.

Oglethorpe wished the Salzburgers to work at their new location communally; but Boltzius, being a better judge of human nature, preferred private enterprise and insisted that the promised land be parcelled out at once. Despite great effort, Jones made little progress with the surveying, mainly because his sickly indentured helpers usually died after a short period of such strenuous work in the miasmic swamps and canebreaks. After he was dismissed and Hugh Ross of Purysburg was engaged in his stead, things went no better. A full year was to pass and many Salzburgers were to die before the land was finally distributed, the assignments being made by lot after humble prayer to God. Like other inhabitants of Georgia, the Salzburgers objected to the law of tail-male, which stipulated that land could be inherited only through the male line. The Trustees had instituted this law for military reasons to ensure that each property would be represented by someone able to bear arms and also to prevent too much land from falling into too few hands.

The Salzburgers' joy at finally obtaining fertile land lasted until late summer, when everyone suddenly contracted malaria. In Old Ebenezer they had been subjected to scurvy, dysentery, and various unidentifiable burning fevers such as typhoid and typhus, yet malaria had not struck. This may have been due in part to the absence of anopheline mosquitoes, which breed less abundantly where dense foliage shades the stagnant water than they do in open areas, such as rice fields, where the trees have been cleared away. Also, it is possible that few malarial people had passed through Ebenezer to infect the mosquitoes. At New Ebenezer, on the other hand, there were open rice fields and infected people across the river in South Carolina; indeed, the malarial epidemic was equally severe in Purysburg and in Savannah.

While dysentery and other maladies had afflicted and even killed many individuals at Old Ebenezer, enough people had remained well to tend the sick and perform some work toward developing the settlement. In New Ebenezer, on the other hand, malaria struck nearly everyone; and at one point Boltzius could not find even four men well enough to row Causton's big barge down to Savannah to fetch the desperately needed provisions. Causton tried to supply English rowers, but they too were usually sick and sometimes could not complete the journey. The flood tide reached only as high as Purysburg, from which point the barge had to be pulled against the river current with the help of a four-oared rowboat out in front, as shown in von Reck's drawing (plate 12).

Various types of malaria appeared in Georgia, but in 1736 the most prevalent seems to have been tertian, which causes the patient chills and fever every other day. Boltzius and

33

Gronau saw God's wisdom and kindness in letting them receive their salutary fevers on different days, so that there was always one minister able to perform the necessary spiritual duties. We should remember that, according to Pietist beliefs, sickness was always salutary, since an omniscient, omnipotent, and all-loving God can do only what is best for us. Healthy days may be welcome to the flesh, but they cause us to forget our dependence on God until He humbles us with a sickness for our spiritual good. Poor Zwiffler, who soon lost the bride he had fetched from Germany, was unable to cope with the malarial epidemic despite his bloodletting and administration of self-concocted medications. Not only was he blamed for the poor state of health in the community, he also received no emoluments, since the Trustees had never granted him a salary and Boltzius considered it unjust for him to demand payment from the poor Salzburgers. At the end of the year, he requested and received permission to return to Europe; but it appears that he went only as far as Philadelphia, from where he wrote letters for several years.

When the main body of the Salzburgers moved from Old to New Ebenezer, they left a few people, mostly sick, to guard their little gardens from wild animals and passersby, with the result that only a pitiful little harvest was gathered to add to what was grown in the communal fields at New Ebenezer. Fortunately, all but the first transport were still receiving some provisions from Savannah whenever transportation could be arranged; and there was a trickle of benefactions from Europe. Despite sickness and hardships, some progress was made at New Ebenezer; and by the end of the summer there were huts for all the widows and two large communal shelters. Whereas many Salzburgers had received sandy garden lots, this inequity was somewhat mitigated by the high death rate, because the fertile gardens of the deceased passed on to those who had received sandy soil.

As if sickness and privation were not enough, Boltzius had

problems with many of his parishioners, mostly with those who were not Salzburgers. Josef Ernst had to be forcibly removed to Savannah and incarcerated there for striking Mrs. Müller, and the English lad Nicolas Carpenter was sent there because of continued naughtiness. Even von Reck, worn out by hardship and humiliated by loss of authority and prestige, had struck a Salzburger woman who had had the effrontery to buy some honey from an Indian woman even though he himself, a nobleman, had wished to buy it. Among the non-Salzburger converts, Boltzius found some with pitifully little knowledge of the Evangelical religion, and even the saintly Salzburgers insisted on keeping their ancient custom of having one godfather stand as sponsor for all children in a family. Because the Catholic church did not permit marriages between co-sponsors, it was inadvisable to choose too many acquaintances in one's village as godparents and thus make them ineligible as future mates for one's family. Boltzius was surprised at the Salzburgers' custom of using coffins only for women who had died in childbirth; all other corpses were merely wrapped in a shroud and carried to their graves on a board.

Boltzius's greatest spiritual fears were caused by the activities of the Herrnhuters, or Moravians, in Savannah, who had come over at the same time as the third transport and on the same ship as Oglethorpe and Wesley, on whom they had made a dangerously good impression. The authorities in Savannah could not understand why the Moravians spoke so well of the Salzburgers, while the Salzburger pastors defamed the Moravians. Urlsperger deleted all references to the Moravians in Boltzius's journal, perhaps for fear that the Salzburgers' orthodox Lutheran patrons in Europe might think that they were being contaminated by these dangerous innovators, who had caused discord enough in Halle. On 19 March 1736 Boltzius wrote that August Gottlieb Spangenberg wished to visit Ebenezer again, which indicates that the

Moravian bishop had already been there and that Urlsperger had suppressed all mention of this fact, just as he
did in this entry, in which Boltzius gives his objections to
these troublemaking sectarians. Jones had interrupted his
surveying at Ebenezer to take Spangenberg up the Ogeechee
River to inspect the five-hundred-acre grant of land he had
received for his people.

By November cool weather had set in and the symptoms
of malaria were alleviated, with the result that there was
relative health again in New Ebenezer and the survivors
could prepare huts to protect themselves from the approaching winter. Mrs. Ortmann, the worldly wife of the old
schoolmaster, had recovered her health sufficiently to slip
away to Charleston, against her husband's orders, to enjoy a
lively Christmas instead of the solemn type celebrated in
Ebenezer. After her return she was not the least penitent;
rather, she soon went to Old Ebenezer allegedly to nurse a
supposedly sick Englishman, much to the scandal of pious
Salzburger women.

3

Progress and Palatines

ompared to the tumultuous year 1736, the following one was relatively calm, serving as a recov-
ery from the past and a preparation for the future. With Vat and von Reck gone and the reins
of government firmly in Boltzius's hands, there was less
bickering and squabbling. Boltzius found considerably more
time for spiritual concerns, as his reports indicate. Although
all his parishioners professed the Augsburg Confession,
namely the articles of faith of the Lutheran church, Boltzius
discovered that some of them had little theological
knowledge, having learned their faith only from their parents and from itinerant journeymen and the devotional
works they managed to smuggle into the country. Besides
that, the Lutherans had been compelled to attend Roman
Catholic services, which must have influenced the impres-
sionable children.

No doubt many of the Salzburgers had seen religious spec-
tacles in which Everyman, when approaching Death, is de-
serted by Wealth, Kinsman, and Friend and is accompanied
on the last lap of his journey only by his Good Works. Such
an idea was of course anathema for Boltzius, who, as a faithful disciple of Luther, believed that salvation could be
achieved by faith alone, not by good works. Consequently,
he never tired of preaching against "work righteousness"

(*eigene Gerechtigkeit*), "self-made piety" (*selbstgemachte Frömm-igkeit*), and "bourgeois honesty" (*bürgerliche Ehrlichkeit*). These ideas were but snares of the devil, which tricked poor sinners into thinking they could win salvation by char-itable acts and good behavior, without recognizing their own depravity and without crawling into the wounds of Jesus to be born again. The Old Adam had to be killed, and this could be done only by the grace of God, not by human efforts.

Boltzius had great difficulty with the "scruples" of some people who were more "legalistic" (*gesetzlich*) than "evangeli-cal" (*evangelisch*), people more concerned with the Old Testa-ment than with the New, more afraid of the law than as-sured of God's mercy through the merits of Jesus. Time and again he had to convince his frightened parishioners that God, through His only begotten Son, would pardon them their sins, no matter how great, if only they would confess them freely, regret them, and resolve not to sin again. A person fortunate enough to come to this great realization had finally "come through" (*durchkommem*).

Boltzius had arrived at Halle during the lifetime of August Hermann Francke, Paul Anton, and Joachim Justus Breit-haupt, the leading Pietists at the time. Even though these worthies had all died soon after his arrival, their teachings remained inviolate. When Boltzius reiterated their dogma in his journal and letters, we may assume that he did so partly to show his mentors in Halle that he had not forgotten their instruction. We should remember that the theologians at Halle had developed theology into an exact science. Even today Germans consider theology (*Gotteswissenschaft*) a sci-ence just like the natural sciences (*Naturwissenschaften*). If one followed the theologians' scripture-based rules carefully, he could achieve salvation, provided, of course, he were ready to renounce the Old Adam.

When jealous people in Savannah complained that all the

Salzburgers did was eat and pray, Boltzius could counter that their prayers must have been effective to enable them to eat so well. Actually, like Luther and his Augustinian monks before him, the Salzburgers knew that a good Christian must both pray (*orare*) and work (*laborare*). They believed that even though good works would not get one into heaven, hard work would make this world less of a hell. Despite Boltzius's primary concern with his parishioners' souls, he was not yet freed from material matters, now being solely responsible for the physical welfare of the settlement and the distribution of all supplies. Because the economy of Ebenezer was generally not quite as bad as elsewhere in the colony, various people wished to move there, giving as their real or feigned reason their thirst for the word of God. Among these were Ambrosius and Johann Jacob Zübli, two Swiss whose wealthy brother in Purysburg, David, refused to help them.

It seems surprising that Ebenezer received any voluntary settlers in view of the unhealthy situation, which had caused half the original settlers to die in a period of four years. On 28 July 1737 Boltzius wrote to Captain Coram, the Trustee who had hosted the first transport at Dover: "The half part of ye Saltzburghers you met with at Dover are translated by Death to a better life, & the rest endeavour themselves at our new Settlement ye utmost of their strength to gain their bread by labour."

In view of the many Swiss settlers in Georgia and South Carolina, it might seem strange that so few settled in Ebenezer. Their absence can be explained, however, by religious preference: the Swiss who came to the colonies were mostly Reformed, being followers of the reformer Ulrich Zwingli. Whenever possible, they tried to settle together or at least with Germans of the Reformed faith; yet Ebenezer did receive some of them, including Bartholomäus Zant, the Helfensteins, the two Züblis, Hans Krüsy and his son Adrian, and no doubt others among the so-called Palatines, a term misused for most German immigrants to Georgia and even for the Romansch-speaking settlers from Grisons.

In theory, the Swiss Confederacy had remained a part of the Holy Roman Empire until the Treaty of Westphalia in 1648, and there was no insurmountable barrier between Reformed persons from Switzerland and from German territories to the immediate north. Also, many Swiss immigrants had resided for some time in the Palatinate before proceeding to America, and some had intermarried with the natives there. It is most probable that some of the later German-speaking additions to Ebenezer from South Carolina had originally come from Switzerland. For example, the Heinrich Fritsee who received a grant in 1759 may well have been the Heinrich Fritschi who had arrived in Georgia in 1735 on the *Two Brothers* en route to South Carolina and had signed a letter praising the good treatment Captain William Thomson had shown his passengers. The Gregorius Stierle who married Maria Rosina Hammer at Ebenezer in 1759 was surely the Gregorius Stierlin, born in 1722 at Birmenstorff in Canton Zurich, who emigrated to South Carolina (43).

The Salzburgers' school also attracted children from Purysburg such as Johann Paul Francke, the son of a poor widow, the four daughters of Theobald Kieffer, and the little son of the hard-drinking cobbler Jacob Reck. Georg Schweiger's new wife from Purysburg, the daughter of a deceased German schoolmaster named Unselt, gradually brought her three sisters to Ebenezer, where they all found husbands. Because it was difficult to earn cash at Ebenezer, some of the inhabitants sought employment elsewhere: Stephan Riedelsperger, Michael Rieser, and Veit Landfelder at the cowpen, or cattle ranch, of the half-breed interpreter Mary Musgrove (called Mosgraf by the Salzburgers); Hans Michael Muggitzer and Georg Bruckner at Causton's estate, Ockstead near Thunderbolt; Josef Leitner and Leonhard

Rauner at Savannah Town, high up the Savannah River; and Friedrich Rheinländer and Gabriel Bach with a party of Swiss. Boltzius was somewhat scandalized when he learned that Thomas Bichler was going to demand unchristian wages for rowing some poor Swiss up the Savannah River to New Windsor; and he was even more scandalized when he learned that Bichler had bought flour in Savannah and sold it to his fellow Salzburgers at a profit.

This party of Swiss from Canton Appenzell spent the night of 7 May 1737 at Ebenezer on their way to New Windsor, a Swiss settlement then being established in South Carolina. These disgruntled immigrants blamed their unhappy decision to emigrate on von Reck's oral encomiums and on letters sent from Ebenezer. They were also particularly embittered against their seventeen-year-old conductor, Sebastian Zoberbiller, and his elderly father, the pastor Bartholomäus Zoberbiller. The most prominent member of this party was Johann Tobler, a defeated governor of Canton Appenzell and a renowned mathematician and compiler of almanacs. Another member of this party was Johann Ulrich Giessendanner, an engraver, who caused a schism and led some of the party to the Orangeburg district in South Carolina, where he served loyally as minister until succeeded by his nephew Johann Giessendanner, who had had no theological background. Here we see that people on the frontier were more concerned with their ministers' personality than with their diplomas.

The land being still unassigned in 1737, little progress was made in agriculture; yet some advance was made in cattle raising, a skill in which the Salzburgers and Swiss surpassed all other inhabitants of Georgia. Whereas most Georgians allowed their cattle to run wild, the Salzburgers kept theirs in herds under the care of paid herdsmen, a practice that greatly diminished the loss of calves to the wolves and bears. Milking cows were, of course, kept in stalls at night.

The most notable event in 1737 was the founding of an orphanage, an institution modeled on the famous Orphan House (Waysenhaus) in Halle and, in turn, the model for George Whitefield's orphanage at Bethesda just south of Savannah. Building the orphanage was a communal undertaking, with some encouragement given to the master carpenters from charities collected in Germany and England. Fortunately, Boltzius found a selfless Salzburger couple, Ruprecht and Margaretha Kalcher, who were willing and able to manage the home, its glebe lands, and the children in it. In addition to the Salzburger orphans and children of poor or sick parents, it also housed widows, school children from Purysburg, and adult patients without families to care for them (67).

During this year the Salzburgers saw much of John Wesley, the Anglican minister in Savannah and subsequent founder of the Methodist movement (plate 14). When Wesley visited Ebenezer, he was astounded by the progress there, which was far greater than that in Savannah; and he reported very favorably about the Salzburgers' economic and spiritual condition. On 27 July 1737 Wesley wrote into his journal: "In the evening we came to New-Ebenezer, where the poor Saltzburghers are settled. The industry of this people is quite surprising. Their sixty huts are neatly and regularly built, and all the little spots of ground between them, improved to the best advantage. On one side of the town is a field of Indian corn; on the other are the plantations of several private persons; all of which together one would scarce think possible for a handful of people to have done in one year." He was, however, far more influenced by the Moravians in Savannah, who were responsible for his true conversion. Boltzius was disturbed by Wesley's intimacy with that dangerous sect and reported it often in his journal, no doubt knowing that Urlsperger would delete all such references before publication. It was probably Urlsperger who deleted the fact that Spangenberg had accompanied Wesley on his visit of 27 July, the good bishop being the other party included in the pronoun "we."

The people of Savannah had generally assumed that Wesley would marry Thomas Causton's niece Sophy Hopkey; but, when he did not press his suit, she married William Williamson. Soon thereafter he repelled her from Holy Communion, and Williamson, Causton, and half the city assumed that it was out of spite. Showing true professional courtesy, Boltzius made only slight mention of the furor reigning in Savannah when Williamson sued Wesley for defaming his wife and thus divided the city into two hostile factions. Against Causton's orders, Wesley soon slipped away from Savannah and out of Georgia history.

On 29 December 1737, Boltzius was called to Savannah to preach to the Lutherans among a shipload of Palatines who had arrived on 21 December on the *Three Sisters,* under Captain Hewitt, and whose passage had been paid by the Trustees. Because so many indentured servants came from the Rhenish Palatinate, the region extending from Heidelberg to France, all indentured Germans were called Palatines, even if they actually came from Alsace, Baden, Württemberg, or even further away. In Savannah the term *Trustees' servants* often meant Germans, for, despite the Trustees' constant complaints against their unsatisfactory service, the Palatines were still the best labor obtainable.

On 7 October 1738 another large cargo of Palatines arrived on the *Two Brothers,* commanded by the previously mentioned Captain Thomson; and they, along with Captain Hewitt's freights, played a large role in the economic life of Georgia. Friedrich Wilhelm Müller, the clockmaker who had joined the third transport in Frankfurt, redeemed Martin Kaesemeyer and his wife to help him run his plantation on shares, this being the earliest known example of "share-cropping" in Georgia. Michael Schneider and Friedrich Nett and their families were donated to Boltzius, who assigned them as herdsmen to guard the orphanage's and community's cattle; and, because the schoolmaster Ortmann was old and weak, Oglethorpe gave him the services of Christian Lewenberger and his wife to help him in his garden. Somewhat later, hearing that Mrs. Boltzius was pregnant, Colonel Stephens gave Boltzius his own servant, the widow Anna Maria Bischoff, because she was a midwife. Receiving little information from Oglethorpe, who preferred the sword to the pen, the Trustees had recently sent Stephens to Georgia as their secretary to send them firsthand reports.

For many years either Boltzius or Gronau would go down to Savannah at least once each month to minister to the Lutherans and also to many of the Reformed among the indentured servants, language being an even stronger tie than dogma. It was better to have a Lutheran sermon in German than a Calvinist sermon in English. Most of the Germans in Savannah, not being religious exiles, turned to Boltzius more for secular than for spiritual help, even if they usually called on him for ostensibly religious reasons. That some of these Palatines were in a deplorable condition is attested by Whitefield's journal entry for 9 January 1740: "Took in three German orphans, the most pitiful objects, I think, I ever saw. No new negroes could look more despicable, or required more pains to instruct them. They have been used to exceedingly hard labor, and though supplied with provisions from the Trustees, were treated in a manner unbecoming even heathens. Were all the money I have collected, to be spent in freeing these three children from slavery, it would be well laid out."

Many of the Savannah Germans asked Boltzius to have them moved to Ebenezer, and sometimes this could be done, with the result that the Palatines at Ebenezer eventually outnumbered the Salzburgers. Nevertheless, by that time they had so intermarried with the older settlers and had so well adopted their pious ways that they were indistinguishable from them and were included in the term *Salzburger*. Today, most of the descendants of these Ebenezer Palatines are also descended on one or more lines from the actual Salzburgers, and no distinction is made, even if a family's patrilineal surname derives from the Palatinate. Palatine origin is suggested by "Salzburger" names like Groover, Hoover, and Stonehevel (from Gruber, Huber, and Steinhebel) because the Palatines tended to pronounce the stop *b* as a spirant *v*.

Because the third transport had refused to settle on St. Simons, Oglethorpe decided to settle other Germans there, knowing them to be the most industrious of all available workers. The bulk of these were brought by Captain Thomson, who found Germans more profitable than ballast when his ship returned otherwise empty from Europe. For these settlers Oglethorpe established German Village, which supplied most of the workers for his fortifications and tillers for the garrison's fields. These people asked Oglethorpe for a minister, and after nearly two years of bureaucratic red tape, he finally obtained a Württemberg pastor named Johann Ulrich Driessler, who found sixty-three souls awaiting him in his parish. It is often stated that these were Salzburgers, but this was not so, since the third transport had resisted all Oglethorpe's cajoling to go there. To be sure, von Reck brought a working detail to help on the fortifications, but there is no evidence that any remained there.

The intelligentsia of Frederica seems to have been largely German-speaking. In addition to Driessler was Samuel Auspurger, a gentleman from Bern who was both surveyor and planter, and Friedrich Holtzendorf, a gentleman from Brandenburg who had settled at Purysburg but was then serving as a physician at Frederica. The most educated of all was a polyglot idealist from Saxony named Christian Gottlieb Priber, who had renounced the trappings of civilization and become an Indian in an attempt to organize a Cherokee

"Kingdom of Paradise" to defend the Red Man from the encroaching whites (46). When the Cherokees refused to extradite this philosopher-reformer to the South Carolina authorities, the commander at Augusta arranged to have him captured by Creek Indians and sold to Oglethorpe (56). Priber's cell in the barracks served as a literary salon until his untimely death. Once, when the arsenal next to his cell exploded and everyone else ran away screaming, Priber remained stoically under a rain of falling shells and grenades. Priber was not a Jesuit, as is so often reported.

Not all the Germans on St. Simons were indentured; a certain Walser had brought his large family at his own expense, and another freeholder named Heinrich Meyer built a fine house and invented a new way of manufacturing tabby, a kind of concrete made of burned oyster shells. Most of the Germans, however, were laborers who worked under the guidance of a certain Shats (Schantz), a man unable to speak a word of English. They appear in the records mostly as the victims of rape and other abuse by the military. When the recorder John Terry intervened to help the victims, Col. William Horton and his cronies caused a Palatine named Samuel Suitor (Seuter?) to accuse Terry of raping his wife, Elisabeth; but the jurors in Savannah noted that Samuel had to prompt his wife when she testified and that her testimony was obviously false. Although the Anglican clergyman William Norris was cleared of malicious charges that he had been intimate with a Dutch girl, time was to prove the charges true. German Village lasted only as long as Oglethorpe's regiment remained; as it was disbanded, the German inhabitants began drifting northward, some of them, like the Gebharts, moving to Ebenezer. By 1747 Terry could report that only two German families remained.

During the year 1738, Boltzius received two bits of good news: the Moravians were planning to leave Georgia and go to Pennsylvania, and a physician, Christian Ernst Thilo, had

46

been procured in Halle to replace the druggist Zwiffler. Boltzius had tried, although in vain, to dissuade the Rheinländers
and Helfensteins, both non-Salzburgers, from apprenticing
their sons to the Moravian cobbler David Tannenberger in
Savannah, since he feared they might bring back heretical
views, such as the fallacy that ordained ministers are unnecessary for salvation. The Swiss laborer Grüning, who had once
visited Herrnhut and had crossed the ocean with Spangenberg, remained with the Moravians for a while; yet, despite
their pacifism, he volunteered to serve as a soldier at Frederica for a year. The old carpenter Michael Volmar, who had
also crossed with the Moravians and had then been accepted
by von Reck, moved to Ebenezer but soon fled, at the Ortmanns' connivance and without fulfilling his indenture. The
true Moravians, on the other hand, were more honorable;
and by 11 August 1738 they had labored for the Trustees to
the amount of 260 £ 0 sh. 10 d., as certified by Causton, and
were therefore free to leave Georgia (49). Their physician,
John Regnier, was a native Swiss who had been robbed by
fellow shipmates on his way to Pennsylvania and had had to
indenture himself to pay his passage. Once free, he supported himself by making pewter spoons until finally joining
the Moravians in Savannah. Urlsperger consistently removed
all references to the Moravians, even the fact that they were
the donors of a barrel of dried apples from Pennsylvania.

Upon hearing that a physician was to be provided, the Salzburgers hastened to prepare a hut and garden for him. This
physician, Christian Ernst Thilo, had studied at Halle, then
one of the leading medical schools in Europe, under Christian Friedrich Richter and Johann Junker, both eminent phy-
sicians, and he arrived bearing impressive credentials in Latin
and English. Nonetheless, his arrival in Ebenezer early in
1738 did little to improve the health of the settlement, to
which the malaria returned that summer, albeit in a somewhat less virulent form. To be sure, only one adult, Maria

Bichler, died of sickness in 1738, as opposed to four in 1737 and eleven in 1736; but that was due less to better medical care than to the "seasoning" of the Salzburgers.

In colonial days it was generally believed that settlers in America gradually built up resistance against the diseases that killed off so many at first. While it is true that some diseases, such as measles, mumps, chickenpox, and small-pox, do induce immunities, it is more likely that the "season-ing" was mostly a matter of the survival of the fittest. Those colonists who had arrived susceptible to certain diseases soon died of them; those who had the proper antibodies resisted them; and, after a given time, only people of the latter cate-gory were still alive. Even after the first settlers had achieved relatively good health, later arrivals tended to die off at the same rate suffered by the earlier ones, despite better circum-stances. In any case, while sickness was still a factor in 1738, mortality had nearly ceased. With today's hindsight, we can see that Thilo's cures were mostly useless, if not harmful. Incidentally, being unseasoned, Thilo himself immediately became chronically ill. The Salzburgers' favorite remedy was Schauer's Balm, a cure-all distilled by Johann Caspar Schauer of Augsburg and supplied to the Salzburgers in many crates.

In addition to a physician, the Salzburgers badly needed a shoemaker, because the deep mud destroyed their shoes. Jacob Reck of Purysburg, who knew his job well and worked for fair wages, was a heavy drinker and set a bad example for the Salzburgers. Nevertheless, Boltzius agreed to let him move to Ebenezer and put his little boy in the school there; but Reck soon reverted to his evil ways, and he and his boy were sent packing. Reck was replaced by a Palatine named Salomo Adde, who had come over with Captain Thomson; but he too misbehaved and had to be removed. In the year 1739 a godly cobbler named Johann Caspar Ulich arrived and did excellent work and led a very Christian, but very short, life. Being unseasoned, he sickened at once, living only long enough to marry a shipmate before dying a few weeks later.

Today, when most shoes are factory made, it is hard to realize how essential a shoemaker was. Two Salzburger boys were apprenticed to David Tannenberger, the Moravian cobbler, but without satisfactory results. Young Matthias Zettler, who apprenticed himself to the ill-behaved shoemaker Reck in Purysburg, learned somewhat more, even though his master was drunk most of the time, overworked him, and made him go off to war. Tailors were also indispensable at a time when all clothes were custom-made. Herrnberger was a skillful tailor, but often sick, whereas Gottfried Christ, also usually sick, had learned the trade very badly. It is not surprising, therefore, that Boltzius constantly requested gifts of clothing for his poor parishioners.

Fortunately, Ebenezer had no lack of carpenters, the best being Georg Kogler, Georg Sanftleben, Stephan Rottenberger, and the clockmaker Müller. The Salzburgers acquired the smithy of a man who had run away from Abercorn, and one of their locksmiths undertook the job of smith. Although game abounded and was free for the taking, Boltzius refused the gift of a professional hunter who could have supplied much venison. The particular man may have been dissolute, but Boltzius's decision was probably influenced by his clerical prejudice against hunters and foresters, who were renowned as inveterate tipplers. Boltzius's aversion to hunters had derived from the Middle Ages, possibly in part because clergymen confused the two meanings of the word *venery* which are hunting and coitus. Despite this, the Moravians in Savannah had not been averse to accepting a gamekeeper named Peter Rose.

Like Nimrod, many of the archbishops of Salzburg had been mighty hunters before the Lord, and woe to any subject caught killing their game. This historical background may account for the Salzburgers' delay in profiting from the game available to them at Ebenezer, for they simply could not grasp their right to hunt. Except when passing Indians gave or sold them venison, they depended for a long time upon the unwholesome salted beef brought up from Savannah, sometimes from as far away as Pennsylvania or even Ireland. It is possible, of course, that they killed more game than they cared to report to Boltzius, or that he suppressed this information so that the benefactors in Europe would continue sending gifts. Only gradually do Boltzius's reports mention the taking of game, and several years elapsed before he mentioned that the Salzburgers had shot a hundred wild turkeys so far that season.

The Palatines in Savannah seem to have taken to hunting much more readily than the Salzburgers; but, if we may trust the English authorities, they most often went hunting at night to shoot other peoples' cattle. A tragedy occurred when two friends went out together and one man's musket fired accidentally and killed his companion. Fortunately, the authorities adjudged it was unintentional and made no charges. Another Dutch servant shot the only "tiger" mentioned in the colony's records. When he shot and wounded the beast, it turned on him and would have done him harm had the man's little dog not distracted it and held it off until the man could reload and fire again. Colonel Stephens's description of the animal reveals it as a puma or mountain lion, a nocturnal predator which, although never mentioned by the Salzburgers until much later, may have caused some of the loss of calves and hogs that was attributed to wolves and bears. Boltzius first mentioned a mountain lion in 1754, when a very destructive one had to be chased away with hounds.

The Salzburgers were also slow to catch fish, and no mention of them was made in the early years, even though the Savannah River abounded with sturgeon, shad, bream, eels, and other nourishing fish. Once, when Boltzius returned to Old Ebenezer, the English miller there drained the millrace and gave him a large string of "trout," which shows that even at that early date the largemouth black bass (*huro floridana*) was erroneously called trout, as it still is in the southeastern United States. When we read of the drab lives led by most of the inhabitants of Ebenezer, it is refreshing to read that the naughty Rheinländer boy and his Helfenstein playmate squandered much of their time in fishing; and it is pleasing to learn that later both became successful and useful citizens despite their indulgence in this worldly sport.

The most important progress made during 1738 was the further distribution and clearing of land. Although the new surveyor, Hugh Ross, frequently interrupted his work at Ebenezer for more rewarding work elsewhere, most of the Salzburgers received some property during the year, and many acquired fertile bottomland that was often flooded in winter and thus replenished with rich alluvial soil. As a result, the crops were sufficient for the Salzburgers' own use, even if there was little left for sale. Those who had sown yellow corn from Pennsylvania lost most of their crop, the foreign seed being unsuited to local conditions; but beans and rice were sufficient, even if damaged by the deer and rice birds.

Francis Moore, who acompanied the third transport to Savannah on his way to Frederica, visited Ebenezer two years later and had this to say of what he saw:

> Fifteen miles from Purysburgh, on the Georgia side, is Ebenezer, where the Saltzburghers are situated; their houses are neat and regularly set out in streets, and the whole economy of their town under the influence of their ministers, Messieurs Bolzius and Gronau, is very exemplary. For the benefit of their milch cattle, a herdsman is appointed to attend them in the woods all day, and bring them home in the evening. Their stock of outlying cattle is also under the care of two other

herdsmen, who attend them in their feeding in the day, and drive them into cow pens at night. This secures the owners from any loss, and the herdsmen are paid by a small contribution among the people. These are very industrious, and subsist very comfortably by their labor. Though there is no regular court of justice, as they live in sobriety, they maintain great order and decency. In case of any differences, the minister calls three or four of the most prudent elders together, who in a summary way hear and determine as they think just, and the parties always acquiesce with content in their judgment. They are very regular in their public worship, which is on week days in the evening after their work; and in the forenoon and evenings on Sunday. They have built a large and convenient house for the reception of orphans, and other poor children, who are maintained by benefactions among the people, and are well taken care of, and taught to work, according as their age and ability will permit. The number computed by Mr. Boltzius in June of 1738, whereof his congregation consisted, was one hundred and forty-six, and some more have since been settled among them. They are all in general so well pleased with their condition, that not one of their people has abandoned the settlement.

Although a bit rosy, this picture is more or less true, except that some of the congregation had left Ebenezer for Pennsylvania.

John Wesley, who had left Savannah so abruptly, was replaced by George Whitefield, a young clergyman of remarkable energy and rhetorical ability, who preferred the preaching circuit to staying home to tend his flock (plate 15). Emulating the Salzburgers, he founded an orphanage at Bethesda, near Savannah, for which he collected large sums of money on his preaching tours in England and the northern colonies, while a young schoolmaster, James Habersham, managed the orphanage. On his tours Whitefield also collected generous donations for the Salzburgers, which he faithfully brought to Ebenezer. Despite Whitefield's largess,

Hanns Klammer aus Bischoffshofen.

Ach Herr laß unsre Flucht im Winter nicht geschehen,
die war sonst meine Bitt und meiner Wünsche Ziel,
doch nun bin ich getrost im Winter auch zu gehen,
weil Gottes warme Lieb uns selbst bedecken will.

1. Salzburger exile with his son. (University of Georgia Libraries.)

Evangelium Iesu Christi Eruditio mea.

SAMUEL URLSPERGER,
Pastor ad D. Annæ et Ministerii Augustani
Senior.
Aᵒ 1723.

2. Samuel Urlsperger, Senior of the Lutheran ministry in Augsburg and Reverend Father of the Georgia Salzburgers. (University of Georgia Libraries.)

3. James Edward Oglethorpe, founder of Georgia and patron of the Georgia Salzburgers. (University of Georgia Libraries).

4. Map of coastal Georgia and South Carolina, from a German
engraving. As Boltzius quickly noted, New Ebenezer was omitted
and Old Ebenezer was wrongly placed.
(University of Georgia Libraries.)

5. Tomochichi and his nephew, whom the Salzburgers first saw in London.
(University of Georgia Libraries.)

6. *Facing page, top:* Uchi Indians passing through Ebenezer, from
von Reck's folio.
(Royal Library of Denmark.)

7. *Facing page, bottom:* Indian camp, as illustrated in von Reck's folio.
(Royal Library of Denmark.)

Indianer welche auf die Jagd gehen. Fig.

Indians going a hunting

1 Ein Indianer mit Bauast die Graß.
2 Ein Bündel worinn allerhand Provision auf Reiß dienen rc.
3 Indianisch Weib.
4 Ein wollenes Deck wie eine Pferd Deck.
5 Ein Bündel worinn allerhand gerät damit und Küssel Geschirr als Pfannen Töpfel rc.
6 Ein Bouteille worinn Sie darinnen Öhl oder Bärenschmer mit sich führen.
7 Indianische Camaschu wie niedt Reisen dann ein Pferd Deck um die Bauch wickeln.
8 Indianische Schug oder ein Stück Leder worüber auf Sie Füß zuschnüren und tretten.
9 Ein Indian Spieß und ein Camaschu guter Ehr gehen.
10 Ein Schlaf Decke.

Ein Indianisch Lager wie sie solches machen wenn sie auf der Jagd sind, ist manchmal völlig und manchmal. Fig.

A Indian Camp.

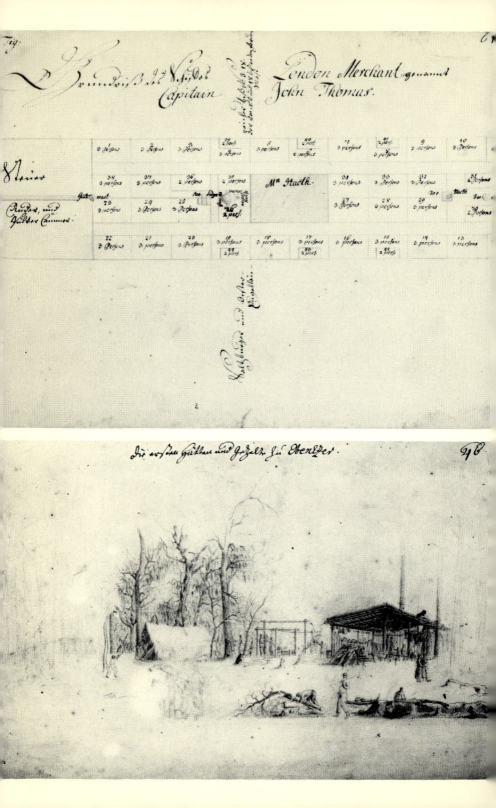

Grundriß B. des Schiffes London Merchant genannt
Capitain John Thomas.

8 Reÿen

Rieder und Felder Commer

1 persons	2 persons	3 persons	4 persons	5 persons	6 persons	7 persons	8 persons	9 persons	10 persons
38 persons	37 persons	36 persons	35 persons	Mr. Hacth	34 persons	33 persons	32 persons	31 persons	
25 persons	24 persons	26 persons	26 2 pers			27 persons	28 persons	29 persons	30 persons
22 persons	21 persons	20 persons	9 persons	18 persons	17 persons	16 persons	15 persons	14 persons	13 persons

Die erste Hütten und Gezelt zu Ebenezer.

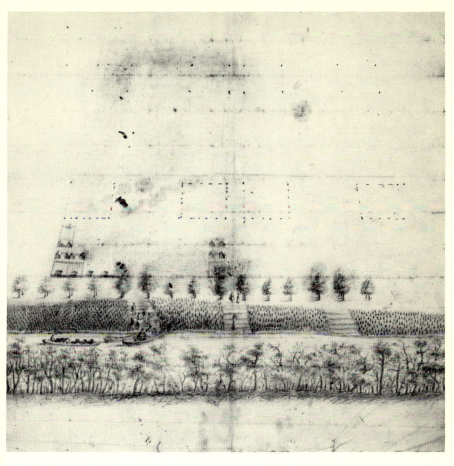

8. *Facing page, top:* Living quarters aboard the *London Merchánt*, from von Reck's folio. (Royal Library of Denmark.)

9. *Facing page, bottom:* The first shelters on the Red Bluff, from von Reck's folio. The original is in color. (Royal Library of Denmark.)

10. Earliest sketch of New Ebenezer, from von Reck's folio. (Royal Library of Denmark.)

11. Indian busk, or harvest dance, from von Reck's folio. The original is in color. (Royal Library of Denmark.)

12. *Bottom right*, Thomas Causton's barge aided by a rowboat; *top right*, bottom view of barge; *top left*, type of boat used by the Indian traders. (British Public Record Office.)

Urlsperger deleted his name from Boltzius's reports, apparently because Whitefield had embraced the wicked doctrine of *decretum absolutum,* or predestination, as taught by the Calvinists.

Whereas the German settlers in America appear to have been generally more literate than the English and much more literate than the Highlanders, some of the Salzburgers were deficient because the archbishops had discouraged the dangerous art of reading, which might tempt them to read scripture and heretical books. Because edifying books are profitable for the soul, Boltzius introduced adult education courses for the culturally deprived; and several adults made good progress in this spiritually (and economically) productive skill. Second in popularity only to the Bible was Johannes Arndt's *Four Books of True Christianity,* a massive volume found in almost every German home in colonial America and among the first books printed in Philadelphia.

Boltzius and Gronau continued their ministry in Savannah, where Boltzius often took the side of the Trustees against the indentured Germans; for, being a good Lutheran, he tended to uphold the authorities and to agree with St. Paul's admonition to the Romans: "Let every soul be subject unto the higher powers. For there is no power but of God: the powers that be are ordained of God." Boltzius believed that if God put a wicked or cruel superior over someone, it was surely to punish that person for his sins. On one occasion Boltzius greatly embittered the German community in Savannah. When a German servant went hunting instead of working for his master, Mr. Causton, Causton summoned the constable John Fallowfield to arrest him, which Fallowfield could do only by clubbing him on the head with the handle of his leather riding crop. The next morning the unnamed servant was found dead in his cell in a puddle of vomit. At the inquest, Thilo agreed with the coroner that the man had not died of the beating, but suffocated in the vomit. When the widow and other Germans would not accept this reasoning, Oglethorpe required Boltzius to handle his delicate public relations for him. This was a thankless task, for even many of the English considered the death unjustifiable. Thomas Stephens, the son of the Trustees' secretary, wrote on 24 November 1739 that the bailiff Fallowfield "had no Reason to strike that German that died, because Several People were at hand, whom the law directed him to command to his Assistance, in Case the man had not been obedt."

Despite his humiliating confrontation with Boltzius in the spring of 1736, when the minister extorted permission to remove his people to the Red Bluff, Oglethorpe had remained a good friend of the Salzburgers and had helped them to the best of his ability. This is understandable: the Salzburgers at Ebenezer and the Highlanders at Darien were the only proof he had that white men could prosper in Georgia without slaves. Despite his busy schedule, Oglethorpe visited Ebenezer several times. On an important mission to the Creek Indians in 1739, he stopped off in Ebenezer and devoted half a day to settling a dispute between Boltzius and the Ortmanns, showing the same patient understanding in this trivial matter that he was wont to show in his important negotiations with the Indians.

With the original settlers somewhat "seasoned" and with sufficient land allotted and cleared, the year 1739 may be considered a new beginning for the Salzburgers. The people were not only industrious, but thrifty, unlike other inhabitants of Georgia, who were mostly in debt. Since settlers in America usually arrived impecunious and in debt for their passage, they had to borrow money to get started, normally at ten percent, and often remained crushed by debts. The Salzburgers, on the other hand, insisted on paying cash, much to the surprise and dismay of the moneylending merchants of Purysburg and Savannah. Moreover, they spent their precious money almost exclusively for cattle, with the result that by the summer of 1739 they owned 250 head. The Koglers, who had not owned a single cow in Salzburg, now had fourteen, as well as other livestock. All heifers were kept for milking and breeding, some calves were kept for breeding, some were altered and trained as work oxen, a few were sold in Savannah, and only a very few were slaughtered for local consumption. The Salzburgers could not yet afford the luxury of veal or beef.

Because of the economic advances, Boltzius at last found some time for the niceties of life. Having previously founded a singing club (*Collegium Musicum*) in Halle, Boltzius was musically trained and could write musical notes; and one of his great regrets was that he could never afford an organ for his church. Although dour and opposed to frivolity, he agreed with Luther that music is a proper offering to God. Consequently, as soon as Thilo arrived with a good bass voice, Boltzius introduced polyphonic singing into the church. However, before the children were allowed to participate, they had to assure him that they were bringing their hearts as well as their voices and that the singing was not for worldly enjoyment but purely an offering to God. Polyphonic music was of course well advanced at the English court, where Boltzius's compatriot Georg Friedrich Händel was then flourishing; yet it does not seem to have been popular in the American colonies, at least not in Georgia. After hearing the Germans sing, one of the English officials is purported to have said, "The Dutch are peculiar people. When four Englishmen sing together, they sing the same song, but when four Dutch sing together, they sing four different songs."

The most important single event of the year 1739 was the return of Georg Sanftleben, a carpenter of the second transport who had gone home to Silesia to fetch his sister and to recruit other unmarried women and tradesmen. Their voyage on the *Charles,* under Captain Haeramond, had been uneventful as far as Charleston; but on the way from there to Savannah they all sickened, and two soon died. The previously mentioned shoemaker Ulich married Margaretha Egger two weeks after his arrival and three weeks before his death; and Gertraut Lackner, the sister of Martin Lackner of Ebenezer, died slowly and miserably, after first persuading Ulich's widow to marry her brother. Seeing how grotesquely hideous the dying woman had become by the end of her protracted illness, Boltzius made the tactless observation that people should look at her to see how ugly sin is. He was not, of course, implying that she was sinful, for she died a very sanctified death, yet she was still as ugly as sin.

Another important event of the year 1739 was the construction of a parsonage for Boltzius, which was built by the congregation with the assistance of £40 from Oglethorpe, who may have had pangs about making Boltzius leave all the lumber of his previous parsonage behind in Old Ebenezer. Boltzius was most grateful for this house and used it for numerous communal purposes; yet, when Heinrich Melchior Mühlenberg, who will be mentioned shortly, visited Ebenezer thirty-five years later, he was surprised at how modest the little dwelling was.

Returning to Ebenezer on 25 June 1740, the benefactor George Whitefield wrote into his journal:

> Went on Monday to, and returned this evening from Ebenezer, which I have seen with no small satisfaction. Surely there is a difference, even in this life, between those that serve the Lord, and those that serve Him not. All other places of the colony seem to be like Egypt, where was darkness, but Ebenezer, like the land of Goshen, wherein was great light. For near four miles did I walk in almost one continued field, with a most plentiful crop of corn, pease, potatoes, etc. growing upon it,—all the products of a few months' labour. But God blesses the labourers; they are unanimous; the strong

help the weak and all seem hearty for the common good. In a few years the Saltzburghers, I believe, will be a flourishing people. Their land is good, and before long, will be capable of providing raiment for themselves. I shall send them up cotton, spinning wheels, and a loom to begin a manufactory for themselves; and next year they hope their own land will produce enough flax, cotton, etc. to carry it on. I had communications with their ministers. Our sister Orphan House is there, is blessed by their means. Yesterday was set apart as a day of thanksgiving for assistance sent the orphans from Germany and Savannah. The people seemed very grateful. They willingly received me into their clean little huts, and seemed proud when I accepted any thing from their hands. As I said formerly, so I say again, they who help the Saltzburghers will do a good work. They want assistance. Lord, raise them up benefactors.

An engraving made in Augsburg at about this time (plate 17), probably a bit optimistic, shows that Ebenezer had increased considerably in size.

Whitefield's favorable view was shared by Thomas Jones, who had been installed as the new keeper of the storehouse in Savannah after Causton had been recalled to London to justify his accounts. On 18 September 1740 Jones wrote:

> Having mentioned Darien, which is a Town inhabited by the Highland Scotch, under the Care of Mr. McCloud, the People live very comfortably, with great Unanimity; I know of no other Settlement in this Colony more desirable, except Ebenezer, a Town on the River Savannah, at 35 Miles Distance from hence, inhabited by Saltzburghers and other Germans, under the pastoral Care of Mr. Boltzius and Mr. Gronau, who are discreet, worthy Men; they consist of 60 Families or upwards.—The Town is neatly built, the Situation exceeding pleasant, the People live in the greatest Harmony with their Ministers, and with one another, as one Family; they have no idle, drunken, or profligate People among them, but are industrious, many grown wealthy; and their Industry hath been

blessed with remarkable and uncommon Success, to the Envy of their Neighbours, having great Plenty of all the necessary Conveniences for Life (except Cloathing) within themselves and supply this Town and other neighboring Places with Bread Kind, as also Beef, Veal, Pork, Poultry, &c.

As Boltzius well knew and often reported to his superiors, the Salzburgers' belated success was owed primarily to private enterprise, which had succeeded where their earlier communal endeavor had failed. Col. William Stephens, the elderly gentleman sent over as the Trustees' representative, soon shared Boltzius's view on private enterprise. On 21 November 1739 he wrote that "the Palatine servants sent over from Holland on board Capt. Hewet are the most lazy of all, but those which went with Capt. Thomson are good, and would have done well, if immediately on their arrival they had been made free, a little land given them, and a tolerable support in the beginning." This, as we shall see, later became the Trustees' policy. The rule to be learned was that human beings seldom work well if they do not profit from their labor.

Once the Salzburgers owned their own land and cattle, progress was rapid, for, as Swiss farmers had discovered long before, cattle fatten best under their master's eye (*Dein selbers aug daz vich macht faiss*). Despite the difficulties incidental to frontier life, many of the Salzburgers had "grown wealthy," to use Thomas Jones's somewhat exaggerated expression. As previously mentioned, Georg Kogler owned fourteen head of cattle besides other livestock. The incentive to clear land also increased as the Trustees became less stringent in enforcing the unpopular law of tail-male, thus making it possible for a man to bequeath his land to his wife or daughters. The obnoxious law was officially rescinded in March 1742.

Despite their desire to work independently, the Salzburgers were still rural enough, and Christian enough, to look out for each other too, as we see from their willing support of the orphanage. Whitefield was to the point when he wrote, "They are unanimous; the strong help the weak, and all seem hearty for the common good." This sense of communal loyalty was splendidly manifest in 1740 in the building of the grist mill on Ebenezer Creek, a feat not equaled elsewhere in colonial Georgia and worthy of an excellent etching by the celebrated engraver Tobias Conrad Lotter of Augsburg, which was printed in 1747 by Matthäus Seuter of that city (plate 16). Needless to say, this cooperation was furthered by Boltzius, who, through Christian and economic arguments, persuaded the church builders to be content with modest wages and used similar arguments later with regard to the mill.

The construction of the mill posed a dilemma for Boltzius. A clergyman devoted to God rather than to Mammon should have put church construction first, especially since Whitefield's contributions had been collected specifically for that purpose. On the other hand, Oglethorpe was urging the Salzburgers to plant wheat, barley, rye, and oats, grains which were of little use to them so long as they had no mill. Putting economic necessity before religious obligation, Boltzius interrupted church construction (after token work to pacify Whitefield) and directed all efforts toward the mill. His chief workers, such as the master-builder Kogler, received "just" wages, whereas the rank and file, with the exception of Josef Ernst and Michael Rieser, contributed their efforts in return for future use of the mill. Work on both projects was discontinued during the spring planting season.

Whereas fieldwork at Ebenezer, unless communal, was usually performed by the proprietor himself, there was one case of an economic system that was later to play a baneful role in Georgia history, that of the previously mentioned sharecropping agreement between the clockmaker Müller and a Palatine redemptioner named Martin Kaesemeyer,

59

who had come over with Captain Thomson. Being an "old" man of about fifty and too weak to work his land, Müller shared it with the landless Palatine in return for half the crop. In this case, however, social and economic equality survived, since Müller's son, Johann Paul, helped the share-cropper in his work. Incidentally, sharecropping does not appear to have been a German custom.

Another evil soon to be inflicted upon Georgia was already in the offing, namely, the slavery that was still illegal but was being advocated by the Malcontents, a group of disgruntled inhabitants in Savannah, mostly Lowland Scots (41). It is sometimes pointed out that Boltzius's objections to slavery (all of which proved valid) were chiefly of a practical rather than a moral nature, since he argued that slavery was uneconomic and dangerous, as he did, for example, in his entries for 23 April and 14 July of 1740. But it should be remembered that his arguments were usually aimed at the British authorities, who, he assumed, would be more receptive to worldly reasons. His entry for 20 July of the same year proves that he considered slavery morally as well as economically wrong.

When the Georgia Trustees held up Ebenezer as proof that white men could subsist in Georgia without African slaves, the Malcontents countered that the Salzburgers were "yearly supported from Germany and England." To this the Earl of Egmont, the leader of the Trustees, rejoined that "their friends may make them presents but they support themselves." There was some truth in the Malcontents' claims, for the Salzburgers did receive funds for building their parsonages, church, and orphanage, to say nothing of liberal donations of clothing. In this regard, 1740 was a banner year. Whitefield arrived in Savannah on 11 January bearing gifts for Ebenezer, which were duly itemized in Boltzius's entry for 16 January, namely, foodstuffs, clothing, £73 18 *s.*, a bell, and a barrel of hardware for the church. On 8

February the congregation received a large chest that had been dispatched two years earlier from Halle and had been lost en route; and on 19 May they received another crate that had been intended for Lutheran missions in Cuddalore, India, but had been misdirected to Ebenezer. A third crate, apparently even larger, arrived on 3 August. These chests held linens, books, and medicines.

The various sums received, including the ministers' stipends, circulated in Ebenezer and served as an economic catalyst, changing hands many times before leaving the community, because the frugal Salzburgers bought little from outside except cattle. However much sacrifice these donations may have cost the charitable donors in Germany and England, they were only a small fringe benefit in comparison to the hard work the Salzburgers themselves performed. It would have been far better for them if they had settled on healthy and fertile land in Pennsylvania or western Maryland without any benefactions.

ᓂ 4 ᓂ

War and Peace

ot so near home as the new grist mill, but potentially far more important, was Oglethorpe's siege of St. Augustine, the Spanish bastion in Florida, of which Boltzius gives interesting secondhand reports. Although these reports tell us nothing new about the campaign, they do show us how it affected his little community. Like the mill, the war posed a dilemma for Boltzius. A naturalized British subject and protégé of Oglethorpe should have supported the British offensive; and the leader of a band of expelled Protestants should have welcomed a chance to take Florida from His Most Catholic Majesty of Spain. However, as a native of war-torn central Europe, Boltzius knew that military life brutalized enlisted men. Officers, often from noble families, were gentlemen who practiced a code of chivalry amongst themselves, whereas the enlisted men, unless draftees, were usually from the lowest level of society and acted accordingly. On 12 April Boltzius expressed this view about military service: "Righteous people do not let themselves be used for this purpose; but rather those who like to roam around and find pleasure in such a life."

Because of Boltzius's stand against military service, only one Salzburger, Gabriel Bach, volunteered, as did two Austrians, Josef Leitner and Peter Reiter. The young apprentice

Matthias Zettler was required to go by his master, the non-commissioned cobbler Reck. It was primarily the redemptioners who saw a chance to free themselves from servitude in the short period of four months, instead of in an equal number of years. It is for this reason that the three orphanage servants, to wit, the English boy Robinson, who had already served five of his nine years of indenture, and the two Palatines, father and son Held, volunteered. It was beyond Boltzius's comprehension that his servants would jeopardize body and soul to win their freedom, apparently unaware of the indignity attached to servitude.

Jacob Reck, the hard-drinking cobbler of Purysburg, had become a noncommissioned officer in Jacques Richard's polyglot South Carolina battalion. He was none too discriminating on 21 April when he accepted the Swiss inhabitant Bartholomäus Zant, who had been almost totally blind the previous year, and the consumptive Jewish convert Johann Gottfried Christ, who was still coughing blood. He soon lost the latter when some pious women dissuaded him from serving and refunded his bonus money. Recruiting was also active in Savannah, as is revealed in the journal of Colonel Stephens, the Trustees' new secretary in Georgia. On 24 April Stephens wrote, "Enlisting Men was now the principal Affair in hand; which had drained the Town, that it was hard to find a Man more to enter." The shortage of able-bodied men in Savannah explains the impudence of Major Richard's soldiers there in impressing one of Gronau's Salzburger rowers into service, as recorded by Boltzius on 9 and 14 May.

Gabriel Bach had enlisted in a pique when Boltzius required his fiancée, Margaret Staud, to perform humiliating church penance before letting them marry. Penance had been done on 3 February, and they were duly married on 4 February; but by then it was too late for Bach to obtain his release, even if he really wished to. He quickly became a skilled and renowned ranger and was one of the first casualties when hostilities began. Boltzius reported on 4 June that Bach had been beheaded by the Indians and that Oglethorpe had retrieved the head and sent it in a box to the governor of St. Augustine with the warning that if he would not restrain his Indians the same fate would be suffered by all Spanish prisoners. This was hypocritical of Oglethorpe, who had had his bloodthirsty Indians attacking Spaniards for a long time.

Bach was Boltzius's only parishioner killed in action. The older Held died of fever on the campaign, and Leonhard Rauner died of dysentery on the way home. Six others, Zant, Robinson, Held, Jr., Leitner, Reiter, and Zettler, returned in varying degrees of ill health. A tenth cannot be identified, unless it was the old schoolmaster Ortmann, who had been a Royal Marine, or else Rauner's wife, who had wished to accompany her husband if only Boltzius would keep her children at the orphanage in her absence. In the eighteenth century women were recruited along with men, and the German woman Maria Ludwig, better known as Molly Pitcher, was not the only woman to serve in Washington's ranks. Boltzius seems to have been almost pleased with the tragic results (tragic, of course, only in a worldly sense but spiritually very salutary), for they confirmed his predictions that the campaign would be a costly affair. However, even though he had tried to dissuade his parishioners from going to war, he saved their donations of linen for them during their absence and later allowed the survivors to settle again in Ebenezer.

It seems that Boltzius made all such decisions himself, for among his many duties were those of administering justice and maintaining law and order. Maintaining law and order meant not only punishing infractions but also anticipating misunderstandings. For example, in April of 1740 he required Elisabeth Sanftleben to postpone her marriage to Hans Michael Schneider, one of the Palatine herdsmen, until her former fiancé, Andreas Grimmiger, renounced all claims on her. It is possible that Grimmiger had already planned to marry the widow Bischoff, as he did in June, but it was still wise of Boltzius to take this precaution. The congregation seems to have accepted the pastor's judgment willingly, knowing full well that he was able, as he often warned, to request a "justiciar" to represent the authorities in temporal affairs. Such a man would surely have been more severe than the benign cleric, for "It's good living under the crozier" (*Unter dem Krummstab ist gut leben*).

It was exceptional when, on 21 June 1740, Boltzius sent an incorrigible thief to Savannah for punishment rather than try him in Ebenezer, as the divine had tried Grimmiger for stealing five pounds from his fellow Austrian Johann Pletter. Three years elapsed after the theft before someone recognized a tool in Grimmiger's hand as one that had disappeared from Pletter's chest along with the five pounds. Knowing his guilt had been discovered, Grimmiger fled across the Savannah River but became lost in the woods, where he nearly died of thirst and exhaustion before being found. After Grimmiger had confessed, repented, and served his very mild sentence, he was welcomed back into the community and no one was allowed to refer to the incident again. It is even probable that the widow Bischoff did not know she was marrying a former thief.

The same tolerance was shown to Margaretha Bach: once she had publicly confessed her sin of whoredom, it was officially consigned to oblivion. Margaretha had cohabited with a fellow redemptioner in Savannah until Boltzius interrupted their common-law marriage, which had been ignored by the more tolerant British authorities, since they, according to the elderly Stephens, often had "housekeepers" of their own. Not long after the Spanish Indians killed her husband Bach, she was married to the pious Christian Leinberger and lived to be the respectable proprietress of a slave plantation.

All in all, 1741 was a productive year. The mill, already completed, had encouraged the planting of hard "European" grains such as wheat, rye, and oats, especially after plow horses were acquired in July and August and after the first plow was constructed in October. A barrel of flour sent to Oglethorpe on 7 January seems to have been well spent, for he soon persuaded the Trustees to refund the £77 spent on the mill and thus contributed greatly to Ebenezer's mercantilistic economy. This was a timely blessing, since high water had caused extensive damage to the millrace and necessitated considerable repair such as raising its walls one foot. Indian corn remained, however, the main crop; and a fair harvest was gathered despite the damage done by worms early in the growing season. Corn was scarce elsewhere in Georgia, partly because many men had abandoned their fields to fight at St. Augustine.

Cattle raising was still the most successful enterprise at Ebenezer, cattle being sent down to Savannah on 14 January, 23 February, and 13 May of 1741 and no doubt at other times too. Already by 3 January a barn had been erected in the Salzburg manner. Unfortunately, Boltzius did not tell enough about it to indicate whether it influenced later barn building in Georgia as much as the Pennsylvania German barns influenced those built in the eastern and middle western states. On May 11 of this year, Georgia welcomed a new industry, that of raising silkworms and spinning silk. Encouraged by a generous subsidy, this undertaking subsequently throve among the Salzburgers and endeared them to the English authorities and also brought modest returns to the widows and girls entrusted with the work (58). On 30 November Oglethorpe contributed £5 for twelve-hundred white mulberry trees, of which each family received thirty-two.

Despite Whitefield's impatient urging throughout the previous year, church construction had been postponed in favor of the mill; but in 1741 a place of worship was finally finished, even though its construction had often been subordinated to the more pressing needs of repairing the mill and cultivating the fields. Jerusalem Church, which was consecrated on 20 November 1741, was the first of any denomination in Georgia, for even the Anglicans in Savannah had to worship in a structure built for secular purposes such as holding court. Boltzius and Gronau continued their ministry with their usual devotion regardless of much sickness. They, particularly Gronau, also preached regularly to the Palatines in Savannah. There, for the first time, they had to cope with black magic, which surprisingly was practiced not by the Germans but by the French, only the victim, a Palatine named Johann Georg Dressler, being German.

Like most ministers, Boltzius was burdened with both consoling and controlling his parishioners in their domestic problems. When Kieffer's daughter, Elisabeth Catherina, wished to break her engagement to the young shoemaker Matthias Zettler on 24 April, he helped the parents dissuade her. On the other hand, he had been less successful when Kieffer's daughter-in-law, Anna Elisabeth Depp, had wished to run away to her mother in Orangeburg, S.C., on 17 March. Little did he realize her reason, being unaware that she had been carrying the child of a Charleston shoemaker when she married Johann Jacob Kieffer; and it is strange that he said so little even after suspecting her of purposely aborting the unwanted child. Another scandal vexed him when a German woman named Elisabeth Penner, who had run away from Frederica, confessed to God and Boltzius that her pregnancy had been caused by William Norris, the Anglican minister at Frederica who had been cleared of the malicious accusation that he had been familiar with a German servant girl.

Equally sordid was the ordeal of two young German redemptioners at Augusta, the children of Boltzius's late and faithful Palatine servant Peter Heinrich, who had been maltreated and sexually abused by two Negro slaves with the connivance, and even the encouragement, of their master. Because the sister cried out for help when about to be raped, her master had her stripped, hung up by the wrists, and thrashed. Hearing of this cruelty, the compassionate Colonel Stephens had the children brought down to Savannah and cared for in his own house before freeing them and sending them back to their family in Ebenezer. The two Negroes, but not their voyeur owner, were brought down at the same time in chains for punishment; but they broke out of jail despite their heavy fetters and escaped to South Carolina, from which the authorities refused to extradite them.

Boltzius's greatest anxiety during this momentous year of 1741 was his fear of wholesale desertion. Having resided three or more years in Georgia, most of the inhabitants of Ebenezer were legally free to quit the colony. Therefore it was hard to hold back some of the discontented souls by appealing to their sense of gratitude to God and the English authorities. So far, Stephan Riedelsperger and Hans Michael Muggitzer had been the only real Salzburgers to steal away; Thomas Bichler of the second transport, whose name appears as Pichler in the earlier records, had planned to accompany Riedelsperger to Pennsylvania at the instigation of his sick wife, who was sure she would die if she remained longer in Ebenezer. Boltzius had, however, persuaded him to stay, whereupon the wife proved her point by dying. Now the Landfelders, the Michael Riesers, and the Spielbieglers, all of whom had sojourned in Memmingen, were secretly planning to depart, having been tempted by an enticing letter from Muggitzer in New York. Rieser's intention to leave Ebenezer seems to explain why he had refused to do his share of the work on the mill. Word of mass desertion would surely have discouraged further immigration to Ebenezer and would also have cooled the ardor of the benefactors of Ebenezer in Europe; consequently, Boltzius reminded the intended deserters that they would have to leave behind them all gifts from the Trustees, including their cattle and tools. Later, while working as a bricklayer in Charleston, Johann Spielbiegler swore out an affidavit that the tyrant Boltzius had robbed him of his property. In former years Boltzius had implied that only his non-Salzburger parishioners were causing him woe, but now he often admitted faults in the real Salzburgers, too.

Sickness still prevailed in 1741, and malaria struck again; in fact, the previous year's quartan fever had lasted all winter. While the older inhabitants had become partially seasoned and could bear their illnesses somewhat better, new arrivals, like the Kaesemeyers, were quickly prostrated. In addition to the usual sicknesses, the Salzburgers suffered the kinds of accidents incidental to frontier life, not the least of which was the dislocated hip suffered by Peter Reiter when a bear he shot in a tree fell and landed on him. The surgeon in Purysburg subjected him to the most dreadful tortures, "Negro-cures" as they were called, before the injury finally healed.

As in other years, Boltzius continued his feud against the Moravians in Savannah, as we see from his letter of 17 April 1741 condemning them. Although he never denounced his benefactor Whitefield for embracing the infamous dogma of predestination (*ex absoluto decreto*), he did combat that heresy in a theological dispute with Habersham and Barber, the manager and the chaplain at Whitefield's Bethesda orphanage. The Salzburgers continued to accept generous gifts from Whitefield, yet Urlsperger still deleted the donor's name. During this year Whitefield was relieved of his ministry in Savannah, not because of his Calvinist heresy, but because he was too often absent from Georgia preaching and collecting money in England and the northern colonies. He was replaced as Anglican minister by Mr. Christopher Orton, who promptly died.

Boltzius maintained his cordial relations with the British authorities, especially after the Trustees promoted their pious old secretary Stephens to the position of President of the Council on 7 October 1741; and he wholeheartedly backed the Trustees against the Malcontents, who wished to subvert the Trustees' idealistic plans for Georgia (41). Boltzius opposed the introduction of slavery not only because of economic theories and moral principles, but also because he saw the difficulties Kieffer was having with his slaves. One of Kieffer's slaves had committed suicide, and one had escaped. A third had been captured while trying to escape, but his feet had to be amputated, purportedly because of frostbite but more probably because they had been bound too tightly. During 1741 the Salzburgers again received not only liberal monetary gifts from England but also several large chests of books, clothes, and utensils from well-wishers in Germany.

In 1739 the Salzburgers had requested that a fourth transport be sent to Ebenezer, where there was now sufficient food for their support. Word arrived on 2 May 1741 that they were coming, and loving preparations were made for housing and feeding them until their own fields would maintain them. The newcomers arrived in Georgia safely on 2 December after a quick and relatively easy voyage on the *Loyal Judith,* under Captain John Lemon, having suffered little sickness and no deaths en route, in contrast to the poor Swiss who crossed at the same time on the *Europa,* under John Wadham, and lost a quarter of their number on the way and another quarter soon after their arrival.

This fourth and last Salzburger transport had been recruited in various towns of southern Germany, mostly in Württemberg, where the Salzburgers had found refuge after being expelled from their homeland and where many had found employment but little chance of advancement. When we read that a certain inhabitant of Ebenezer was from Lindau or Memmingen or some other Swabian city, this does not mean he was not a Salzburger; it probably means that he had sojourned in that city after leaving Salzburg and before departing for Georgia. By referring to him as being from that city, Boltzius was able to identify him for the inhabitants there who had supported or employed him during his stay. It will be noted that the exiles who had sojourned in the same town often remained united even after reaching Ebenezer. Very probably they were most often groups of relatives or friends who had stopped off together in the same town and had therefore already shared ties and commitments.

Whereas the earlier Salzburgers had been mostly farmers, the fourth transport had sojourned long enough in the south German cities to learn various urban skills and trades, which were most needed in Ebenezer. Being sufficiently burdened by their own indigent, the mayors and town councils encouraged their Salzburger guests to accept the opportunity of the better life that Ebenezer seemed to offer. Led as far as London by Johann von Müllern and the rest of the way by Johann Friedrich Vigera, this expedition was well planned and skillfully conducted by the two commissioners, who kept a detailed diary of their journey (31). When the fourth and last Salzburger transport reached Ebenezer on 3 December, Kalcher served them a fatted ox instead of the biblical fatted calf.

As seen from the Salzburgers' perspective, in the year 1741 God showed His great works in many ways: He erected a temple to His glory, He gave a bountiful harvest to His chosen people, and He brought the fourth transport safely across the ocean. But, to judge by the space Boltzius allocated to it in his journal, God's greatest work was the humbling of a impenitent sinner. Josef Ernst, like the wicked Georg Bartholomäus Roth before him, had been the villain of the community, questioning God's will and Boltzius's authority. But God is not mocked, as Boltzius often warned his congregation. Ernst dislocated his thumb, which Thilo and the surgeon in Purysburg could not set with even the most torturous methods used earlier on Reiter; and already by 13 March the thumb was unusable. Gangrene had set in, and by the time Boltzius agreed that surgery was necessary, too much time had elapsed and the hand had to be amputated four inches from the armpit. This divine chastisement opened Ernst's eyes to his perdition and his danger of eternal damnation, a bit of which he had already experienced; soon he was asking Boltzius for spiritual help. Boltzius accompanied him to Purysburg for the amputation and stood by him in his ordeal. The operation was a success, but complications arose and the patient died, apparently of pneumonia. If we may trust Boltzius, the poor sinner died truly penitent and forgiven, and for this shining example of God's merciful chastisement and forgiveness Boltzius had to pay £11 medical fees.

The Salzburgers' major task in 1742 was integrating the fourth transport into the Ebenezer community. Whereas the earlier transports had tended to be clannish, marriages soon occurred with the newcomers. Theobald Kieffer, Jr., now a resident of Ebenezer, married Maria, the widowed daughter of Matthäus Bacher; and the Palatine herdsman Hans Michael Held, who had obtained a good plantation after returning from St. Augustine, married the widow Kunlin, whose husband had died immediately upon his arrival.

The older inhabitants' kindness toward their friends and kinsmen of the fourth transport was rewarded, for the latter proved a financial benefit. Instead of the provisions given the earlier settlers, they received cash support amounting to £6 per man and only a little less for each woman. To be sure, a good deal of this they saved for buying cattle; yet some was spent in Ebenezer for food and shelter, and this new cash stimulated the economy. Besides that, the fourth transport brought gifts from Augsburg and Württemberg for themselves and for the older inhabitants. Boltzius not only distributed these most conscientiously, giving the clothes mostly to the established inhabitants and the iron tools to the new settlers, but also recorded all these numerous gifts, along with the names of the recipients, so that the donors might see how their gifts had been distributed. Whereas Urlsperger, and even the Trustees and their representatives, sometimes covered up or altered unhappy information, there is one type of report on which we can rely with confidence, namely, financial records. All expenditures, both charitable donations and government grants, are fully recorded and preserved, often in duplicate, in English and German. Because of accountability, these reports had to be accurate, with the result that even today a patient auditor could reconstruct nearly all the Salzburgers' financial transactions.

Later in the year 1742 a Salzburger named Matthäus Kurtz arrived with his family, having been sent to Georgia by the Trustees after spending years of misery in Holland and England. These were the last Salzburgers to reach Ebenezer; after them came only Palatines, as all German immigrants were then called, or else German Swiss, and, still later, Swabians. Among the so-called Palatines who joined the Salzburgers in 1742 was the previously mentioned Swiss widow Magdalena Meyer, who found employment at the orphanage while her young daughter Ursula took in sewing and cared for an infant. Gottfried Christ, the consumptive convert, married the widowed daughter of the Palatine tailor Jacob Metzger of Purysburg and brought her and her three young children to Ebenezer. One of these, a bright and willing little girl, could walk only on her knees, apparently as a consequence of rickets. Johann Georg Dressler, who had been the innocent victim of the recent witchcraft in Savannah, was now well established in Ebenezer and proving invaluable as a mill expert. Johann Georg Meyer, the younger brother of the Swabian surgeon with the fourth transport, had been discontented with Ebenezer at first, but he soon came to like it and settled there and married Magdalena Roner, also of the fourth transport.

The most stirring event of 1742 in Georgia was Oglethorpe's repulse of the Spanish invaders at the battle of Bloody Marsh near Frederica; yet Boltzius scarcely mentions this great victory. Being off the beaten path and trusting in God's providence, the Salzburgers seem hardly to have realized that an English defeat would mean the end of their settlement, for the Spanish commander had strict orders to devastate the entire colony. Whereas Boltzius had not supported Oglethorpe's offensive against the Spaniards, he seems to have approved of self-defense, if we may believe a letter written by William Ewen, a neighbor of the Salzburgers, on 21 August at the very height of the Spanish alarm: "Mr. Boltzius offer'd his People to come down with what arms they had there, and Join the English and Dutch that were in Savannah, they would then have made about two hundred, men, who under the conduct of a good Commander might have repulsed six or seven hundred of the enemy, if any had come."

Despite this willingness to defend his new homeland, Boltzius made almost no reference to the war in his journal until a flood of refugees from Frederica filled all the houses in Ebenezer and proved a great burden. The refugees' assumption that they would be housed and fed was Boltzius's first acquaintance with the obligation of "Southern hospitality." The Salzburgers seem to have been more afraid of the savages, especially after Spanish Indians captured Fort Venture on the Savannah River and massacred the English captain's German wife and their children and after Creek and Uchee Indians began killing each other near Ebenezer.

Boltzius opened his journal for the year 1742 with the report that, during the previous year, twenty-four children had been baptized, two men and four small children had died, and six couples had been married, thus suggesting that the seasoned Salzburgers could at last cope with the climate. The fourth transport, on the other hand, fared less well. Despite their unusually healthy crossing and the care and shelter furnished by the older inhabitants, they soon sickened and suffered almost the same rate of mortality as the first arrivals. In the month of August alone Johannes Maurer, Johann Paul Müller, Simon Rieser, Veit Lechner, Johann Scheffler, and Johann Schwartzwälder, recently of Old Ebenezer, all lost their wives; and many children died too, as did some children of the older settlers. Müller replaced his wife with another in a very few weeks, the haste probably necessitated by having a sickly infant in need of care.

The only unusual injury during the year was the snakebite suffered by Ruprecht Steiner, who fortunately survived the cure: he was buried up to the chin, naked, to draw out the poison. Ever since the Garden of Eden, snakes have aroused fear and superstition. The Salzburgers were no exception, living as they did amidst rattlesnakes and water mocassins. One of the settlers became grieviously sick because of a snake: immediately after drinking a hatful of water from the Savannah River, he saw a serpent swim away from the spot and realized that it had poisoned the water. Like many Georgians today, the Salzburgers believed that rattlesnakes can spring through space, whereas in reality they can only thrust their heads a fraction of their body-length, having to leave part of their bodies coiled. Boltzius tried to be objective in his tales of snakes. On one occasion he reported a seven-yard-long rattlesnake that had been killed near Savannah; but after his next visit there he hastened to correct himself; it had been seven feet, not seven yards, long. But even that was a considerable exaggeration on the part of his informant. Boltzius himself would have been bitten by a snake, if a little dog had not been running ahead of him and received the bite instead. Although people were bitten every year or so, the first fatality seems to have been Valentin Depp, who died on 24 June 1758 as a result of a rattlesnake bite, or perhaps of the treatment. Snake oil was, of course, a cure for many ailments.

Despite sickness and rumors of war, Ebenezer's economy continued to flourish in 1742. To be sure, silk production brought only £14 because a disease afflicted the worms, but the wheat crop was good even though only a small area had been planted. Far more important were the harvests of corn, beans, sweet potatoes, and rice, of which the lately arrived fourth transport raised a good part. In the official crop report for the northern division of Georgia for 1742, Ebenezer was credited with 3,048 bushels of corn, 527 bushels of peas, and 566 bushels of potatoes, for a total value of £178 18s., which was far more than half the total. In this connection it is to be remembered that in Georgia field peas were actually beans, much like soybeans, and potatoes always referred to sweet potatoes, or yams, a nutritious tuber introduced from Africa to feed the slaves.

A planter who brought two hundred head of cattle to Ebenezer from South Carolina agreed to sell cheaply because a cattle disease was raging in Purysburg and Savannah. Therefore the fourth transport, having cash in lieu of provisions, could buy cheaply even if at risk. During this year the Salzburgers also received seven horses from the Trustees. These were actually for reconnaissance, but this did not prevent their use for practical purposes. Besides that, the men who were to ride them received modest wages as rangers.

Because the fourth transport introduced money but little small change, Boltzius issued notes in his own name, which circulated freely in Ebenezer and could be converted into lawful money by those who wished to make purchases in Savannah. The relative prosperity in Ebenezer is indicated by the purchase of windowpanes for the church, eight panes for each of its twenty-four windows. It was also shown by the consecration of several cottages, such as those of Georg Brückner and Thomas Gschwandl, which replaced the crude huts built during the first years. The poor box could even afford to engage Johann Georg Köcher of the fourth transport as teacher on the plantations. The greatest undertaking of 1742 was a three-hundred-foot bridge over a stream, now known as Lackner's Creek, wide enough for a wagon and secured with railings, which greatly shortened the journey to the plantations.

Important for the history of the Lutheran church in America was the arrival of Heinrich Melchior Mühlenberg, a young theologian from Halle whom Francke had sent to organize the scattered Lutherans in Pennsylvania, who were being proselytized by Count von Zinzendorf and his Moravians. Mühlenberg was supposed to visit Boltzius long enough to learn how to function in America and then to travel with him to Philadelphia. Boltzius did accompany him as far as Charleston; but Mühlenberg's late arrival in America precluded Boltzius's journey to Philadelphia and back before winter, and for this reason he returned from Charleston by land to his congregation and sick family. Since both divines described the journey from Ebenezer to Charleston in their journals, we can compare their reporting styles (19, 33). While in Charleston, Boltzius visited the German painter Jeremias Theus, who later painted him as an older man. The painting is now lost, but Urlsperger had an engraving made from it in Augsburg (plate 18). Mühlenberg summarized his impressions of the Ebenezer congregation by writing, "The dear Salzburgers sing accurately and beautifully, conduct themselves reverently during the hearing of God's word, and behave courteously toward each other."

Ebenezer would have had another notable, in this case notorious, visitor, if Theobald Kieffer of Purysburg had not refused to extradite his guest, the "Prince of Württemberg," to the new constable of Ebenezer, Thomas Bichler. Declaring himself a royal prince, a questionable character calling himself Carl Rudolf claimed to have been kidnapped in London and sold by Captain Thomson as an indentured servant at Frederica. Some highly educated person must have believed this royal redemptioner, because he was furnished with exceptionally well composed credentials, neatly written and well translated into English. However, we later hear that a man fitting his description preached to several Lutheran congregations in Virginia and Maryland until chased away, usually after having seduced a parishioner's daughter. As incredible as it may sound, this con artist seems to have had the audacity to return to Georgia fifteen years later, for on 11 February 1757 Boltzius wrote in his journal that the deceiver Carl Rudolph was up to his old mischief and had been accepted as a minister by some Lutheran and Reformed people in Vernonburg, a town of which we shall hear more.

In his final report for 1742, which he submitted on the first of the following year, Boltzius reported twelve children born, of whom seven still lived, nine marriages, and twenty-four deaths, fourteen of them adults and ten children; but he does not mention that most of the adult deaths occurred among the last transport. As a grand total for the nine years in America, he reports one hundred births, one hundred and twelve deaths, and fifty-seven marriages. Unfortunately for present day genealogists, he did not give the names in his journal, and the reports he submitted to London cannot be found.

The year 1743 marks a new era for Ebenezer: by then all the Salzburgers had arrived and all major enterprises were well underway, such as the production of dairy products, beef, corn and other grains, lumber, and silk. The next few years were to bring large acquisitions of pasture and farming land and an expansion of the lumber business through enlargement of the saw mills. A steady influx of Württembergers would soon add a Swabian accent to the

Salzburgers' Bavarian and the Palatines' Rhine-Franconian dialects. Nevertheless, the large addition of newcomers would do little to change the religious orientation of the community: the new arrivals who could not adjust to such a godly city either refused to join it or left, sometimes without even completing their indentures.

For the first eight years Boltzius had maintained law and order through his flock's voluntary submission to his judgments, which were inspired by God and approved by the congregation's elders. It was exceptional for him to appeal to the authorities in Savannah to handle unruly people like the Roths. Mrs. Rheinländer had been excommunicated and expelled for misbehavior and readmitted after feigning penitence, but in 1743 Boltzius had to send her down to Savannah to be reprimanded by the magistrate Charles Watson for injuring the character of Theobald Kieffer. The following year two indentured Palatines at Old Ebenezer, then the Trustees' cowpen, or cattle ranch, caused serious disorder in Ebenezer and defied the pastor. When the new constable, Thomas Bichler, attempted to arrest them, Heinrich Meyer escaped up the Savannah River to Augusta, where he later killed an Indian in a drunken brawl. Bichler succeeded in taking Martin Dasher down to Savannah along with the necessary witnesses; but, although Dasher had blasphemed the Sabbath by debauching a Salzburger's serving girl while everyone was at church, the lenient judge merely put him on probation for a year and made him promise not to annoy Boltzius any more. Outraged by such clemency, Boltzius accepted the office of justice of the peace so that he might try future crimes himself and punish more severely. The naughty Heinrich Meyer of this episode is not to be confused with the industrious worker by that name at Frederica. Dasher was a Swiss named Taescher when brought over as a servant in 1735 by William Cooksey. The "Swish" girl whom he seduced was none other than the previously mentioned Ursula Meyer.

All this time Boltzius was fighting his rearguard action against slavery, much to the anger of the Malcontents, who charged that he was merely currying favor with the Trustees and that none of his parishioners really agreed with him. When the Malcontents claimed that Boltzius's favorable reports were inconsistent with truth, the Earl of Egmont angrily retorted that "it is an outrage scarce to be paralleled thus to defame the character of Mr. Boltzius. There is not a person in the Colony more eminent and more esteemed to piety, integrity and prudence than this clergyman. . . ."

The Malcontents claimed that Boltzius was alone in opposing slavery, while all his congregation favored it, and that he was only toadying to Oglethorpe. Robert Williams, a Savannah merchant and leader of the Malcontents, had the audacity to state in Parliament that Boltzius ruled the Salzburgers as their "God, king, and priest." Although Boltzius reacted indignantly to this calumny, he may have been flattered by it; at least he mentioned it in his correspondence. John Tobler, the Swiss almanac maker of New Windsor, said of Ebenezer: "They are all Germans there, yet they are in a flourishing state. They have two ministers. One of them, who is my esteemed friend, is named Martin Boltzius. He spares no pains to make the people there happy in both this world and in the next. There are, to be sure, people who claim that he meddles too much in secular matters, but who can please everybody?"

John Dobell, who had come over as a servant to Charles Wesley, was the other chief opponent of slavery. He defended Boltzius against such accusations; the threats Boltzius began receiving made him realize why Dobell had fled from Savannah and taken refuge in Charleston. Matters culminated in 1743 when the previously mentioned Thomas Stephens, the ungrateful son of the dutiful Colonel Stephens, visited Ebenezer to obtain signatures on a petition requesting the introduction of slavery. Thomas Bichler and the troublesome old schoolmaster Christopher Ortmann were the only two who signed; and even they retracted after a thorough tongue-lashing from the indignant pastor.

Two years later Boltzius wrote a long letter to his benefactor Whitefield arguing against slavery, even though Whitefield owned a plantation in South Carolina where blacks toiled to support the orphans at Bethesda. One may suspect that this letter was really aimed at the Trustees, whose secretary, Benjamin Martyn, wrote to Boltzius on 18 July 1746 that the Trustees "are much pleased with your Letter to Mr Whitefield; Your reasons against admitting Negroes into the Colony are good ones, and they are glad to find that they had a proper effect on Mr Whitefield."

Being really directed at the British authorities, this letter, like most of his others, gave primarily practical arguments; yet it was clear that Boltzius also saw the immorality of slavery. Unfortunately, all his dire predictions came true as soon as slavery was introduced; coastal Georgia lost many of her Germans along with other yeoman farmers. Boltzius's stand against slavery and his success in the lumber business even without slaves may have prompted Harman Verelst, the Trustees' accountant, to write to Colonel Stephens on 24 March 1746: "You did well to assist Mr. Boltzius with the Timber Chain he wanted, and you cannot recommend your Selves more to the Trustees Favour, than by encouraging and countenancing him and the Saltzburghers under his Care, who are become an Example of Industry worthy of Imitation of every Inhabitant of Georgia."

5

New German Settlements and Swabian Transports

he Lutheran congregation in Savannah was steadily growing, and a year after Mühlenberg visited these Lutherans, they collected £4 from their paltry earnings and sent the collection to Philadelphia to help build a Lutheran church there, possibly to show their Pennsylvania kinsmen that they were not faring too badly in Georgia. After serving their time, most Lutheran redemptioners were pleased to settle with their coreligionists in Ebenezer, but the larger part of the Savannah Germans, being Swiss and Palatines, were of the Reformed faith and wished to organize their own congregation. Thomas Jones wrote to Verelst chiefly about these Germans on 1 July 1741:

> The Trustees *German* servants in general behave well, and are industrious: Of these, eight or ten Families are more remarkably so, and have this last Year purchased a good Stock of Cattle, some having six Cows, the least two; and each having a Garden, where they raise some Corn, Pease, Pompions, Potatoes, &c. which with the Milk of their Cows is the chief Part of their Food: They are at little Expence in Cloathing; but this exposes them to the Envy and Hatred of our Negro-Mongers, and such who seek the Extirpation of the Colony, as well as of the drunken, idle Sort amongst us.
>
> I am informed by Francis Harris and William Russell (who

are very conversant with them, and can talk the German Tongue)
That they have lately joined, in a Letter writ and sent to their
Friends and Acquaintances in Germany, persuading them to
come to Georgia, where they may, by their Industry, live in
greater Plenty, and more comfortably than they can elsewhere.

These Servants are very desirous, That (when the Time of
their Service is expired) they may have Lands allotted to them
within twelve or fifteen Miles of Savannah, where they may bring
Things by Land-Carriage in Vicinage, and that they may make
one common Fence (as the people of Ebenezer Have done) and
be assisting to one another.

On 27 October 1741 the surveyor, Joseph Avery, wrote
that forty Dutch servants who had served their time wished
contiguous plantations, and he proposed a site at the head of
the Vernon River about nine miles from Savannah and just
south of the German hamlet of Hamstead, which the inhabitants germanized as Heimstatt. At Hamstead the Germans
first proved themselves to be the best farmers in Georgia. In
describing the state of that village in July 1738, William Byrd
listed the many residents who had left and then added the
footnote: "N.B. Burgholder, Holstatler, Houlster, and Des-
ter are all industrious and Laborious men; the Rest of little
Account." (This Burgholder was actually Michael Burckhalter, a Swiss who had fled secretly from his home in
Lützelflüh in Canton Bern to avoid paying an emigration tax
and who later became prominent in Georgia.) The region
that Avery proposed to develop was to be divided into Acton
to the north and Vernonburg to the south, both places to be
settled exclusively by German-speaking people. Avery must
have started his project at once, because already by 31 January 1742 he could write to Vernon:

> Sir: in my last of the 27th: Ober I signefied that I was going
> to run out the Dutch Town at White Bluff upon Vernon
> River, since that I have done so and have given out the Town
> and farm lots, and have settled the people upon their farm

lots so that they may clear the land and plant a crop this Season, by which they will be supply'd with provision for the next year, and therefore be no farther an expence to the Trustees and publick.

He then continues that there are now only thirty families containing a hundred people but that there are lots laid out for eighty families, all excellent for plantations. He next mentions that, while the people are kind to one another, they are not so to strangers. Also, this year in Georgia there is little planting except by the Germans.

On 11 November of the same year, after visiting Vernonburg, Boltzius recorded in his diary:

The Lord Trustees have freed all the children of the German servants in Savannah who still have some years to serve after their parents have won their freedom so that they can move with their families at Christmas to the plantations that are now being surveyed for them on a large river near the orphanage. Together they should found a big city. As long as they live, these servants should never forget what the Lord Trustees have done for them. Their work is insignificant, and at the same time they and their families have received better provisions than they will have on their own land. But most of them have sinned against the Lord Trustees through disloyalty and unrighteous behavior, and because of that they have already felt the heavy hand of God through the cattle disease but have not yet become any better. Divine truth is freely dispensed when we come to minister to them; but they just listen to it, there is no true penitence or withdrawal from unrighteousness.

The Trustees' decision to free the children of the indentured servants eventually applied to Ebenezer too, so that the herdsman Hans Michael Schneider could regain the services of his sons.

Boltzius and Gronau visited the Vernonburgers occasionally; but the Vernonburgers still wished a Calvinist minister,

13. Probably the portrait made of Oglethorpe in 1736 at Frederica by von Reck's servant, Christian Müller. It is now hanging in the Chatham Club in Savannah. (University of Georgia Libraries.)

14. John Wesley, friend of the Salzburgers. (University of Georgia Libraries.)

15. George Whitefield, popular preacher and benefactor of the Salzburgers. (University of Georgia Libraries.)

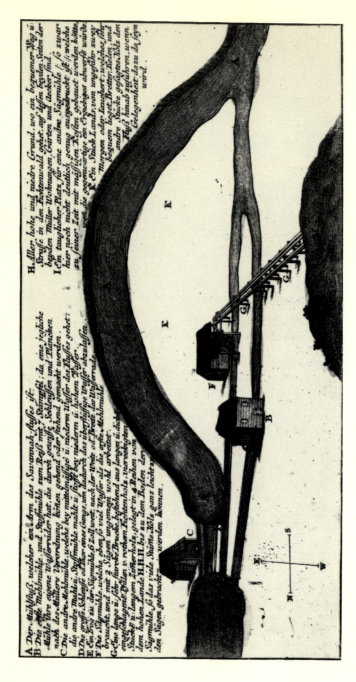

16. The grist and lumber mills on Ebenezer Creek, from a German engraving. (University of Georgia Libraries.)

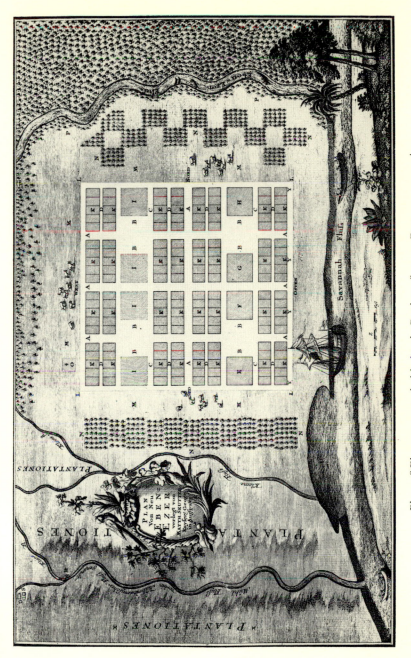

17. Plan of Ebenezer, probably by de Brahm, from a German engraving. (University of Georgia Libraries.)

18. Johann Martin Boltzius, Salzburger pastor, engraved after a painting done in Charleston by Jeremias Theus. (University of Georgia Libraries.)

19. *Left:* James Habersham,
schoolmaster, merchant,
president of the Council, and
patron of the Salzburgers.
(University of Georgia
Libraries.)

20. *Below:* Jerusalem Church,
the oldest house of worship
in Georgia.
(University of Georgia
Libraries.)

21. Salzburger cottage showing mortised construction. (University of Georgia Libraries.)

even if it were to be Henri François Chiffelle of Purysburg, whose broken German was, in Boltzius's opinion, hardly better than his Christianity. Although Boltzius, applying his own otherworldly standards, wrote scathingly of Chiffelle's greedy and worldly nature, the inhabitants of Vernonburg signed an enthusiastic recommendation for the Swiss clergyman, apparently valuing his relaxed attitude toward sin more highly than Boltzius's fulminations against drinking, dancing, and banqueting. Some six months later, after his first visit, Boltzius wrote: "In this first year the German people have not made a good beginning on their land on the White Bluff, for their cattle are still perishing from the cattle disease. Because their corn is growing so poorly and they have little hope for their harvest, some of them are again working for daily wages."

Only a month later, however, Boltzius discovered that he had been too pessimistic, and this time he wrote in his diary:

> The German people have already expended much labor in this first year on their new land, which they are to call Vernonburg because it will be built on the Vernon River, and they will get more grain and other crops than they recently expected. They have very good land, and their city can be situated very advantageously. The souls who heard God's word were very pleased at my visit and would have shown me much love if I let them. I had come, however, only to serve them with my office through Christian encouragement and prayer. They greatly wished to hear something for their edifcation and assembled for that purpose in a hut, where we prayed together and took affectionate leave. I hope to remain a couple of days with them in the future and to edify myself with them longer.

This more favorable estimate was confirmed by the annual crop report of 1743, which showed that Acton and Vernonburg were second only to Ebenezer in the production of grain. Whether or not the Lord sent the cattle distemper to punish the Vernonburgers for their sins, the Trustees eventually saw fit to replace twenty-two of their cows.

Because of their success, the Salzburgers of Ebenezer were naturally a model for the people of Acton and Vernonburg, and Boltzius and Gronau occasionally preached at the newer settlements for want of a Reformed minister. Because Ortmann had been unable to maintain his sick servants Christian and Margaretha Lewenberger, they had reverted to the Trustees; and within two years they owned a fifty-acre farm at Dutchtown, as Vernonburg was commonly called, and they offered to adopt a pair of orphans, apparently the Halter children, whose parents had died on the *Europa*. In 1745 the Trustees set aside two acres between Acton and Vernonburg for a temple, which, in view of the inhabitants' persuasion, would be used most often for Reformed services. When Boltzius dismissed Ortmann from Ebenezer in the same year for conspiring with Thomas Stephens, the latter's father, Colonel Stephens, created a position for the old schoolmaster at Vernonburg at £12 per annum. The Trustees refused at first to confirm the appointment; but they finally consented, probably feeling an obligation to the old marine veteran who had given up a pension to go to Georgia. Stephens and his assistants even shamed Boltzius into forgiving the old sinner, who became very well loved by the Vernonburgers and often served as witness in their business transactions.

The settlers at Dutchtown wished to imitate the Salzburgers' method of measuring out their parcels of land in long strips, thereby giving equal shares of good and bad land to all the owners and allowing friends to live near each other at the same end of the strips and to build communal fences around adjoining farms. The surveyor, Joseph Avery, refused to survey such long strips until threatened with bodily harm, whereupon he acquiesced. Today many of the lots at Vernonburg are still long and narrow. The waterfront at Vernonburg was called White Bluff because of the color of its steep bank, just as the site of Ebenezer was called Red Bluff. White Bluff is still the usual name for the region.

When the *Europa* brought its disease-ridden cargo to Georgia at the end of 1741, some of the survivors were sent directly to Acton and Vernonburg. The Swiss newlander Hans Jacob Riemensperger had organized his expedition in Bern, but it had been detained in Frauenfeld, where the authorities believed his passport a forgery; hence he had to slip away secretly and return to Bern to get better identification. His party, which was destined for Saxe-Gotha in South Carolina, was initially all Swiss, but he had picked up so many Germans along the way that he arrived in London with twenty-six more people than requested by the South Carolina authorities. The Georgia Trustees welcomed this opportunity to engage the extra twenty-six for Georgia, and the survivors of this group were sent directly to Vernonburg and Acton without having to serve for their passage. As previously mentioned, the Trustees, like Boltzius, had discovered that free men work better than bondsmen.

Another large addition to Acton and Vernonburg arrived early in 1746 aboard the *Judith,* which also brought the Reverend Hermann Lemke as replacement for Gronau, whom he replaced as assistant pastor and also as husband for his widow Catherina. Gronau had never really recovered from the malarial epidemic of 1736 but had remained in varying degrees of ill health during his arduous work, which included most of the trips to preach to the Germans of Savannah. He finally died at the beginning of 1745 after a long illness, much of it spent at Bethesda, where the sea air was known to be healthier. His death was a dreadful blow to Boltzius, who loved him as a brother. Fortunately, his successor, Lemke, also proved retiring and long-suffering and therefore equally able to get on well with the autocratic first pastor. By having Lemke marry the widow Gronau, the benefactors in the SPCK avoided having to pay her a pension; and in time Lemke's salary was supporting her two surviving children and three of his own. Lemke, who was twenty-five years old when he arrived, hailed from Fischbeck in the county of Schaumburg and was therefore a North German like Boltzius and Gronau. He too had been an instructor at the famous Francke school in Halle; but, unlike them, he had also been a pupil there.

The German passengers aboard the *Judith* had set out a year earlier at their own expense on the *Two Brothers* but had been captured by two Spanish corsairs and taken to Bilbao, where they were robbed of all their belongings and suffered the indignity of being proselytized by zealous Dominicans. Brought back to England on a cartel ship, those who could afford to do so returned to Germany, while the remainder were stranded at Gosport on the charity of the townsfolk until the Trustees engaged a hundred of them as servants and put them aboard the *Judith,* under Capt. Walter Quarme. Their second voyage was scarcely better than the first: a burning fever afflicted both crew and passengers; and because the captain died and the first mate nearly died, the ship might never have reached Frederica if a passenger named Bartholomäus Zouberbühler, himself a landlubber from St. Gall in Switzerland, had not known enough geometry to plot the ship's course with the help of an illiterate sailor. Zouberbühler, later to play an important role in Georgia, was the son of the old Reformed minister Zoberbiller, who had died in Purysburg, and the brother of the newlander Sebastian Zouberbühler, who later led Germans to Maine. Finding no Reformed parish in South Carolina able to support a minister, Bartholomäus, now Bartholomew, had returned to England to be ordained an Anglican minister, after which Boltzius always referred to him as the "English" minister.

The servants aboard the *Judith* were assigned for further

distribution to Boltzius at Ebenezer and to Michael Burck-halter, the previously mentioned Burgholder and now the leading inhabitant of Vernonburg. Among Ebenezer's share were the Bohrmanns, Ihles, Wiesenbachers, two girls named Zorn, a very large family of Walthauers, a girl named Leine-bacher and her very pious brother, who soon died, and three boys named Richard (Ritschart?), who promptly ran away to Congarees in South Carolina, where they were joined by their two brothers who had been indentured in Savannah and, later, by their parents, who served out their time there.

Among these redemptioners sent to Vernonburg were sev-eral who later found their way to Ebenezer, such as the large family of Adam Straub, who had married the widow Häfner and taken on her children. Most important was Johann Adam, a twelve-year-old who was to play a major role in Ebenezer history. He was listed under the unrecognizable family name Frideling, an incredible distortion of the name Treutlen. His mother, Maria Clara, who had lost her hus-band during the Spanish captivity, was redeemed by the British along with her three sons and brought to Gosport, where they spent nearly a year and a half and where she apprenticed one of her sons to John Carver before sailing to Georgia with Johann Adam and his brother Friedrich. Not long after their departure Carver and his new apprentice drowned in Gosport harbor (54).

Arriving at Vernonburg, the Treutlen family was inden-tured to Burckhalter, who signed a florid English letter thanking the Trustees for the gift of four servants, the num-ber suggesting that Maria Clara had adopted an orphan dur-ing the ill-starred voyage. Johann Adam so impressed his master, Burckhalter, that the magnanimous Swiss, although himself Reformed, sent the lad to Ebenezer for a proper Lutheran education. There the boy prospered as pupil, teacher, storekeeper, planter, and politician. In addition to its passengers, the *Judith* also carried for them "20 Plow Shares & Coulters made to Jethro Tull's Pattern, 4 dozen Scythes Sorted, 3 Brass Plates for Watchmakers, 2 Groce of Shoemakers Awl Blades, & 6 Cutting Knives with Handles." This record suggests that the Trustees were truly concerned with the welfare of their indentured servants.

Because his congregation was steadily increasing, Boltzius soon had to look for more land. The neighboring area of Abercorn, once a Scottish settlement but subsequently depopulated by death and desertion, was gradually being germanized by inhabitants from Savannah and Ebenezer; for already by 1745 Martin Dasher, the once unruly indentured servant from Old Ebenezer, had taken up land there, as had also Friedrich Helfenstein, the son of the Swiss widow at Ebenezer. Mrs. Helfenstein, who was of the Reformed faith and had been contaminated by sectarians in Heidelberg, had often argued with Boltzius about theological matters and had never bowed to his better judgment. Friction finally became so bad that she left Ebenezer with the intention of moving to Pennsylvania, but she and her son got only as far as Abercorn. Just as Hamstead had been germanized to Heimstatt, Abercorn also suffered a folk-etymological change to Haberkorn (oat grain).

By July 1750 there were enough Germans at Abercorn to hold regular Lutheran services. Beyond Abercorn lay Parker's Mill, an unsuccessful and abandoned sawmill built by Robert Parker. Because Parker's son, Robert Parker, Jr., insisted on importing slaves, Causton and Noble Jones had not let him assume ownership of the land. Consequently Boltzius's request for it was granted in the summer of 1746. In his journal entry for 22 June 1738 Boltzius calls the mill builder Purker and says he was a native-born Swede. Because of Boltzius's usual accuracy, we may believe this statement, even though Parker was recommended by Sir Robert Walpole and no English records make any mention of his foreign birth. Perhaps Parker, like John Terry and many others, recognized the insularity of the British and realized that it was advantageous to anglicize foreign names.

In 1746 the Salzburgers also received some cast-iron ovens from Germany, which were a great improvement over the open fireplaces used by the British settlers. Such German stoves, miscalled Franklin stoves after the Philadelphian who first popularized them in America, were far more effective and efficient than open fireplaces because they warmed the entire room, instead of merely scorching the near side of the person standing at the hearth. Boltzius lists the advantages of these iron stoves in his journal for 18 December 1749.

The year 1747 proved uneventful yet productive. Köcher, the schoolmaster on the plantations, constructed a loom, for which he obtained flax from Bethesda and wool from South Carolina. Hans Michael Held, the Palatine herdsman who had served at St. Augustine, had also become a weaver; but in this year some South Carolina planters persuaded him to move to their area, where he could profit from slave labor. Henry Bishop, Boltzius's former servant and husband of Friederica Unselt, seems to have preferred slave labor likewise, for in the same year he too left Ebenezer to live on a Carolina plantation. Ruprecht Zittrauer had already moved there and was supporting himself as a slave driver.

Three years earlier Boltzius had requested lands near the Ogeechee River, a blackwater river roughly paralleling the lower reaches of the Savannah. His request had been refused for being too vague; but now he at last acquired these lands, which had been reserved for the Uchee Indians. The crops were good in 1747, and the peaches so bountiful that the Salzburgers made a great quantity of brandy with newly arrived stills. One man had already made a good quantity of brandy by cooling the vapor with only the barrel of a musket. Sheep were introduced this year for the first time. Unfortunately, the Salzburgers lost many cattle, which eluded the herdsmen and joined the wild cattle in the swamps.

Although England had now been at war with Spain for eight years and the Spaniards had seized many English ships, the Salzburgers had not lost a single piece of mail, as Boltzius could write to his benefactors as late as 21 July 1747. In that same year, however, he did lose some mail from Philadelphia on a coastal vessel that was captured by a Spanish privateer off the Carolina coast and taken as booty to St. Augustine, and during the following year some mail was intercepted on its way from Europe. This war had started in 1739 as the War of Jenkins' Ear when an English captain lost an ear as punishment for smuggling goods to one of the Spanish colonies; but already by 1740 it had fused into the War of the Austrian Succession, in which England supported Austria against Spain and France until the war ended in 1748.

During 1747 four adults and seven children died in Ebenezer, and seventeen babies were born. Several of the children died of pica, or "clay-eating," a strange malady that baffled Boltzius and Thilo even though it had struck several times before. The victims of this illness, usually small children or at least young people, were afflicted by an uncontrollable hunger for inedible matter, such as dirt and raw corn or rice. No amount of admonition or threats of punishment in this world or the next could stop them. The clay-eating was obviously the result rather than the cause, which was apparently a dietary deficiency such as a lack of iron; but in the eighteenth century it was customary to treat the symptoms rather than the sickness.

George Schweiger, who lost a seven-year-old child to this disease on 7 January 1748, had already lost seven children in Ebenezer and was left with only one sickly one. Soon thereafter Stephan Rottenberger lost the last of his three children to pica, which had also taken the other two. Boltzius usually put the blame on the parents for not watching their children. If the children had reached the age of reason, he preached to them that eating such things was a form of suicide and therefore against God's commandment; but even that did not deter them. Something even worse must have occurred about this time, because Urlsperger saw fit to delete the entire month of February from his edition of Boltzius's journal. One tragedy was barely avoided when a child was pulled out of the millrace just as he was about to go under the wheel, the heavy wheel which had recently crushed an immense alligator.

Because Boltzius's duties had increased with his growing parish while his health had declined, the Trustees had persuaded the surgeon of the fourth transport, Johann Ludwig Meyer, to serve along with him as conservator of the peace, and Thomas Bichler had been appointed constable at Ebenezer to assist them in their office. By 1747 Meyer was, in theory, responsible for all secular matters. After 1750 the conservators were able to share some of their responsibilities with seven tythingmen elected by the people.

In 1748 the Salzburgers produced 464 pounds of silk. The following year their silk was acclaimed by the experts in London, and the Trustees gave twenty families £2 each to build huts for raising the worms. By this time the mills were self-supporting, and the milling business was advanced even further when the Salzburgers received two heavy millstones for their grist mill. The Salzburgers also won the contract for supplying lumber for the church in Savannah, where Boltzius acquired an eighty-five-foot landing place under the bluff next to Habersham's wharf so the lumber could be loaded on ships without being carried up and down the steep bank. The price of rice, which had dropped during the partial embargo caused by the Spanish war, had risen again, and Boltzius tried to coax his people to clear and cultivate the rich alluvial soil on Abercorn Island. However, he found them reluctant to undertake this strenuous task without servants, as all hired hands and employees were then called.

This need for hired hands was partially remedied when Capt. Peter Bogg brought a party of Palatines to Georgia on the *Charles Town Galley* on 2 October 1749, forty-eight of whom were sent to Ebenezer. These people had been recruited by the newlander Riemensperger. Some, like Jacob Kübler (Kiebler) and his family, had paid their passage; but many who had expected to do so had run out of money on the long journey down the Rhine and had arrived penniless in London, where they agreed to serve the Trustees four years for their fare. Soon after reaching Ebenezer, several of them absconded, including their spokesman, Balthasar Zoller, and also Balthasar Kuhn and Friedrich Scheffer. Like the Richard brothers before them, these redemptioners fled to Congarees, from where the governor of South Carolina would not extradite them; but most of the new redemptioners served out their time loyally and became respected Salzburgers. Included in the loyal group were families that later played an important role in Ebenezer, such as the Gugels, Heidts, Mohrs, Schneiders, Schubdreins, Seckingers, and Zieglers, most of whom were from the vicinity of Nassau-Saarbrücken. Jacob Kübler and his family settled in German Village on the River Ness, as did Michael Bohrmann and his half brother, Georg Philip Portz. Johann Christian Seelmann, a physician, was unhappy and useless at Ebenezer, so Boltzius permitted him to move to Pennsylvania after promising to refund his passage money. The records do not tell whether he ever did so.

Of all the passengers aboard the *Charles Town Galley,* the man who made the greatest mark was Johann Caspar Wirtsch, a baker's apprentice from Ansbach who was indentured to Johann Flerl as schoolmaster on the plantations. Subsequently he became shopkeeper and economic leader of the town and married Gronau's daughter Hanna Elisabeth.

As keeper of the store many years afterward, he donated a greatcoat to Mühlenberg when that venerable cleric returned to Ebenezer thirty years later. Wirtsch, who later spelled his name Wertsch, would probably have risen even higher if he had not met his match, and superior, in the above-mentioned Treutlen. The relative popularity and influence of Wertsch and Treutlen are indicated in the church records by the number of their godchildren (35); for, despite Boltzius's admonitions, the Salzburgers persisted in choosing godparents for political rather than religious reasons, sponsors in baptism being as closely bound as blood kinsmen.

Although many of the old settlers in Ebenezer had shared grants and were therefore crowded together on insufficient land, they were reluctant to go to better and larger tracts elsewhere. Because of this confusion, on 28 September 1750 the President's Council resolved to find someone capable of putting things aright, and they agreed

> that no Person in the Colony was better qualified to execute this weighty Trust, than Mr Noble Jones, who, notwithstanding it had not been his proper Business, had kept a private Register, and had always been ready to assist with His services therein, when desired; Therefore it was now proposed to Mr Noble Jones to undertake it, who willingly accepted it and engaged to perform the same carefully, the Board not doubting but the Trustees will approve of, and confirm him therein.

This was the same Noble Jones who had been dismissed from Ebenezer for failing to survey to Boltzius's satisfaction.

Even after the arrival of the passengers aboard the *Judith* and the *Charles Town Galley*, many Salzburgers still needed hired hands, because all free men in the colony preferred to take up land themselves rather than work for wages. The first Salzburgers had now been in the colony for fifteen years and had aged thirty; and many had lost the staff of their old age. To forestall requests for Negro slaves, Boltzius did all in his power to obtain white servants; he appealed often to the Trustees who in turn consulted with Urlsperger in Augsburg. Since Augsburg was then a Swabian city, and since Urlsperger was acquainted with many Lutheran ministers in Württemberg, most of the later servants were Swabians. It was apparently in order to further such immigration that, on 19 March 1747, "Mr Chretien Von Munch & Rev^d/Mr Samuel Urlsperger [were] appointed Corresponding Members of the Trust for the Service of the Salzburghers and Other Germans Who may be inclin'd to go to Georgia." In 1752 von Münch, who seems to have had great mercantile plans for Ebenezer, asked Pastor Kleinknecht of Leibheim in the territory of Ulm to help recruit emigrants for Ebenezer in order to save them from going to areas without Lutheran ministers; but the Ulm authorities told Kleinknecht that this was a secular, not a spiritual, matter (50).

On 29 October 1750 the *Charming Martha*, Capt. Charles Leslie, brought sixty Swabians, twenty-seven of them servants, from the vicinity of Ulm, these being known as the "first Swabian transport." They had undertaken to cross the ocean at their own expense; but, like so many other immigrants, they had not reckoned with the greed of the customs collectors along the Rhine and the exploitation of soul-catchers like Zacharias Hope in Rotterdam, so they arrived in London without funds. Consequently, they had to appeal for aid to the Trustees, who sent them as servants for the inhabitants of Georgia. Among the additions to Ebenezer were the Bollingers, Fetzers, Heinles, Helmes, and Hubers. Jacob Huber, from the territory of Ulm, had brought Catherina Michel (Michler) from Nerenstetten, and Barbara Oechsle from Langenau, small towns in the same territory. Neidlinger, a sixty-six-year-old tanner from Ulm, soon died;

but his family survived and prospered. Of all these new arrivals, Boltzius commented most favorably about the Heinles. Being still unseasoned, all these Württembergers were fever-ridden by the following summer, and several died.

The next two years brought two large parties of Würtembergers, each numbering 160 souls. On 21 August 1751 Benjamin Martyn, the secretary of the Trustees, made the following entry in their journal:

> Several German Protestants attended the Board, and expressed their Desire of going over to Georgia at their own Expence, in order to settle with the Saltzburghers at Ebenezer. And the following Seven Elders viz Michael Walliser, Michael Wienkraft, Daniel Renshard, John George Gwant (Gnann), John Neidlinger, and John Peter Shubdrein, being Conductors of the Embarkation were called in, and They acquainted the Board that their Number would amount to One hundred and fifty Seven, Whereof fifty four Men, forty six Women, twenty seven Boys, and thirty Girls.

In this case the Trustees' secretary did an unusually good job with the German names, misspelling only Weinkraft, Schubdrein, and Gnann. Like Jacob Huber and Catherina Michel, and possibly encouraged by them, this group had also come from the territory of Ulm, an Imperial Free City on the Danube whose wealth was manifested by one of the highest cathedrals in Europe. Most of this transport came from small towns belonging to the city: Hans Georg Winkler from Nierstotzingen, Anna Schroter from Langenau, and David Unselt and Peter Zipperer from Bernstadt. This "second Swabian transport," aboard the *Antelope,* Capt. John McClelland, was led by Wilhelm Gerhard von Brahm, an artillery officer from Koblenz who had served Emperor Charles VI until converting from Catholicism to Protestantism (47). Von Brahm, who usually signed himself as de Brahm, had not inherited his title of *von* but had assumed it as befitting his earned rank of commissioned officer. De Brahm settled his people on the Blue Bluff just above Ebenezer, so that by now the Red Bluff, White Bluff, and Blue Bluff of Georgia were all occupied by Germans.

The Salzburgers had long desired this fertile region but could not have it as long as it belonged to the Uchee Indians. Eventually, disease, rum, and war had decimated the Uchees, and the few survivors had moved farther up the Savannah River. Colonel Stephens finally offered the area to Boltzius in the summer of 1749; but Boltzius preferred to reserve it for the expected settlers, who would be better able to defend it. Boltzius's hesitation to encroach on the Uchees' land may be explained by a letter Oglethorpe had written on 18 May 1736 to the Trustees stating that a certain Captain Green had "advised the Uchee Indians to fall upon the Saltzburghers for settling upon their Lands, the occasion of which was an indiscreet Action of one of the Saltzburghers who cleared and planted four Acres of Land beyond the Ebenezer contrary to my Orders and without my knowledge." As late as 25 September 1741 Oglethorpe had written a strong letter to Colonel Stephens declaring that the land west of Ebenezer Creek belonged to the Uchee Indians who had served well at St. Augustine, where thirty had been killed and where those taken prisoner had remained loyal to the British despite generous offers from the Spaniards. Oglethorpe never broke his word to the Indians, and the debated land was occupied only after there were no more Uchees to complain. Even if the Uchees had attacked, the settlers on the Blue Bluff would have been in little danger, for de Brahm was a military man of considerable experience, intelligence, and energy.

Although the Blue Bluff had been reserved for the newcomers, Boltzius saw fit to order fifty-five-acre plots surveyed for some of the older inhabitants of Ebenezer who were having difficulty in finding fertile land, such being found only along the river. Among those so provided were Matthias Zettler, Georg Meyer, Ruprecht Schrempff, Christian Rottenberger, Valentin Depp, Johann Paul Francke, and Ruprecht Kalcher, and also Jacob Meyer, who had recently moved from Purysburg to Ebenezer in 1750 to be with his sisters. Boltzius also had similar plots surveyed for seven heads of families of the first Swabian transport who had paid their own fare on the *Charming Martha.*

Johann Paul Francke, who received a grant on the Blue Bluff, was the son of a poor widow in Purysburg who had struggled to send him to school in Ebenezer, where he performed well. However, after his confirmation, Boltzius heard the distressing news that he had run away to live with the Indians. Actually, he had gone into the service of an Indian trader. When he finally returned to civilization, he had forgotten not only his Christian dogma but even the German language, which he had to relearn. Fortunately, his sojourn among the heathens and even worse Christian traders did not prevent his becoming a good and God-fearing member of Jerusalem Church. We hope that his self-sacrificing mother lived to see the return of the prodigal son.

The population of the Blue Bluff grew even more in 1752 when a third Swabian transport arrived on the *Success,* under Captain Isaacs, being conducted by Stückhauptmann Krauss. Werner Hacker has shown from emigration records that in the spring of 1752 forty-four individuals and heads of families in the territory of Ulm requested permission to emigrate to Ebenezer, this being more than wished to go to South Carolina or anywhere else in America, even Pennsylvania (50). This choice was surely due to the efforts of Samuel Urlsperger, a man whom the emigrants and the authorities could trust. At the same time a man named Gottfried Jacob Müller was jailed in Heilbronn for tempting people to emigrate. He would have been flogged had he not been too sick. All these people came from small towns belonging to Ulm, more than half from Langenau and Altheim, as can be seen in the appended list of Ebenezer residents.

The severity of the German and Swiss governments against the newlanders was, in theory, to protect the emigrants from exploitation; but one senses that the wealthy ruling classes feared that if too many impecunious people emigrated, those who remained could demand higher wages. Therefore the authorities tried to prevent emigration except in those places and at those times in which the population had increased too much and the unemployed were becoming a burden on the local government. The Swiss cantons were particularly zealous in prohibiting emigration and placed all sorts of financial barriers in its way, a fact that explains why Michael Burckhalter had seen fit to abscond. The cantons required the pastors to report all people who had emigrated, and their lists have been well preserved (43). To free themselves of the onus of having let useful subjects escape, the pastors would often add some negative remark, such as that the person in question was worthless or a good riddance.

A few of the immigrants to Ebenezer from Ulm were serfs who had to pay for their manumission; yet all had the means to pay for the voyage, save two who needed aid to make the journey possible. In order to emigrate, nearly all had to forfeit the right ever to return home. In the eighteenth century the German principalities, and even free cities, looked upon their subjects as a national resource. If a subject served another lord or land in his prime years, they did not wish him to return later and expect his native lord or land to support him in his old age.

The authorities in Savannah had wished to settle this contingent at Briar Creek, some miles farther up the Savannah River, but most of the immigrants did not wish to be so far from their church or kinsmen in Ebenezer. Also, they arrived without funds or sufficient tools to start a new colony; consequently many settled on the Blue Bluff or at Ebenezer, and some found employment in Savannah, where they were tempted by the high wages. Only a few settled at Briar Creek, or Halifax, as the general area was called. The third Swabian transport was the last organized migration, but individual Germans and their families continued coming to Ebenezer from Savannah and South Carolina. Because the Swabian servants had often failed to justify the money spent on them, Boltzius began discouraging their importation as servants and preferred to have them come as free men. After observing the efforts made by the free and the unfree Palatines who had come over on the *Charles Town Galley,* Boltzius had written to Benjamin Martyn, the Trustees' secretary, that "the Difference in Labour of such freed Persons & of the Servants is surprisingly great, the latter reckoning it hard & unjust to Serve for their Passage some years, therefore are very burthensome to their masters, tho' used almost like Children."

Another factor may have discouraged the formation of a fourth Swabian transport. Two of the first immigrants from the territory of Ulm, weavers from the town of Langenau by the name of Barthel and Martin Botzenhardt, wrote discouraging letters from Ebenezer, which were published in an Ulm weekly named the *Ordentlich-Wöchentliche Anzeigszettel.* The Botzenhardt brothers must have been shiftless fellows, because they could give no real grounds for warning against emigrating to Ebenezer. They also made inaccurate statements: Barthel claimed that no land was given, whereas, as the appended list of Ebenezer inhabitants shows, all the Swabians received grants soon after arriving, including the Botzenhardts. Martin claimed that no one could catch fish because there were no boats, whereas there were boats and one could also fish with the line or trap from the shore. He also stated that Ebenezer was forty miles from Savannah, without explaining that he meant English miles, they being only about a sixth of a German mile. Their propaganda served to ingratiate them to the Ulm authorities so that they might return home, which they were allowed to do, but only as serfs. Matthias Neidlinger also returned from Ebenezer as bearer of one of their letters.

6

Slavery, Prosperity, and the Death of Boltzius

uring the time the three Swabian transports were arriving, major changes were occurring in the colony of Georgia. On 16 March 1746 Secretary Martyn had written that the Trustees would never permit slavery and that the "industry of the Saltzburghers will furnish a constant & prevailing Argument for the Prohibition." As late as 28 May 1748 the Trustees had assured Colonel Stephens that "the introduction and Use of Negroes in Georgia will never be permitted by the Trustees," yet the clamor and threats of the Malcontents prevailed. In less than a year even Boltzius reluctantly signed their petition of 10 January 1749 to be allowed to import slaves. To be sure, he insisted on certain reservations and stipulations, even though knowing in his heart that they would be ignored, as were all similar restrictions in South Carolina. Thus, the newcomers on the *Charles Town Galley* settled not in a free colony but in a slave colony.

James Habersham, now a prosperous merchant, was soon offering the Salzburgers his African slaves on credit; Boltzius said he would neither approve nor disapprove of their purchase. The Trustees granted land only to those able to clear and cultivate it, and the ownership of a slave was considered evidence that one could do so. The Salzburgers, who had previously paid cash for their cattle, were now sorely tempted to buy slaves on credit rather than wait until they were able to pay cash; for the land cleared by a slave could then be used as a collateral for buying another slave on credit. Habersham aided in this process: for example, he advised giving a grant to Jacob Caspar Walthauer when the latter's father gave him £30 toward buying a Negro. Slaves were quickly acquired by Matthias Zettler, the son-in-law of the slave-owning Theobald Kieffer, and even by Christian Leinberger, who had married the widow of the scalped Gabriel Bach. When the Zettlers' slave bore a baby, they had it baptized and served as its godparents (66).

Ill-informed in their rear-echelon headquarters in London, the benevolent but misguided Trustees continued urging the Salzburgers to cultivate silk, a product scarcely suitable for a country with a chronic labor shortage. At the same time they discouraged the weaving of flax and cotton, both of which grew well in Georgia and would have been far more useful for the economy. As it turned out, even though the Salzburgers far surpassed all other inhabitants of Georgia in producing silk, the industry survived only so long as it was subsidized by Parliament.

Of far greater potential than silk raising was the lumber industry, especially after the completion of the second sawmill in 1751, because vast primeval cypress swamps provided a wood that well withstood the ravages of water and weather. At first the Salzburgers could not raft the great cypress logs to their sawmill because they sank; but eventually the settlers discovered that the felled trees would become buoyant if left to dry out for a year. Boltzius constantly urged his parishioners to devote more of their time to making barrel staves for the rice planters, an activity they could practice in the shade; he even advised the redemptioners that they could pay their £6 passage money by making six thousand staves. The West Indies offered a ready market not only for barrel staves but also for masts, spars, oars, and cypress shingles.

Boltzius tried in vain to dissuade the Salzburgers from depending entirely upon agriculture just because their fathers had been farmers; rather, he encouraged them to adapt themselves to the nature of their new homeland, which favored the lumber industry rather than farming. However, tradition was strong, and the Salzburgers continued to consider it the highest goal in life to own a farm, be it ever so humble; besides that, as farmers they could feed their families regardless of economic fluctuations. Boltzius's insistence upon export products was surely inspired by Habersham, who made it clear that the British authorities were more interested in trade than in self-sufficient farming.

The longleaf pine, which stood all around as high as church steeples, offered an unlimited supply of wood suitable for shingles, clapboards, and other building materials. Should the forests around Ebenezer ever become depleted, the Savannah River would furnish an easy means of rafting additional timber from the hinterland. In the sugar islands of the West Indies, the forests had long since given way to cane fields, so there was a great demand for lumber. To oblige the sugar planters and to provide the Salzburgers with a market for their lumber, the Trustees had decided on 13 April 1747 to permit the importation of rum and thus make it easier for the sugar producers to pay for the lumber. Boltzius said nothing against this decision even though he had previously backed the Trustees in opposing the importation and consumption of rum. About this time lawyers began to make an appearance in Georgia too, and thus the Trustees' paradise lost its three main safeguards: prohibitions against slaves, rum, and lawyers. Having seen all their idealistic endeavors thwarted, the Trustees at last gave up the fight and let their colony revert to the crown to be managed, like the twelve older colonies to the north, by the Lords of Trade and Plantations.

The year 1750 was significant in several ways. A start was made in manufacturing bricks, for which there was unlimited clay and firewood. Also, the old Salzburgers were allowed to increase their holdings from fifty to one hundred acres; and, even more important, settlers were now permitted to select their own land instead of having it assigned according to maps that indicated the location of the land but not its fertility. In July of this year the Trustees sold the Salzburgers all the cattle at their cowpen at Old Ebenezer for only £350, that being £50 less than first demanded; and by 8 August 1751 the Salzburgers had paid £150 of their bond. This not only increased the Salzburgers' herds considerably, but also removed the difficulty they had experienced in keeping their cattle from joining those of the Trustees. The Trustees themselves had experienced no end of trouble with their cowpen, in part because of the shiftlessness and dishonesty of their managers. For example, in 1743 the German redemptioners Christoph Ryländer and Georg Held, servants at the cowpen, had attested that the manager, Joseph Barker, had starved the Trustees' horses while feeding his own hogs and, for pay, the horses of strangers. Christian Rump and Henry Miers (the Heinrich Meyer who so annoyed Boltzius) added evidence. Boltzius himself had complained mightily about Barker's claiming unfair rewards for "finding" the Salzburgers' unlost cattle and also about working one of his horses nearly to death.

Ebenezer received some soldier settlers about this time, and on 7 January 1750 Benjamin Martyn, the Trustees' secretary, sent a reprimand to Colonel Stephens for not having paid the disbanded soldiers in Ebenezer the £5 promised to each of them for settling in Georgia. At about the same time Boltzius reported in his journal that he had visited two soldiers who had recently settled on Ebenezer Creek and were behaving themselves well. It is not clear whether they were both Germans, but at least one was German and another had a German wife. The English regiment at Frederica had been disbanded; it was not long before most of the inhabitants of German Village on St. Simons folded their tents and drifted northward, some, like the Gebhards, to Ebenezer. In 1747 John Terry wrote that only two German families were still at Frederica, and he must have been right, for on 8 November a certain Davis had transported sixty-four "freights" of Germans from Frederica to Savannah. One freight equaled one adult or two children, an infant carried at the mother's breast not being counted.

The year 1750 was a banner year for silk raising; President Stephens and his assistants in Savannah even scolded Boltzius for paying the silk raisers too little. Boltzius was farsighted enough to distrust all subsidies, and he did not wish to expand the industry greatly as long as it depended upon them. A year after the second Swabian transport reached Bethany, Boltzius provided them with five thousand mulberry trees for £1 5 s., which was one-twentieth the price demanded in Savannah. Matthias Zettler's wife Elisabeth Margaretha, née Kieffer, produced seven pounds and fifteen ounces of silk, as James Habersham, now the Salzburgers' staunchest champion, wrote to Benjamin Martyn the following year. This additional income obviously helped the young couple buy their slave woman. Impressed by the Salzburgers' industry, Habersham wrote Martyn on 5 March 1750:

> I have had the Opportunity for some Years past of knowing these People, as well, or perhaps better than any Person in the colony, and have always thought them deserving of every Encouragment, which has induced me, as well from a Sense of Duty, as Inclination, to represent their Situation relating to their Lands as fully as I can; and I wish those on Blue Bluff, as well as those vacant on Black Creek may answer their Expectation.

Black Creek was an area southeast of Ebenezer near Joseph's Town that was then being settled by Germans.

For Boltzius, all this prosperity was darkened when two of his four children died of fever within a single week; yet he did not let this tragedy hinder his performance of duty in any way, except that Lemke gave the funeral addresses for the two children. Boltzius was not the only parent to suffer this tragedy: three other children died of the same ailment in one day, and they were followed a few days later by three more and by still others throughout the year. They all seem to have recovered from the measles before succumbing to the *rote Friesel,* which the English called "military disease" or the "purples."

Health on the coastal plain of Georgia did not really improve until the twentieth century with the introduction of artesian wells, sewage facilities, vaccines, malaria control, and wonder drugs, all of which have made the region so salubrious that many Salzburger descendants now attain a remarkable old age. During the colonial period mortality from disease, especially among children, was most appalling. Although Thilo was a highly trained physician for his time, his diagnoses are of little help in recognizing the diseases he treated, since he describes general symptoms that would fit dysentery, typhus, typhoid, and other illnesses. Boltzius, also armed only with the medical knowledge of his time, attributed sickness primarily to the weather and warned his parishioners not to exhaust themselves in pursuit of worldly gain. Although ahead of most of his contemporaries in medical knowledge, Boltzius himself was somewhat dumbfounded by the improvement of a withered arm after the application of a belt of human skin. Strangely, he did not ask the origin of the human skin.

With so many ailments at Ebenezer, it was fortunate that yellow fever and smallpox never struck, even though these plagues ravaged Charleston several times during the colonial period. An English servant by the name of Sommers, who contracted smallpox in South Carolina, continued to function at the Trustees' cowpen, yet the infection did not spread to New Ebenezer. One Ebenezer inhabitant may have benefited from the climate. Gottfried Christ had been in an advanced stage of consumption when he joined the third transport at Frankfurt; yet, even though he continued to hemorrhage frequently, his condition does not seem to have worsened. Surely he would not have survived as many winters in crowded northern European quarters as he did in the milder climate of Georgia, where the huts were better ventilated.

When we read of the tragic infant mortality at Ebenezer, we should remember that people of the eighteenth century as a whole were forced to react differently from us. Having so little certainty that her child would live, a pregnant woman could not give it all her love. Until relatively recently, the Negroes on the Georgia coast called a newborn baby a "come-see," because it came only to see whether it wished to remain, which it often did not. We should remember that thousands of pregnant women and mothers of suckling children embarked for America, fully aware that the voyage was almost certain death for the child; and even in Ebenezer the inhabitants seemed more alarmed by mortality among their cattle than among their children. The Salzburgers were not the only people in Georgia to lose children. Habersham lost two daughters at about the same time that Boltzius lost his two children, yet both had some children left, unlike poor Schweiger and Rottenberger. Infant mortality struck in Europe also; Urlsperger survived all his children but one, and Good Queen Anne lost all eighteen of hers.

Despite so much sickness and the prevailing malaria, there may be some truth to de Brahm's contention that the German children born in America were better specimens than their parents, who had been crushed, physically and spiritually, by hard labor and petty tyranny. He was, of course, a romanticist and quite intoxicated with his own verbosity; yet his quaint observations justify quoting the following two sentences:

> The author has made a peculiar observation of those Germans, with whom he made the settlement of Bethany, among which were very few well built Attitudes, and much less likely faces, and very few of them has to this day, learned as much English as to make themselves tolerably understood, nor is there any English family settled among them, & their Schools as also divine Services are all in the German Language. This notwithstanding the Children born there, are all of a genteel attitude of likely & some very handsome countenances and what is as peculiar all speak ye English as easy as the German Language, for which the Author allows the following causes: that the Parents when in Germany their native Country, they laboured under hard oppressions in time of War, more then in time of peace, also under great cares and anxieties to raise their Taxes & Quit Rents which kept their minds always pressed with a gloomy downcast, to which they became so familiar that they even printed them on their features where they served as Characters or Hieroglyphics to indicate the condition of their minds to those, as are Connoisseurs, but coming to America, where, they enjoy the sweets of Peace, & the Bounties of Liberty, where they have all things in abundance surrounding their houses, & but small Taxes to pay the Legislator and a smaller Quit Rent to their humane King, their minds are raised & elevated with Joy & Gladness, which, altho' it cannot be so lively embossed on their own worn out & callous Countenances, yet it is printed with full & sweet Characters on the delicate features of their Babes. which as they are growing without being compelled by their parents (as they were by their Ancestors) to submit their tender shoulders to a share of hard domestic Burdens, in order to help acquiring what must pay the preemptory demands of their Princes, Lords & Nobles, they therefore have an uninterrupted & unpressed procession in their growth; & as their minds are not perplexed, consequently not weakened in their liquid Spring, as those of their parent's have been, their

Memories, like soft Wax, take & retain all the impressions of sound & words they receive from those English; which peradventure pass through the Settlement & are necessitated to enter one or two hours conversation now in one, then in another family.

As soon as de Brahm arrived, he took out five-hundred-acre grants for himself and for several members of the von Münch family of Augsburg. Apparently unmindful of England's strict mercantilist policies, these enterprising philanthropists seem to have harbored hopes of large-scale commercial and industrial development in Ebenezer, and it was probably for their benefit that Boltzius prepared detailed answers to eighty-eight questions concerning the establishing and operating of slave-labor plantations (22). There is evidence that Christian von Münch, the head of the family, had already circumvented some of the British import restrictions by making a charitable donation of merchandise, which was sold to pay for the mills; this transaction probably explains the £200 that Boltzius, in a letter of 29 January 1748, requested the Trustees to repay him.

De Brahm quickly made a name for himself among the English, and Habersham wrote to Martyn that de Brahm was one of the most intelligent men he had ever met. Promoted to Surveyor General of the Southern District of North America, de Brahm produced a superb map of South Carolina, Georgia, and Florida; he also erected fortifications in all those regions. Although his home, Koblenz, was far from the sea, he was the first to plot the course of the Gulf Stream.

Soon after building Fort Loudon on the western frontier, de Brahm had the good fortune to be transferred just before the garrison was massacred by the Indians. Later, after the death of his wife Wilhelmina, he married a wealthy South Carolina widow, the relict of Edward Fenwicke, spent the Revolutionary period in England, and subsequently settled at Bristol, Pennsylvania, where he, now a Quaker, devoted himself to mystical and metaphysical writings (47).

Among the servants on the *Charles Town Galley* in 1749 were three brothers named Schubdrein, whom Zouberbuhler had picked out in Savannah for his own use on 12 January of the following year; but Boltzius, seeing their good qualities, advanced them money to pay their passage and thus become free. As free men, the brothers served willingly and well in Ebenezer and won all hearts. One year later, in January 1751, the youngest, Johann Peter, returned to their home at Weyer in Nassau-Saarbrücken to persuade other members of their family to come to Georgia, and he even visited Augsburg before returning with the second Swabian transport. Soon after the other members of his family arrived, Boltzius wrote, "All the Schubdreins are right Christian, industrious, practical, and contented people, who are useful to us and whom God blesses in their profession."

By this time Ebenezer was so prosperous that it could be recommended despite the high mortality rate. Already by 1744 the orphanage was no longer necessary as such, either because adult mortality had decreased or because child mortality had increased, so it was put to other uses such as sheltering the strangers who came to have their grain ground at the mill. Thus the saintly orphan-father Kalcher became a tavern keeper, while continuing to cultivate his grain fields with horse and plow. By now most of the Salzburgers had riding horses, a luxury enjoyed in their fatherland only by the very wealthy. Of course, the horses were not only a luxury, but also a necessity in rounding up cattle, for Georgia was then on the wild west frontier, where cattle ranged free.

Black magic annoyed Boltzius again in 1750, this time in his own parish; he had to reprimand a widow for allowing her servant to exorcise her cattle. More important that year was the founding of Goshen, an outlying settlement of Salzburgers southeast of Ebenezer and "behind" Abercorn. The settlement was called Goshen because it was considered as fertile as the Israelites' home in Egypt. (When Johann Adam Treutlen's brother Friedrich bought fifty acres at Goshen on 23 July 1755 from Johann Caspar Both, he was listed as Frederick Trith, which was hardly more recognizable than the name Frideling on the passenger list of the *Judith*.) Abercorn was also growing; on 13 July 1750 Friedrich Helfenstein and two other Germans petitioned for an island in the Savannah River across from Abercorn. This developing area was served by Zion Church, a substantial house of worship, which had already been built in 1743 by the Salzburgers on the "plantations" between Ebenezer and Abercorn.

In 1751 Boltzius received a five-hundred-acre estate near Goshen, which he named Good Harmony. However, unlike the Swiss ministers Chiffelle, Zouberbuhler, and Zubly and the English officials Causton and Stephens, he never attempted to develop it for his own enjoyment, always putting the good of his congregation before any personal gain. Lemke was even more abstemious, willingly living in virtual penury and turning his three-hundred-acre estate over to three deserving Salzburgers. Despite their easy opportunity to amass wealth, the Ebenezer pastors lived hardly better than their parishioners, and their dwellings scarcely differed from those of their flock. A cottage recently restored in Ebenezer reveals the mortised-timber construction then being developed by the Salzburgers (plate 21).

Because the population of Ebenezer was rapidly expanding with the arrival of the Swabian transports, the Reverend Fathers in Germany decided that Boltzius and Lemke needed help. Consequently, while organizing the third Swabian transport in 1752, they agreed to send a chaplain with it; for this purpose they selected Christian Rabenhorst, a thirty-year-old minister who was from Pagenköpp in Pomerania and therefore a North German like Boltzius, Gronau, and Lemke. Also like them, Rabenhorst had studied and taught at Halle. The SPCK being unwilling to furnish a third salary, the Reverend Fathers in Germany collected funds to buy and develop a plantation in Ebenezer to support the third pastor. Unfortunately, they did not make the matter of seniority clear, and the more aggressive and somewhat greedy Rabenhorst soon had the docile Lemke up against the wall.

The bachelor Rabenhorst was to dine at the home of David Kraft, a merchant who had arrived with the second Swabian transport and had opened a store in Ebenezer; however, Kraft had died before Rabenhorst's arrival, and the latter married his well-established widow. Rabenhorst did not take charge of the "third minister's plantation" immediately but let Lemke assume the responsibility until the winter of 1756/57. Then, enjoying both his wife's plantation and the minister's plantation, Rabenhorst was financially ahead of his salaried seniors, especially since his wife was not only a competent manager of the two plantations but also a grasping businesswoman who made her husband accept all benefits due him. At first Rabenhorst succeeded in alienating Boltzius from Lemke; but in time Boltzius saw his error and was reconciled with his unassuming colleague. It was probably because of this friction that Urlsperger failed to edit and publish the pastors' reports for the years 1755 through 1758.

Having fought manfully against slavery for fifteen years, Boltzius resigned himself to it once it had been introduced. Because free labor could not compete against unfree he realized that, once slavery was established, his congregation would have to come to terms with it. Also, all his efforts to obtain hired hands for his old and worn-out Salzburgers had failed. Some of the Palatine and Swabian servants had died before repaying their passage, others had remained too sick to earn their keep, a few had run away, and the rest completed their service before becoming really useful. As a result, Boltzius gradually saw the need of Negro slaves, which he justified in his journal entry for 3 January 1753.

In the spring of 1753 Habersham brought in a shipload of blacks from St. Kitts and St. Christopher and auctioned them on 18 April after having washed and fattened them for sale. At this cash auction Boltzius bought a twenty-six-year-old Catholic man and two other men and two women, who pleased him with their behavior and the skill with which they rowed him back upriver to Ebenezer. Boltzius soon noted that blacks had the same native intelligence as whites and differed only through their lack of civilization; he was convinced that, with proper treatment and training, they could be equally good Christians.

As mentioned, money had been collected in Germany for Rabenhorst's support; it was decided that the capital could be most safely invested in a plantation operated by a white man using Negro labor. For this purpose Boltzius surrendered his estate Good Harmony near Goshen in return for land on the Blue Bluff, and it is not clear whether the five slaves he bought remained on the "third pastor's plantation" or stayed with him. By now the Germans in the area were increasing so rapidly that by 1755 the Lutherans of Abercorn, Joseph's Town, and Goshen were able to build a church and school at Goshen.

Boltzius's twenty-year bout with malaria had taken its toll, and his energies had greatly decreased. Besides that, his eyes were failing, especially his left one, which was nearly blind. Lemke gradually took over most entries in the journal; but this can be detected only by occasional references to Boltzius in the journal, since Lemke closely followed the style of his predecessor. As long as there had been only two pastors, God had usually kept one well enough to function; but now that there were three, there were periods in which not one was well and the necessary duties devolved on the one who was least sick. In time Rabenhorst became seasoned and strong enough to assume his share of the chores, thereby easing Boltzius's task.

The mortality of the old settlers and the influx of new is well illustrated by the names of the children confirmed on 5 May 1754. Representing the earlier families we find Christian Steiner, Hanna Elisabeth Gronau, and Maria Kogler, while the later families were represented by Johannes Remshardt and Jacob Bächle from Langenau, Maria Rosina Hammer from Lausnitz, Ursula Unsold from Giengen, Barbara Schneider from Trimbach, Anna Maria Zürcher from Purysburg, and Anna Maria Häfner from Vernonburg, she being the step-daughter of Adam Straub. The next confirmation class had a similar ratio. Among the Salzburger children we find Johannes Gruber, Hanna Flerl, Maria Kalcher, and Elisabeth Maurer; among the newcomers we find Benjamin Friedrich Stähele from Württemberg, Johann Jacob Heinle of Gerstaetten, Elisabeth Gnann from Ulm, Angelica Heck from Langenau, Anna Margaretha Rosch of Purysburg, and Maria Elisabeth Schwarzwelder from Old Ebenezer.

Like most Germans in colonial America, those in Savannah shunned politics and left such worldly concerns to the Englishmen, partly because they did not understand the English language or political system, but mostly because they were more concerned with the City of God than the city of man. This, however, did not hold true for Ebenezer, where Germans had to engage in political functions because there were only Germans there. English democracy prevailed at Ebenezer; the congregation selected its officials before they were appointed by the crown. In a letter of 16 February 1755 to Urlsperger, Boltzius wrote:

> A right good arrangement has been made at our place by our Lord Governor John Reynolds (who is a well-minded regent and a patron of the Ebenezer ministers and congregation) for

the furtherance of good order and the administration of justice. Namely, four justices of the peace have been appointed, who are Mr. Rabenhorst, Mr. Mayer, John Flerl, and Theobald Kieffer, who are to hold a court of conscience every two weeks on Thursday and are to take three knowledgeable inhabitants in turn from our three main districts and quickly settle all sorts of disputes that are not capital crimes and all debts that do not amount to more than two pounds Sterling according to local laws, equity, and their best knowledge and conscience. They are to punish all recalcitrant and disorderly people with prison and fines and other legal means, and there will be no appeal to any other court.

On 20 February 1755 "John Ludwig Meyer, Clement Martin, and John Flert [Flerl]" were appointed collectors for the town and district of Ebenezer; and on 7 March of the same year Mathias West, John Flerl, Ludwig Meyer, Theobald Kieffer, Christian Riedelsperger, and Mathias Zettler were appointed surveyors of the highways. One soon notes that, year after year, certain names appear and reappear on the rolls of public servants.

All in all, the year 1756 was prosperous; the population of Ebenezer continued to grow as indentured servants who had served out their terms at or near Savannah requested grants in the all-German community. The silk industry was still flourishing; as William Little wrote to the Board of Trade in London, "in the year 1756 there was raised at Savannah 1024 lbs. and 14 oz. of cocoons—at Ebenezer 1232 lbs. 11 oz." In the early years of the industry, the Salzburgers, like the other silk producers in Georgia, had been held back by the Piedmontese expert Mary Camuse (Maria Camuso), who had maliciously kept her secrets from the Salzburg girls sent to her in Savannah to learn the business; now Joseph Ottolenghe, an Anglican convert from Judaism who managed the silk industry in Savannah, insisted that all cocoons in Georgia be brought to the filature in Savannah for processing. Naturally this restriction on their freedom deprived the Salzburgers of much of their profit, but it did shorten the time they needed to devote to business. The industriousness of the Germans, particularly of the Swabians, caught the attention of Governor John Reynolds, who wrote to the Trustees on 29 March 1756 that "the Germans in this Province are a very Industrious People" and that "more of them should be brought from Württemberg, who would come at their own expense with only a little support, perhaps 4 £ for the first year."

By 1757 the Salzburgers served as public servants not only for Ebenezer but also for Abercorn and Goshen. On 4 February the collectors and assessors for the town and district of Ebenezer were David Montaigut, Theobald Kieffer, and Charles Thilo, and after 28 July they were John Flerl, John Goldwire, and John Caspar Wertsch. On both dates the collectors and assessors for Abercorn and Goshen were John Morell and Mathias West. On 19 July the following were appointed commissioners for Ebenezer: "William de Brahm, Robert Hudson, John Thomas, Ludowick Mayers, John Flerl, and Theobald Kieffer, Esquires." By now Ludwig Meyer, Johann Flerl, and Theobald Kieffer were prominent enough to consort with de Brahm and his English associates. Three years later, on 24 April 1760, these three were serving again, along with John Goldwire; in the same year Meyer, Flerl, Wertsch, and William Ewen were appointed commissioners for erecting forts in Saint Matthews Parish. Needless to say, the military engineer de Brahm was in command of this undertaking, which was a heavy and unnecessary burden for the Salzburgers because, even though the French and Indian War had begun in 1755, there were no French and few Indians anywhere near Ebenezer.

During the brief period from 27 January to 27 July 1757, the following people registered grants in Ebenezer: "Christian Rabenhorst, heirs of David Kraft, Mathias Brandner,

Christian Riedelsperger, Ludwig Meyer, Michael Weber, Christian Birk, Thomas Gschwandel, Simon Reutter (Reiter), Ludwig Weidman, Hannah Elizabeth Gronau, Mary Frederick Gronau, John Cornberger, Christian Leimberger, Christian Stainer (Steiner), Christian van Munch, Thomas van Munch, Charles van Munch, George Heckall, Michael Snyder (Schneider), John Michael Herse, Veit Leckner (Lechner), John George Snyder, Christoph Cramer, Frederick Bruckner, Daniel Schubdrien, Veit Landfelder, Charles Sigmund Ott, Daniel Burgstainer, George Swyger (Schweiger), Elizabeth Hunold, John Martin Boltzius."

In the following six months, additional grants of land at Ebenezer were issued to "Balthasar Backer, John Reutter, Ezekiel Backler, Valentine Depp, John Pletter, John Hangleiter, Ruprecht Erschberger (Eischberger), Ludwig Ernst, Gabriel Maurer, John Maurer, Nicholas Cronenberger, George Fowl (Faul), John Sheraus, John Jacob Metzger, Davis Ashperger (David Eischberger), George Dressler, John Gaspar Walthour, Peada (Pieta!) Clara Stroub, Conrade Rahn, Paul Fink, John Gugell, Martin Lackner, Sr., Martin Lackner, Jr., Matthias Zettler, Peter Arnsdorff, Joseph Schubdrein, Nicholas Schubdrein, and Maria Catherine Cranwetter." In addition, we find in Goshen: "Gotleb Stayley, Jacob Ports, John George Henry, John Staley, Jr., Michael Borman, Matthias West, Matthias Zettler, Peter Arnsdorff, and Jacob Walthour."

These lists reveal that, despite twenty years of high mortality, a number of the early inhabitants of Ebenezer were still active, among them Arnsdorff, Bacher, Brandner, Burgsteiner, Cornberger, Eischberger, Gschwandl, Heinrich, Landfelder, Leinberger, Maurer, Ott, Pletter, Reiter, Riedelsperger, Schneider, Schweiger, Steiner, and Zettler. It also shows that some succeeded in rearing children old enough to take up land. Most of the Salzburgers, having no slaves, were satisfied with small grants of fifty or a hundred acres, which were as much as they could operate and as much as they could obtain close to their church. There were some exceptions, however. For example, on 3 July 1759 the governor and council of Georgia granted John Helvenstine fifty acres, in addition to his previous two hundred, on an island above Abercorn and adjoining land of Frederick Helvenstein. Newcomers were sometimes even more ambitious. On 7 February 1758, Stephan Millen requested and received 150 acres on Ebenezer Creek eight miles west of Old Ebenezer; on 3 February 1761 he had 250 acres and received 150 more; and on 3 July 1764 he received an additional 200, making a total of 600 acres. This may help explain why Mühlenberg always referred to him as Squire Millen.

Although it was the largest such building in Georgia, Jerusalem Church was quite inadequate for the Salzburgers when they came in from the plantations and outlying villages on special occasions. Well aware of this fact, the benefactors in Germany collected funds for a new structure, this one to be of brick, since the previous wooden ones had rotted so quickly in the semitropical climate. Unfortunately Boltzius did not live to see this dream come true, for he died on 19 November 1765 and the new church was not completed until 1770, delayed in part by a dishonest or incompetent mason who began building with poor quality mortar. The new church, built of large bricks, still stands today, the only vestige of the once promising town of Ebenezer (plate 20). Boltzius's death was a double blow to Ebenezer; the congregation lost a devoted, self-sacrificing, and effective spiritual and secular leader, and he was replaced by a man who was destined to sow fatal dissension in the congregation.

7

Dissension and Destruction

pon hearing of Boltzius's death and knowing that Lemke would soon follow, the Reverend Fathers conducted a search for a replacement, but this proved more difficult than expected. They found few qualified young men and hardly anyone willing to undertake the difficult and dangerous mission to Georgia. Because Samuel Urlsperger was then retiring at the age of eighty, he delegated the search to his son and heir, Johann August Urlsperger, who was henceforth one of the Reverend Fathers. After several candidates had declined the call, only two remained, both of whom the younger Urlsperger found unsatisfactory. A certain Mauer was too sullen and phlegmatic; the other candidate, Christian Friedrich Triebner, was selfish and unstable. Urlsperger judged Triebner well because he had known him as a teacher at the Francke Foundation; yet less-informed people gave him good recommendations and he was chosen.

As had been the case of Boltzius and Vat and later the case of Lemke and Rabenhorst, the Reverend Fathers did not clarify Triebner's rank; he was allowed to believe himself Lemke's replacement and therefore Rabenhorst's superior. This was of course not so, since Rabenhorst had seventeen years seniority and was well liked by the congregation. Soon after his arrival in 1769, Triebner married Gronau's daughter

Friederica Maria, thus becoming the brother-in-law of Wertsch, the husband of Gronau's daughter Hanna Elisabeth. Now allied with a strong Ebenezer faction, Triebner accused Rabenhorst of trying to misappropriate the mills.

Boltzius had already transferred control of the mills to Lemke in 1757, and Lemke had passed it on to Rabenhorst ten years later. The mills having become unremunerative under communal management, Rabenhorst had leased them to a tenant, who was able to make them profitable once again. Instead of investigating the situation carefully, Triebner hastily wrote his suspicions to the Reverend Fathers; the younger Urlsperger believed them and made Triebner the manager of the mills. The mill board in Ebenezer, being well acquainted with the facts, rejected the distant and misinformed benefactor's decision; soon open friction broke out between the two pastors. Being an emotional man, Triebner raged even in the pulpit, from which he made scurrilous accusations against his opponent; the supporters of both pastors bombarded the benefactors in Europe with scathing denunciations.

Although the dispute was more economic than theological, Triebner denied Holy Communion to Rabenhorst and his party; Rabenhorst, feeling himself abandoned by his superiors in Germany, even offered to retire to Savannah rather than split the congregation. But the congregation was already split; Jerusalem Church found itself with two sets of church wardens. On Triebner's side were Wertsch, Johann Flerl, Christopher Krämer, Matthäus Biddenbach, Johann Paulus, and Paul Müller, while Rabenhorst was backed by Treutlen, Ulrich Neidlinger, Christian Steiner, Joseph Schubdrein, Samuel Krause, and Jakob Caspar Waldhauer. Thus upright citizens were found on both sides. This schism almost ended when Rabenhorst and his wife nearly died of rat poison, apparently administered by a demented old slave woman. It could have been judged an accident if other slaves had not said that the old woman boasted of her deed. Triebner naturally thought her the instrument of a righteous God; but according to one report, she "fell into the hands of the authorities and was burned alive."

The English laws of the time did not allow for such punishment, yet there had been a precedent, for in 1741 fourteen blacks and whites had been burned in New York for fomenting a Negro rebellion. Since the time of Spartacus and long before, servile insurrections had been put down with the greatest cruelty, otherwise slavery and serfdom would not have been possible. After Wat Tyler's men were suppressed in 1381 and the German peasants were crushed in 1524, the English and German peasants had remained docile. Similar brutality had been dealt the slaves who revolted at Stono in South Carolina soon after the Salzburgers settled at New Ebenezer. Since the Rabenhorsts' slave had not been tried by due process of law, her burning must be judged a lynching, perhaps the first of the many in Georgia.

Confused by conflicting reports of the clerical squabble from Ebenezer, the European benefactors requested Heinrich Melchior Mühlenberg, the Lutheran patriarch in Philadelphia, to make the arduous journey to Ebenezer to reconcile the two warring pastors. Apprised of Mühlenberg's approaching visit, the congregation made one last attempt at reconciliation, but Triebner repeated all of his old accusations. The next day, when the members of Triebner's party tried to enter Jerusalem Church, Treutlen, Jenking Davis, and Johann Niess drove them away with drawn swords so that Rabenhorst could preach unmolested.

Arriving in Savannah on 28 October 1774 after an exhausting voyage, the aged Mühlenberg lodged with Stephan Millen, the previously mentioned Lutheran landholder, and summoned the two feuding pastors to come to him individually and acknowledge his authority in the dispute. He then went to Ebenezer and forced the two ministers to make up;

but it soon appeared that, even if they themselves had been willing to reconcile their differences, their adherents were not. Armed with the power to confiscate the third minister's plantation and return the capital to the donors, Mühlenberg finally compelled the factions to make peace, on which occasion he caused all adult male parishioners to sign new rules for governing the church (*Kirchenordnung*). These rules were exceptionally well formulated, perhaps with the help of Treutlen, the astute and well-trained justice of the peace, yet in substance they hardly differed from the procedures arduously developed by Boltzius in his thirty years of tenure.

After many long sessions, which are vividly reported in Mühlenberg's journal (20), harmony was restored and the congregation returned more or less to its former condition. Against Triebner's protests the mills were again rented out, this time to Christian Steiner. An important result of Mühlenberg's visit was his discovery that, apparently innocently, Triebner and Wertsch had almost let Jerusalem Church and its glebe land escheat to the established Anglican church, since the words *Evangelical Lutheran* had somehow been omitted from its new charter.

Through his great wisdom and experience, Mühlenberg aided the people of Ebenezer in many ways and endeared himself both to them and to the authorities in Savannah. Before sailing from Savannah, he paid his respects to James Habersham, now a wealthy planter and vice-governor (plate 19), whom Mühlenberg had known thirty-two years earlier as a slim young schoolmaster. Meanwhile, Habersham had become portly and was suffering dreadfully from gout. Seeing his agony on his "torture rack," Mühlenberg remembered the words of a German divine who had asked God to keep him and his children from ever becoming members of the nobility. Apparently Mühlenberg shared the current belief that gout resulted from high living.

Not long after Mühlenberg's departure from Ebenezer,

Triebner, a married man with three children, was accused of familiarity with the late Lemke's younger daughter. Upon his refusal to obey Court Chaplain Ziegenhagen's command to stand trial, he was dismissed from office. Consequently, after Rabenhorst died in 1776, Ebenezer had no pastor at all; the senior vestryman, Ulrich Neidlinger, conducted services.

All this time Ebenezer continued to grow, mainly through the addition of new inhabitants from the North, most of them from Pennsylvania, as was a certain Mr. Schrind who suddenly appears in the church records. The Jerusalem Church records list a woman named Reinier, whose husband appears to have been none other than the Moravians' physician, John Regnier. This Swiss, who had already joined various sects, had broken with the Moravians in Savannah and had returned to Europe. Later he moved to Philadelphia; from there he returned to Georgia, an older, more practical, and less idealistic man who could acquire both slaves and land. Although he used a French spelling for his name, he seems to have been German by tongue. Mühlenberg sent a diligent young man named Israel Heintzelmann down from Philadelphia to help Treutlen in his store, and Treutlen was so pleased with him that he would have given him his daughter Rachel in marriage if Heintzelmann had not been thrown from a horse and killed. By an odd coincidence Treutlen, who thus lost a son-in-law, had previously gained his second wife through a similar accident when David Unselt was thrown from a horse in a "hateful" race, leaving his wife Anna as an available widow. Had Boltzius still been alive, such a worldly amusement as racing would never have taken place.

Partly because of the new settlers from the North, Georgia, so well treated by the crown, began to make common cause with the rebellious inhabitants of the older and discontented colonies; it was not long before Treutlen and most of the other Georgians embraced the Whig or revolutionary party. James Habersham, a Loyalist to the core, died at about this time, thereby freeing his three sons to join the rebels. Triebner may have shown as much insight as malice in stating that young John Habersham joined the rebels to cancel his debts to his London creditors, for most colonial merchants received their wares on credit, for which they paid usurious interest. Having been favored and almost coddled by the royal government, the Salzburgers had little reason to rebel, other than because the crown's mercantilist policies had sometimes interfered with their proper economic interests, as Boltzius intimated in his journal for 11 October 1754.

Treutlen, who spoke excellent English, had had legislative experience and was familiar with the colonial leaders; in May 1777 he was elected as the first governor of the new state of Georgia. Treutlen's term of office, less than a year, was not spectacular; he did, however, succeed in obtaining a large grant of money from the Continental Congress, and also prevented some Carolinians from persuading the Georgians to join their struggling colony to their wealthier neighbor to the north. A price set on the instigators' heads kept them from returning to Georgia. Because Triebner refused to swear allegiance to the new republican government, he was arrested and declared a prisoner by John Holtzendorff, the speaker of Georgia's House; eventually he was forced, at swordpoint, to abjure his oath to the king.

Triebner's day was soon to come. The British commander, Col. Archibald Campbell, captured Savannah near the end of 1778, along with much of its garrison and all of its supplies; as he approached Ebenezer behind a horde of refugees, he was met by the Loyalist pastor, who urged him to occupy Ebenezer and protect her loyal inhabitants, who were ready and anxious to reaffirm their allegiance to the king. As long as the British and Hessian troops remained in Ebenezer, Triebner dined at the colonel's table; he preached freely in Jerusalem Church to those of his parishioners who had not fled with the Whig party or later slipped away to serve with the rebel troops.

Ebenezer was again in American hands for a short period after Count D'Estaing landed a French army at the late Colonel Stephens's plantation at Beaulieu in September 1779 to help the Americans retake Savannah, causing the British there to withdraw all outlying garrisons. Unfortunately for the American cause, the allied assault of 9 October failed, the French army sailed away, and the battered American survivors withdrew across the Savannah River at Zubly's Ferry, leaving Ebenezer once again in British hands. Triebner soon lost the use of Jerusalem Church because the king's men, being unseasoned, were sick much of the time and needed it as a hospital. The British commanders were then in the process of transferring their British troops from the South to the healthier climate of the northern colonies, leaving the poor Hessians to swelter in the malarial South, where far more of them died of disease than of bullets.

Ebenezer had deteriorated so far by this time that the Hessian colonel Friedrich von Porbeck could refer to it as "an insignificant place," as compared to Abercorn, which had meanwhile become a thriving rice plantation when an Englishman named William Knox bought up the small German farms and consolidated them into a large slave-operated agribusiness, thus fulfilling Boltzius's dire predictions. When, in 1774, Knox had wished to convert his slaves, he turned to the Moravians, who sent him two missionaries, Ludwig Müller and Johann Georg Wagner. These missionaries arrived in Georgia in the same year and took up residence in Knoxborough, as Abercorn was sometimes called, and preached there and in Goshen, where some Lutheran families still resided. Needless to say, their presence in Goshen was most unwelcome to Mühlenberg, who feared they would fish in troubled waters. Actually he did not need to worry, for Müller died within the year and Wagner returned a few years later to England, having accomplished little.

Legend says that Jerusalem Church served the British not only as a hospital but also as a stable; by the end of the war nearly all the floors, windowsills, and other woodwork had been destroyed. For years after the Revolution a weather vane representing Luther's swan showed a small hole, which was said to have been made by a Hessian soldier's bullet. Most serious was the destruction of the millrace, which the British cut through to bring their boats closer to Ebenezer, thereby putting an inglorious end to the chief industry of Ebenezer.

While Ebenezer stagnated under British occupation, the war raged on in up-country Georgia and the Carolinas. Augusta and Charleston fell, and Cornwallis cut a swath through the heartland of the Carolinas before being penned up at Yorktown in Virginia, where he surrendered to the French and American besiegers. The internecine strife in Georgia eventually ended, and the Hessian garrison withdrew again from Ebenezer and remained bottled up in Savannah, where, according to von Porbeck, "slatternly women" from Ebenezer tempted many to desert by distributing a proclamation promising land and livestock to all who would change sides. In the summer of 1782 the last of the Hessians in Savannah were transferred to New York and Nova Scotia, leaving Georgia for the victorious Whig party. Several inhabitants of Ebenezer were accused of having collaborated with the British and were sentenced to redeem themselves by serving a period in the Continental Army. This sentence, which was never enforced, was soon repealed, either because the accused proved their innocence or because the army no longer needed them or was unable to maintain additional troops.

Treutlen did not live to see the final victory. The British invasion had forced him to withdraw to a plantation in the Orangeburg district of South Carolina next to that of his son. In the spring of 1781 he was elected to represent his constituency at the state assembly in Augusta, but he failed to attend, having been dragged out of his house at night and brutally murdered. Family legend says he was murdered by Tories; but, since the Tories were not very active in Orangeburg at the time, he may have been murdered by personal enemies, perhaps by a jilted suitor, he having just married for the third time. In any case, Treutlen's place of burial, like his place of birth, remains a mystery. The death of such an intelligent, energetic, and capable leader was a dreadful loss for Georgia and especially for Ebenezer (54).

During the British occupation of Ebenezer, Sgt. William Jasper performed the second feat by which he endeared himself to the Patriot cause, if we may believe the account by Parson Weems, from which all later accounts are derived. Upon occupying Georgia, the British determined to punish all prisoners who had broken their parole and fought again after being released. A party of these poor victims, followed by their grieving wives and children, had been collected at Ebenezer before being taken under guard to Savannah for execution. This was the very sort of situation to catch the fancy of Sergeant Jasper, who had arrived in Philadelphia in 1767 as a German indentured servant and had been recruited in Georgia eight years later at Halifax for a South Carolina regiment. After distinguishing himself at the Battle of Fort Moultrie in Charleston Harbor in 1777, he had excelled in guerrilla tactics in the South Carolina backwoods. According to Weems, and subsequent legend, Jasper and a comrade named Newton accompanied the British guard, ostensibly for protection, and marched with it to within a mile of Savannah. There the troops stopped to drink at a spring after tying their prisoners to trees and stacking their arms. Although unarmed, Jasper and Newton overpowered the sentry, seized the muskets, shot the guards, and freed the prisoners. Although this daring rescue smacks of fiction, it concurs with what Gen. Benjamin Lincoln and other trustworthy observers had written about Jasper's previous exploits. In any case, Jasper proved his courage by his heroic death while rescuing his regimental colors during the tragic assault on Savannah, where his heroism is now immortalized by a handsome monument (55).

As the last of the Hessians evacuated Ebenezer, the Tory pastor accompanied them, taking his family and Wertsch's daughter, Mrs. Triebner's niece, with him. Poor Wertsch had recently died, shunned by the Whigs and ignored by the British, yet wealthy enough to leave generous charitable legacies. When Savannah too fell to the rebels, the British and Hessian troops moved to St. Augustine, where Triebner served as von Porbeck's chaplain. From there he innocently wrote asking whether he might return to Ebenezer. According to legend, the Whigs replied that he was most welcome to return, but that he would hang from the nearest tree if he did. Early American historians, more concerned with edification than fact, wrote that the traitor had died in shame and want; but historical documents show that he returned with the troops to England, where he served first in military and then in civilian positions and was granted a £40 pension plus £20 per annum to begin as of the date that the SPCK discontinued his salary. In addition, he received £700 compensation for the £2,260 he claimed was confiscated because of his loyalty to the king. If he had really amassed such a fortune in only ten years in such an impecunious colony, then he cannot have served his congregation very selflessly. Credit should be given him, however, for paying back to his superiors in Europe all funds entrusted to him, funds which his enemies claimed were stolen. His basically contentious character is shown by a defense he inserted in an English newspaper to protect his good name during a later quarrel. Triebner's hasty departure and the Whigs' return to Ebenezer mark the end of the colonial history of the Georgia Salzburgers, which has been the subject of this saga.

✑ Epilogue ✑

ot all Salzburgers returned to Ebenezer at the close of the war. Many young refugees had found healthier and more fertile land in the interior of the country, where they would not have to compete with slave labor; those who had served in the Continental Army received generous grants on the frontier. Because these settlers were scattered among an English-speaking majority, they soon lost their German language. Also, finding no Lutheran churches nearby, many joined Methodist and Baptist congregations, these being the most numerous on the frontier, where, in order to preach, a man needed only the Lord's call, not a diploma from a theological seminary.

Those Salzburgers who returned to Ebenezer found little to encourage them: many plantations had been burned and were plundered of cattle and slaves, while the remaining buildings in the town were dilapidated. Undeterred, all hands pitched in to restore some semblance of order, and the town regained a measure of prosperity. As was always the case with German settlers, as soon as the basic requirements of life had been met, the Salzburgers yearned for spiritual guidance. The activities of the SPCK now being restricted to British subjects, the newly elected vestrymen again approached the Reverend Fathers in Germany, where steps were immediately initiated to supply a minister. Word had reached Germany of the deplorable situation prevailing in Ebenezer, and few young ministers considered giving up the security of their fatherland for a questionable future in Georgia. Yet a volunteer was at last found in the person of Johann Ernst Bergmann.

Bergmann, who had been born into a very poor family of Peretz in Saxony and had studied theology in Leipzig, was then serving at the Halle orphanage while being prepared for service in Pennsylvania. After much decision and revision, he left Halle in May 1786 for Augsburg, where he was ordained; from there he proceeded to Altona, a little port near Hamburg, to meet Johann Gotthilf Probst, who was to serve with him in Ebenezer. They arrived in Charleston on 1 December; three weeks later they reached Ebenezer, where conditions must have discourged Probst, who promptly disappeared.

Like all other newcomers, Bergmann quickly contracted malaria; yet he still saw fit to get married, namely, to Catherine Herb of Savannah. This was a happy marriage, even though three of their four children died very young. Bergmann was a fine man, but not a good choice for Ebenezer. Scholarly, withdrawn, and unable to relate to his rough-and-ready parishioners, he preferred the intellectual companionship of the other divines of the area, regardless of their dogmas. Such tolerance in confessional matters may have emboldened some of his flock to associate with other churches, for he allowed ministers of all persuasions to preach in Jerusalem Church and even allowed a Roman Catholic monk to take up a collection at Ebenezer for his monastery in Switzerland.

The decline of the Jerusalem Church congregation was mainly due, however, to the unwise retention of the German language. For the older generation, German was the language of God and English the language of the world and the devil; but not so for the younger generation, as de Brahm had asserted so many years earlier. The first inhabitants of Ebenezer had spoken only German, be it of a Bavarian, Palatine, Swabian, or even Swiss variety. Knowing the importance of English in an English-speaking colony, Boltzius had immediately introduced English instruction into his school program, using the services of Ortmann, Bishop, and Henry Hamilton, a wigmaker who had lived in Breslau. Against Boltzius's wishes, some Salzburgers had worked at Savannah, Bethesda, Augusta, and elsewhere, where they had picked up a working knowledge of English; a few immigrants, such as Treutlen, had acquired rudiments of the language during their sojourn in England. British troops disseminated their language in Ebenezer for three years, while those Salzburgers who had fled during the war or had served with the American troops had of necessity acquired its use.

In any case, already in the early nineteenth century many young people preferred English and considered German suitable only for old and backward people. Consequently they wished their sermons to be in English; but Bergmann, as a purist, refused to insult the Lord with his broken English. In this he differed from another colonial German pastor who acceded to the wishes of the young people and preached in English, as best he could. An Englishman, who chanced to hear him preach, later expressed amazement that German was so much like English, because he had been able to understand much of the sermon.

The result of Bergmann's retention of German was that he, like many other German Lutheran pastors in America, saw his flock dwindle as the younger members drifted away to English-speaking congregations, especially to those that enjoyed the more emotional brands of religion cherished by frontier people. One Ebenezer pastor is purported to have boasted sadly that the Lutheran church at Ebenezer had produced many of the most outstanding Methodists and

Baptists in Georgia. When Bergmann's only surviving child, Christopher F. Bergmann, succeeded his father as pastor of Jerusalem Church in 1824, he immediately introduced English into the church and thus ended the steady loss of members and ensured the survival of the congregation.

Perhaps encouraged by his father's tolerant and ecumenical views, the younger Bergmann had studied for the Presbyterian ministry; yet, upon accepting the position in Ebenezer, he returned entirely to the Lutheran fold. Unlike Savannah, which had had a series of most disparate ministers and long periods with no minister at all, Ebenezer had enjoyed thirty-five years with ministers who preached the same message. This is not surprising, since the first and foremost, Boltzius, had served for nearly the entire period and had been assisted by men who had received the same Pietistic training at Halle. Even when Triebner arrived and caused a rift, the friction was personal and economic, not theological.

After the Revolution, the economy of Ebenezer fared even worse than her church. The evils of slavery manifested themselves exactly as Boltzius had predicted. While some Salzburgers acquired slaves, this helped them very little and only demeaned the value of hard labor for the other workers. Also, there was no longer any real need for Ebenezer as a market town; Savannah could furnish all market services more efficiently, especially after the introduction of steamboats on the Savannah River. Boltzius and Gronau had both made arduous shopping expeditions to Charleston to bypass the markups demanded by the Savannah merchants (29, 33). A century later the farmers of Effingham County could trade directly with Savannah and thereby avoid the markups required by the merchants in Ebenezer. Thus the merchants remaining in Ebenezer served the same function as "Ma and Pa" stores in large American cities, which fill immediate needs at high prices to customers who do their bulk shopping at distant and less expensive shopping centers. As a result, many Ebenezer merchants and tradesmen moved their businesses to Savannah.

To be sure, the Revolution had hastened the demise of Ebenezer, but the town would surely have died anyway like other towns described by Charles C. Jones in his *Lost Towns of Georgia.* The wonder is not that it died, but that it lived so long, far longer than Purysburg, Hardwick, or other unneeded centers. When Mühlenberg returned to Ebenezer after an absence of thirty years, he noted that the town had not grown very much; and, as mentioned, in 1781 von Porbeck had considered it an insignificant spot. Before the end of the nineteenth century nothing remained of Ebenezer but Jerusalem Church, standing alone among the forests as a monument to the faith for which the Salzburgers had left their homeland (plate 20). The church is still used and is well maintained by its distant congregation; in recent years it has been joined by a handsome museum, a Lutheran retreat, and a fine example of a mortised-log home brought in from nearby (plate 21).

While Ebenezer was vanishing, many of its inhabitants joined their kinsmen across Ebenezer Creek in the area where Springfield now stands. There they continued their agrarian lives and retained not only the blood and names but also the virtues and mores of their German ancestors. Through their work ethic they competed so well against slave labor that Effingham County remained one of the few counties on the coastal plain in which whites continued to outnumber blacks. Even though other people have moved into Effingham County, the Salzburgers remain the dominant element there, and most people bearing English names have at least one Salzburger strain. Nevertheless, far more descendants live elsewhere in Georgia, to say nothing of other states, than in Effingham County, but their number cannot be ascertained.

Epilogue

Since World War II the yeoman farmer has all but disappeared from Ebenezer. Many former farmers have allowed their land to revert to forest, particularly to pulpwood. Some have rented out their arable land to large-scale operators, who cultivate and harvest with expensive laborsaving equipment. Others maintain small plots but earn their major income in nearby businesses and industries. In the mid-nineteenth century Pastor Strobel stated that the Salzburgers had produced no professional men, not even any ministers for their own parish. This situation has changed as the Salzburgers have entered the mainstream of American life. They now produce their fair quota of professionals, not only ministers but also lawyers, legislators, educators, doctors, and military officers. A Salzburger descendant, W. Lee Mingledorff, Jr., was mayor of Savannah from 1955 to 1960.

The pine barrens around Ebenezer, which once produced only low-grade lumber, turpentine, and scrawny "piny woods" cattle, have now become a gold mine for those Salzburgers lucky enough to have held onto them, since they can produce a stand of pine for pulp paper every fourteen or fifteen years, which two large nearby paper mills are quick to consume. This cord wood, which also produces naval stores as byproducts, has made Boltzius's wish come true, that more of his people would devote themselves to the timber business.

With the recent popular interest in "roots," many urban Salzburgers are becoming proud of their exiled forebears, and more and more of them are discovering and acknowledging their ancestry. This process was greatly speeded by the publication of Pearl Rahn Gnann's remarkable genealogy, *Georgia Salzburger and Allied Families* (Savannah, 1965), which was revised in 1970 by her daughter, Mrs. Charles Lebey (38). Compiled when records were hard to find and the general public was still apathetic, this genealogy has alerted thousands of people to their Salzburger heritage, with the result that the Georgia Salzburger Society now numbers fifteen hundred active members, many of them young and vigorous people.

It is hoped that this Salzburger saga will imbue the descendants with a proper admiration for their brave and persevering ancestors.

↬ Appendix 1 ↫
Salzburger Names

Salzburger surnames often terminated in the ending *er,* so much so that in East Prussia, where such names had been uncommon before the arrival of the Salzburger exiles, anyone whose name ended that way was assumed to be an exile. A major subdivision of this category consists of names ending in *berger,* like Berenberger, Braunberger, and Leinberger, which indicate that the first bearer of the name must have lived on or near a mountain named Berenberg, and so forth. Similarly, names like Bach, Biddenbach, Bacher, Wiesenbacher, and Schoppacher suggest that the first bearers once lived on or near a certain brook, just as names like Stein, Helfenstein, Steiner, and Mittensteiner suggest that their ancestors lived on or near a particular rocky mountain. Another large group of names end in *inger,* like Deininger, Ebinger, Eppinger, and Paulinger.

Except for the prevalence of *er* names, the Salzburger names differed little from other South German names, many of which denote a profession, such as Bauer, Baumann, and Meyer (farmer), Fischer (fisherman), Geiger (fiddler), Gerber (tanner), Kieffer (cooper), Krämer (huckster), Maurer (mason), Müller (miller), and Schmidt (smith). Personal characteristics are indicated by names such as Gross (tall), Lang (tall), Kurz (short), Klein (small), Weiss (blond), and Schwarz (brunet).

First names are almost exclusively scriptural. In the Middle Ages most Germans (like most Western Europeans in general) had Germanic names like Albert, Anselm, Bernard, Charles, Henry, Lewis, Roger, and William; but during the Counter-Reformation such secular names were largely replaced by saints' names, except in the case of royalty. Consequently the Salzburgers, including the crypto-Protestants, usually bore saints' names, the most popular for men

139

being Andreas (Andrew), Bartholomäus (Bartholomew), Christoph, Gabriel, Georg, Jacob (James), Johannes (John), Josef, Martin, Matthäus or Matthias (Matthew), Michael, Sebastian, Stephan, and Thomas. A few Germanic names like Bernhard, Lorentz (Lawrence), Ludwig (Lewis, Louis), Ruprecht (Robert), and Wilhelm (William) were acceptable, having been borne by saints. The very few secular names like Conrad, Friedrich, and Heinrich were mostly the names of popular emperors.

As a Protestant, Boltzius accepted only the scriptural saints, and then not as deities but only as exemplary humans; like other Protestants of the time, he seems to have preferred Old Testament names like Abraham, Adam, Benjamin, Daniel, David, Israel, Jacob, Jonathan, Joshua, Nathaniel, Solomon, and Tobias. He often rejected "meaningless" names; he approved of Friedrich and Ulrich only because he mistakenly interpreted them as "Prince of Peace" and "Rich in Grace, " instead of as "Master of the Kinship" and "Rich in Allodial Lands." He was especially fond of German names echoing Hebrew ideas, like Gottfried (God's Peace), Gotthilf (God's Help), Gottlieb (Dear to God), and Leberecht (Live Right).

Feminine names were chosen similarly. Among those from saints we find Agatha, Agnesia, Apollonia, Barbara, Catherina, Dorothea, Elisabeth, Gertraut, Juliana, Magdalena, Margaretha, Maria, Regina, and Ursula, and the Germanic name Waldburga. From the Old Testament we find Eva, Hanna, Rebecca, and Susanna.

The names of men and women were often compounded, the most popular being Johann Adam, Johann Jacob, Johann Martin, and Johann Peter and Maria Dorothea, Maria Elisabeth, Maria Magdalena, and Maria Margaretha.

Most inhabitants of Ebenezer were from South Germany, yet they generally wrote their names as in the standard language. However, they continued to pronounce them according to their particular dialects; this explains why names like Bühler, Kübler, Mück, Oechsele, and Schüle were anglicized as Beeler, Keebler, Mick, Exley, and Sheely, that being the way the English officials heard them. The South German dialects often confused *b* with *p* and *g* with *k*, with the result that Bichler, Biltz, and Gugel also appear as Pichler, Piltz, and Kugel. Likewise, the diphthongs *ei* and *eu* were interchangeable, thus letting Reiter and Treutlen vary with Reuter and Treitlen (misspelled in the records as Tritelen).

Although the dialect pronunciation is most often reflected in the official English records and in the later spellings of many names, the list of names appended here gives only the standard literary forms used in the Ebenezer records and in the archives of the inhabitants' home countries. Those readers who know German should pronounce the names as they are spoken in that language. For others, suffice it to say that *w* and *z* were *always* pronounced as *v* and *ts*, so that Zwiffler was pronounced *Tsv*iffler and Boltzius (even when written Bolzius) was always pronounced Bol*ts*ius. *Ei* was pronounced like English "eye," *eu* like *oy*, and *ie* like *ee;* therefore, Reiter was pronounced like "writer," Treutlen like Troytlen, and Kieffer like Keefer. *Au* resembled *ow* in "cow," and *ü* (=ue) was much closer to *ee* than to *oo*, so that the name Kübler developed into Kiebler and Kieffer could be written as Küffer. The letter *ö* (=oe) resembled the vowel in "girl." *Berg* (pronounced bairk), meaning mountain, should not be confused with *burg* (pronounced boork), meaning castle. *Th* was always pronounced as *t*, so that the name Both was pronounced like "boat."

❦ Appendix 2 ❧
Inhabitants of Ebenezer and Its Dependencies

This appendix attempts to list all the German residents of Ebenezer, Abercorn, Goshen, Bethany, and the areas between them. It also lists a few Lutherans from Purysburg, Halifax, and even Savannah, Acton, and Vernonburg if they sometimes worshiped at Jerusalem Church or later became allied with the Salzburgers, but it does not attempt to list all the many children who died in infancy or adolescence. The list is practically complete for the first seven years; after that some omissions and duplications result from the loss of records and also from the German practice of bestowing two Christian names, either or both of which could be used. For example, Johann Schmidt and Ulrich Schmidt may turn out to have been the same person if a document comes to light recording a Johann Ulrich Schmidt. On the other hand, if Johann Ulrich Schmidt received grants in 1751, 1755, 1761, and 1774 but died in 1768, then the name must have been borne by two people, presumably, but not necessarily, by father and son, (for example, Jacob Gnann II was not the son of Jacob Gnann I but of his brother Georg). It is also probable, but not certain, that a son survived his father and was therefore the recipient of the later grants, but this is not always so. In some families several sons bore the name Johann and several daughters bore the name Maria. In such cases it is obvious that family and friends (but not necessarily the British authorities) called the children by their second name. When this appears to be the case, the less frequently used name appears in parentheses and the more significant name is alphabetized.

To avoid confusing the generations, the year of birth is given when recorded or when deducible from the age given on indentures, ships' manifests, or other sources. Years other than the year of birth have been abbreviated. For example, 47 means 1747. Also given, when known, is the individual's home in Europe. The number following the letter *t* is the number of the transport with which the person arrived, the number following the letters *gr* indicates the year of a grant, *m* follows the year of marriage when known, and *w, s,* and *d* indicate wife, son, and daughter respectively. The letters *dd* indicate "died in" or "dead by" the year given. If a woman married, she appears twice; but her maiden name is in parentheses so it will not be counted twice. In the case of multiple marriages, only the last entry is not in parentheses.

Sometimes a landholder is further identified by the location of his residence or property, be it in Ebenezer (Eb), Abercorn (Ab), Goshen (Go), Bethany (Beth), Purysburg (Pbg), Savannah (Sav), or Vernonburg (Vern). Such identification is not always reliable, since some people exchanged their grants or did not reside on their property. Besides that, in the grant records the name "Ebenezer" is sometimes used specifically to designate Ebenezer as opposed to Abercorn, Bethany, or Goshen, and at other times it is used generally to include Ebenezer and its dependencies as opposed to Savannah. Properties, but not necessarily residences, for the year 1755 and those following are given in the *Cattle Brand Book*, cited here as "55 CB Mil Dis" to show that a brand was registered in 1755 for a person with property in the Mill District (4). The Mill District was a large rectangle of farms reaching from Ebenezer all the way to the mills, with the result that Michael Rieser belonged to the Mill District even though he lived on the very edge of Ebenezer at a considerable distance from the mills. Grants registered in 1755 may have been granted previously and merely reaffirmed in that year, thereby causing duplication.

Birthdates, although not always precise, tend to be fairly accurate, as can be seen by comparing European records with those Egmont received from the various ship captains, who in some cases may have misunderstood the immigrants or guessed their ages from their appearance. Until 1752 discrepancies of one year may have resulted from the German's use of the new Gregorian calendar while the British were still using the older Julian calendar, which was then two months off and assigned January and February to the previous year. Nationalities too are sometimes unreliable, unless confirmed by European records, because the passengers brought over by Yoakley, Hewitt, Thomson, Quarme, and Bogg were classified as "Palatines," in the sense of German redemptioners, even though many were from elsewhere, as was Salomo

Adde, the shoemaker from Tübingen in Württemberg, who arrived with Thomson. Likewise, among Wadham's "Swiss" transport were many Palatines and Württembergers, whom Riemensperger had picked up on his way through Germany.

Abbreviations

Christian Names

Ab	Abraham	Jha	Johanna
Ad	Adam	Jo	Josef, Joseph
Ag	Agatha	Joac	Joachim
Agn	Agnesia	Joh	Johannes, John
An	Anna	Jon	Jonathan
And	Andreas, Andrew	Jsa	Josua, Joshua
Apol	Apollonia	Jul	Juliana
Balt	Balthasar	Leon	Leonhard
Bar	Barbara	Lor	Lorentz, Lawrence
Bart	Bartholomaeus,	Luc	Lucas, Luke
	Bartholomew	Lud	Ludwig, Lewis
Ben	Benjamin	Mag	Magdalena
Bern	Bernhard	Mar	Maria
Casp	Caspar	Marg	Margaretha, Margaret
Cath	Catherina	Mart	Martin
Chna	Christina	Mat	Matthaeus, Matthew
Chph	Christoph, Christopher	Mati	Matthias, Matthew
Chrn	Christian	Mich	Michael
Con	Conrad	Nath	Nathaniel
Dan	Daniel	Neh	Nehemia
Dav	David	Nik	Nikolaus, Nicholas
Dor	Dorothea, Dorothy	Pet	Peter
Elis	Elisabeth	Ph	Philipp
Fr	Friedrich, Frederick	Reb	Rebecca
Fran	Franz, Francis	Reg	Regina
Fried	Friederica	Ros	Rosina
Gab	Gabriel	Rup	Ruprecht
Geo	Georg, George	Sab	Sabina
Gerh	Gerhard	Sal	Salomo, Solomon
Gert	Gertraut, Gertrude	Sam	Samuel
Gotf	Gottfried	Seb	Sebastian
Goth	Gotthilf	Sib	Sibilla, Sybilla
Gotl	Gottlieb	Sim	Simon
Greg	Gregorius, Gregory	Slm	Salome
Han	Hanna, Hannah	Soph	Sophia
Hans	Johannes, John	Step	Stephan
Hr	Heinrich, Henry	Sus	Susanna
Is	Israel	Theo	Theobald
Jac	Jacob, James	Tho	Thomas

Appendix 2

Tim	Timothaeus, Timothy	Val	Valentin
Tob	Tobias	Wal	Waldburga
Ulr	Ulrich	Wilh	Wilhelm, William
Urs	Ursula		

Place Names

Ab	Abercorn	Pa	Pennsylvania
Aust	Austria(n)	Pal	Palatine
Bav	Bavaria(n)	Pbg	Purysburg
Beth	Bethanien, Bethany	Salz	Salzburg
Bl Ck	Black Creek	Sav	Savannah
Eb	Ebenezer	SC	South Carolina
Go	Goshen	St Math	St. Matthews Parish
Hali	Halifax	Swab	Swabian
Mil Dis	Mill District	Vern	Vernonburg

Miscellaneous

ar	arrived	mo	mother
bro	brother	pres	present
conf	confirmed	s	son
d	daughter	sis	sister
dd	died, dead	spon	sponsor, godparent
dep	departed	sur	surveyed
fr	from	sv	servant to
gr	grant	w	wife
h	husband	wid	widow
m	married		

Transports

Units	Ship	Captain	Date of Arrival
1. 1st Salz.	Purysburg	Tobias Fry	12 March 34
2. 2d Salz.	Prince of Wales	George Dunbar	28 Dec. 34
3. 1st Moravian	Two Brothers	Wm. Thomson	6 April 35
4. 1st Pal.	James	John Yoakley	1 Aug. 35
5. 2d Moravian	Simonds	Joseph Cornish	17 Feb. 36
6. 3d Salz.	London Merchant	John Thomas	17 Feb. 36
7. 2d Pal.	Three Sisters	—— Hewitt	20 Dec. 37
8. 3d Pal.	Two Brothers	Wm. Thomson	7 Oct. 38
8a. Sanftleben Party	Charles	—— Haeramond	27 June 39
9. 4th Salz.	Loyal Judith	John Lemon	2 Dec. 41
10. 1st Swiss	Europa	John Wadham	4 Dec. 41
11. 4th Pal.	Judith	Walter Quarme	22 Jan. 46
12. 5th Pal.	Charles Town Galley	Peter Bogg	2 Oct. 49
13. 1st Swabian	Charming Martha	Chas. Leslie	29 Oct. 50
14. 2d Swabian	Antelope	John McClelland	23 Oct. 51
15. 3d Swabian	Success	Wm. Isaacs	23 Nov. 52

Inhabitants

Because the compilation of this list is still in progress, the author would appreciate being informed of any documented additions or corrections.

Ade (Adde), Fr, s Sal, 41 pres
Ade, Joh (Hr), 1735, Pal, t8, s Sal
Ade, Marg, 1706, Pal, t8, w Sal
Ade, (Hieronymus) Sal, 1708, t8, Swab fr Tuebingen, 47 dep for Saxe-Gotha
Almann, An Mag, née Folcker, 56 m Mati
Almann, Mati von, 56 m An Mag Folcker
Alther, Amalia, née Schiermeister, 54 m Jo, 55 wid
Alther, Jo, Swiss fr St. Gall, butcher in Sav, 54 m Amalia Schiermeister
Alther, Ulr, 56 petition rejected
Arnsdorff, And Lor, 1677, Pal, t6, h Dor, dd 37
Arnsdorff, Bar, 2nd w Pet, 57 d Dor, 59 s Joh Geo, 61 s Jon,
Arnsdorff, Cath, née Holtzer, Aust, t6, 1st w Pet, dd 51
(Arnsdorff, [An] Dor, Pal, t6, wid And, 41 m Jo Leitner)
Arnsdorff, Dor, 1757, d Pet
Arnsdorff, Dor (Cath), 1733, t6, d And
(Arnsdorff, Mag, t6, d And, 40 m Sanftleben)
Arnsdorff, Marg, 1727, t6, d And
Arnsdorff, Mar Marg, d And, 41 pres
Arnsdorff, (Joh) Pet, 1723, Pal, t6, s And, h Cath, h Bar, gr 57
Arnsdorff, Soph, 1725, Pal, t6, d And, 41 pres
Aschberger (Ash, Aschpergh), Han, w Mati, gr 60 Go
Aschberger, Mati, h Han, gr 60 Eb, 61 Eb, 73
Austeter (Offsteter), Casp, gr 57 St Math

Bach, Gab, Salz, t2, 40 m Marg Staud, dd 40
(Bach, [Han] Marg, 75 m Ben Glaner)
(Bach, Marg, 1718, Pal, t7, née Staud, 40 m Gab, ca 41 m Leinberger)
Bacher, An Mar, 1709, née Meyer, Swab fr Augsburg, t9, w Balt, dd 48
Bacher, Apol, 1724, Salz, t2, d Tho, 41 pres
Bacher, Balt, Salz fr Gastein, 1710, t9, bro Tho, h An Mar, m Gert, gr 50, 57 Eb

Bacher, Chna, née Langecker, 1693, Salz fr Gastein, t9, w Mati, gr
    50, dd 53
Bacher, Gert, 2nd w Balt, 49 d, 58 d Chna Elis
Bacher, Mar, Salz, t2, née Schweiger, w Tho
(Bacher, Mar, Salz, 1722, t2, d Tho, 41 pres, 52 m Balt Rieser)
(Bacher, Mar, Salz, d Mati, wid Meyer, 42 m Theo Kieffer II)
Bacher, Mati, 1686, Salz fr Gastein, t9, h Chna, dd 42
(Bacher, Sib, m Bart Zant)
Bacher, Tho, Salz, t2, bro Balt, h Mar, dd 48
Backler, Balt, gr 57
Backler, Ezekiel, gr 57 Eb, 59
Bader, Mati, gr 52
Baechle. *See* Bechtle
Bassinger, Bar, w Joh, 73 s Dav
Bassinger, Joh, h Bar
Bauer, And, 1708, Aust, t6, dd 36
Baumann, Con, fr Wuerttemberg, t12, sv Mati Brandner, dd 50
Bechle. *See* Bechtle
Bechtle, (Eva) Bar, w (Joh) Geo, 57 d Mar Mag, 59 d Mar Cath, 61
    d An Mar, 64 s Jon, 65 s Obadjah, 67 d An Mar, 70 s Dav
(Bechtle [Bechtol], Chna Elis, 73 m Jac Buehler)
Bechtle, (Joh) Geo, t12, h Eva Bar, gr 60 Beth; 79 spon, 83 pres
Bechtle, Jac, fr Langenau by Ulm, s Geo, dd 54
Beeler. *See* Buehler
Beltz. *See* also Piltz
Beltz, Elis, 1739, Swiss, t10, d Hans Ulr
Belz, Hans Ulr, 1711, Swiss, t10, gr 41, h Marg
Beltz, Marg, 1718, t10, Swiss, w Hans Ulr
Beltz, Sig, gr 54, 60
Beltzenhagen, Mart, gr 51
Bentz, Hr Lud, 74 pres
Bentz, Mark, gr 50 Eb, 53 Eb
(Berenberger, Marg, Salz, t8a, 40 m Zimmerebner)
Berger, Pet, gr 61 St Math
Betz (Pates), (Joh) Casp, land at Ab
Betz (Petts), ———, wid, property at River Ness
Bichler, (Joh) Gotf, s Tho, 41 pres
Bichler, Mar I, 1708, Salz, t2, 1st w Tho, dd 38
Bichler, Mar II, d Tho & Mar, 41 pres
(Bichler Mar III, née Bacher, 1727, Salz, t9, d Mati Bacher, 42 m
    Tho)

Bichler, Marg, née Kieffer, 2nd w Tho

Bichler, Tho, Salz, t2, h Mar, 38 m Marg Kieffer, 42 m Mar Bacher, dd 51

Biddenbach, An, 1741, née Paulus, 70 m Mat, 73 d Cath, 75 d Marg, 77 s Mat, dd 78

Biddenbach, And, 74 pres, 82 pres

Biddenbach, An Marg, w Mat, 57 s Chrn, 60 s Nath, 62 d An Cath, 67 d An Marg, dd 70

Biddenbach, Apol, wid Rieser, 78 m Mat

(Biddenbach, Cath, 63 m J J Grabenstein)

Biddenbach, Chrn, 1710, gr 59 Beth, dd 70

Biddenbach, Mat, h An Marg, gr 59, 62 Beth, 65; 70 m An Paulus, 78 m Apol Rieser, 74 pres

Biltz. *See* Piltz

Binninger, Jha Egger, 73 m Joh, 79 d Han

Binninger, Joh Rudolf, 73 m Jha Egger, 75 spon

(Birckholt[zer], An Reg, d Joh Geo, 64 m J Jaeckli)

Birckholt[zer], Joh Geo, t13, gr 51

Birk. *See* Buerck

(Bischoff, An Mar, 1699, Pal, t8, m Grimmiger)

Bischoff, Hr. *See* Bishop

Bishop, (Sib) Fried, née Unselt, Pal fr Pbg, w Henry

Bishop, Henry, Eng sv Boltzius, t2, m Fried Unselt, 47 dep for SC, 48 wishes to return

Blessing, Joh, gr 52

Blessing, Leon, Pal, t12, sv Joh Maurer, gr 52,

Blunt, Jac, gr 75

Bohrmann, Mar Eva, w Mich, Pal, t11, 57 s Goth, 59 d Chna

Bohrmann, Mar Mag, 2nd w Mich, 74 spon

Bohrmann, (Joh) Mich I, Pal, t11, h Mar Eva, m Mar Mag, gr 48, 55 CB Go, gr 57 Go, gr 57 Skidoway, gr 60 Go, gr 61; dd 71

Bohrmann, Mich II, Pal, s (Joh) Mich, 57 CB Go

Bollinger, Bar, Swab, t13, w Geo, 56 d Fried Marg, 59 d Fried Marg, dd 67

Bollinger, (Joh) Geo, Swab, h Bar, t13, gr 52, 59 Beth, 74 pres

Bollinger, Jac, t13

Bollinger, ———, w Jac

(Bollinger, Mag, 1740, Swab, t13, 65 m L F Ebinger)

Bollinger, Wal, 1740, d Geo, dd 69

Boltzius, Cath Mar, d Joh Mart, dd 78

Boltzius, Chna Elis, 1743, d Joh Mart, dd 50

Boltzius, Gert, Salz, née Kroehr, 1718, t1, 35 m Joh Mart, dd 66

Boltzius, Goth Is, ca 1738, s Joh Mart, 53 dep for Halle, dd by 74

Boltzius, Joh Mart, 1703, Forst, Lusatia, t1, 35 m Gert Kroehr, gr 47, 50, 55 CB Eb, gr 55, 60

Boltzius, Sam Leberecht, 1736, s Joh, dd 50

(Bornemann, Carolina Mag. *See* Greiner)

Bornemann, Cath, Swab, w Chrph, 57 d Louise

Bornemann, (Joh) Chph, Swab, t15, h Cath, gr 52 New Goettingen in Halifax, dd by 58

Bothe (Booth), Eva Mar, née Ziegler, 54 m Joh Casp

Bothe, Joh Casp, 49 pres, 54 m Eva Ziegler, gr 53 Go, 55 sells to Fr Treutlen, gr 58

Botzenhardt, Bart, fr Langenau by Ulm, t13, gr 52, returns to Germany

Botzenhardt, Geo, fr Langenau by Ulm, t13, gr 52, returns to Germany

Brachfeld, Elis, Pal, t11, w Joh, 48 sur Go

Brachfeld, Joh Wendel, Pal, t11, h Elis

Brahm, (Joh) Wilhelm (Gerhard) de, fr Koblenz, t14, gr 52, 58 Eb, 61; 64 dep. dd 99

Brahm, Wilhelmina de, t14, w Wilh, gr 52, 64 dep, dd 75

(Brandner, Han Elis, d Mati, 64 m J Flerl, dd 73)

Brandner, Mar I, née Herl, 1703, Salz, t2, w Mati, 36 d Mar, dd 68

Brandner, Mar II, 1736, d Mati, 49 pres, 52 conf

Brandner, Mati, Salz, t2, h Mar I, 56 CB Eb, gr 57 Mil Dis, 59

(Brandwein, Cath, 61 m J G Zittrauer)

Braunberger, Mati, Bav, 1703, t2, dd 34

(Brickl, Bar, 1717, Salz fr Saalfeld, t9, m Schrempff, dd 42)

Briest, Joh Fr, 69 m wid Reb Faul

Briest, Reb, wid Faul, 69 m Joh Fr

(Brueckner, An Marg. *See* Brueckner, Jha Marg)

Brueckner, Fr, s Geo, gr 57 Eb

(Brueckner, Fried Cath, d Geo, gr 57, 63 m J M Rheinlaender)

Brueckner, Geo, Salz, t2, h An Marg, 39 m Jha Marg Mueller, gr 50, dd 52

(Brueckner, Jha Marg, née Mueller, 39 m Geo, 57 m Chph Kraemer II)

Buehler (Beeler), Chna Elis, née Bechtol, 73 m Jac, 74 s Jac, 78 d Jha Jul, 81 d Jul Chna

Buehler, Jac, 73 m Chna Elis Bechtol, 74 pres

(Buehler, Mar Elis, 66 m J A Freyermuth)

Buehler, Pet, gr 43 Ab

Buehner, Mar, w Mich, fr Halifax, 70 spon

Buehner, Mich, h Mar, fr Halifax, 70 spon

Buerck, Chrn, h Urs, 57 spon, 57 land in Beth

Buerck, Urs, 1735, w Chrn, 57 s Jac Is, 60 s Dan, 63 s Tim, 65 d Mar

Buntz, (An) Bar, Pal, t12, w Geo I, 56 s (Joh) Geo, 59 s Chrn, 61 s (Joh) Geo, 64 d Mar, 66 d Chna, 69 d An Mar, 80 spon

Buntz, Bar, w (Hr) Lud

Buntz, (Joh) Chph, s Geo, 74 pres, 78 m Elis Hangleiter, 80 spon, 83 pres

Buntz, (Han) Elis, née Hangleiter, 78 m Chph, 79 s Joh Chph, dd 78

Buntz, (Joh) Geo I, Pal, t12, sv Mati Burgsteiner, gr 54, 59 Beth, 60

Buntz, Geo II, gr 65 Beth

Buntz, (Hr) Lud, h Bar, gr 54, 59 Beth

Buntz, Mar, Swab, t15, w Urban, 58 s Joh Chph, 60 d An Bar, 66 s Hr Lud

Buntz, Urban, Swab, t15, h Mar, gr 54; 55 CB Eb, gr 59 Beth, 61, 64, 74, dd 74

Burckhart, Mart, Pal, t12, sv Chrn Leinberger, 50 pres, gr 52

Burgemeister, Chph I, Swiss, h Elis, 1709, t10, gr 51

Burgemeister, (Hr) Chph II, 1737, Swiss, t10, s Chph I, h Marg, 77 spon

Burgemeister, Elis, 1707, t10, w Chph I

Burgemeister, Marg, Swiss, w Chph II, 77 spon

Burgemeister, (Joh) Mart, 1735, t10, s Chph I, 65 m Mar Elis Mengersdorff

Burgsteiner, Ag, Salz, t2, w Mati, d 36, dd 58

Burgsteiner, Dan, s Mati, 69 m Mar Dasher, gr 57 Eb, 66 Cb Eb, 74 pres

Burgsteiner, Joh, Salz, t2, s Mati, 41 pres

Burgsteiner, Mar, née Dasher, 69 m Dan, 72 d Slm

Burgsteiner, Mati, 1695, Salz, t2, h Ag, dd 52

Burgsteiner, Rup, 1735, Salz, t2, s Mati, dd 40

Busch, Joh Hr, fr Sav, h Scholastica

Busch, Scholastica, w Joh Hr, 61 s Joh Wilh

Christ, (Joh) Gotf, t6, convert, 42 m wid, née Metzger, fr Pbg

Christ, ———, née Metzger, d Jac I, w Gotf, dd 50

Cornberger, Gert, Aust, t6, née Einecker, 36 m Joh
Cornberger, Joh, Aust, t6, 36 m Gert Einecker, 55 CB Eb, gr 57
    Mil Dis, 58, dd 70
Cornberger, (An) Mar, d Joh, 41 pres
Craemer. *See* Kraemer
Crauber, Geo (?), gr 60
Crause. *See* Krause
Crell, Wal, 1723, Salz, t9
Cronberger. *See* Kronberger
Crowber. *See* Crauber
Cusmol. *See* Kusmaul
Custobader, Cath, 1688, Pal, t8

Dansler, Hr, gr 67 (= Hr Denzler, 1728, Pal, t7, gr 54)
Dasher (Taescher), An Chna, née Meyer, 54 m Chrn I, 54 s Chrn,
    58 d An Chna
Dasher, Chrn I, Swiss, 35 ar Ga, 54 m An Chna Meyer, gr 45, 48
    sells lot, 52 buys lot, 55 CB Bl Ck, gr 58 Go, 60, 71, 74 pres
Dasher, Chrn II, s Chrn I, gr 54, 67 CB St Math
Dasher, Elis, w (Joh) Mart II, 72 spon, 74 d Dor
(Dasher, Mar, d Mart I, 69 m D Burgsteiner)
Dasher, (Joh) Mart I, Swiss, h Urs, 55 CB Eb, 56 spon, gr 59 Beth,
    60, 62, 65, 67, 68, 72; 72 spon, 74 pres
Dasher, (Joh) Mart II, Swiss, s Mart I, h Elis, 55 CB Eb, 67 CB Eb
    (probably received some of grants listed under father's name), 76
    2nd Lt, 81 magistrate
Dasher, Urs, née Schwinkhofer, wid Paulitsch, w Mart I, 57 s Jsa,
    60 d An Cath, 62 s Ben, 64 s Jsa, 72 spon
(Daumer, Apol, d Mich, 64 m Leinberger)
Daumer (Dauner), Mich, fr Langensee by Ulm, 57 m wid Wal
    Oechsele, gr 52, 60, dd by 58
Daumer, Wal, wid Oechsele, 57 m Mich
de Brahm. *See* Brahm
Deininger, An Bar, w (Joh) Geo, 59 s Joh, 60 s Con, 62 d Cath, 66
    d Mar
Deininger, Con, 1760, s Joh Geo, dd 70
Deininger, (Joh) Geo, h An Bar, gr 59 Beth
Dellinger, Chph, t12, sv Zimmerebner, 49 sick
(Depp, An Elis, Pal fr Pbg, 40 m Joh Jac Kieffer)
(Depp, Mar Marg, w Val, 58 s Dan, 59 m J Gnann)
Depp, Val (Fallentine Tap), Pal, gr 50, 57 Beth; 55 CB Eb, dd 58

Dieter, Reb, 79 spon
Dohart, Joh, gr 63
Donner, Mich, gr 60 Go
(Dopp, Jha, 73 m Chph Preisier)
Dressler, Cath, Pal, 1710, t7, w Geo I
Dressler, Elis, d Geo I, w John Stephen, 77 d Marg
Dressler, (Joh) Geo I, Pal, 1704, t7, h Cath, gr 52, 57
Dressler, Geo II, s Geo I
Dressler, ———, w Geo II, 77 s Geo

Eberhard, Joh, gr 52
Ebinger, (Leon) Fr, 65 m Mag Bollinger, gr 66 Beth
Ebinger, Mag, née Bollinger, 65 m Fr
(Ecker, Urs, sv Kraft, 52 m Veit Landfelder)
Eckhart, Albrecht Lud, 1757, s Con
Eckhart (Etchard), An Mar, wid Huber, 57 m Con, 57 s Albrecht
    Lud
Eckhart, Con, fr Frankfurt, 57 m An Mar Huber, gr 59 Blue Bluff
Eckhart, Mart, gr 52
(Egger, Jha, 73 m J R Binninger)
(Egger, Marg, t8a, 39 m Ulich, 39 m Mart Lackner)
(Ehrhardt, Elis, 74 m Joh Holtzendorff)
Eigel, An Mar, 1733, Salz fr Duerrenberg, t9, d Geo
Eigel, An Theresia, 1728, Salz fr Duerrenberg, t9, d Geo
Eigel, Geo, 1701, Salz fr Duerrenberg, t9, h Urs, gr 56 Mil Dis, dd
    56
Eigel, Joh Fran, 1737, Salz fr Duerrenberg, t9, s Geo
Eigel, Joh Lor, 1735, Saltz fr Duerrenberg, s Geo
Eigel, (Lor) Lud, 1730, Salz fr Duerrenberg, t9, s Geo, 49 pres, 55
    CB Eb, dd 62
Eigel, Urs, 1700, Salz fr Duerrenberg, t9, w Geo, dd 62
(Einecker [Einweger], Bar, 1704, Salz, t6, 36 m Leon Krause)
(Einecker, Gert, 1708, Salz, t6, 36 m Joh Cornberger)
Eischberger (Ashberger), An Mar, 1711, Salz, t9, w Dav, dd 68
Eischberger, Cath, Salz, 1736, d Rup, 41 pres
Eischberger, Cath, Salz, t9, d Dav, 41 pres, 44 s Chrn Tho
Eischberger, Chrn Tho, 1744, s Dav, dd 63
Eischberger, Dav, 1717, Salz fr Werffen, t9, h An Mar, gr 57 Mil
    Dis, dd 57
Eischberger, Joh, Salz, t9, s Dav, 41 pres
Eischberger, Mar, née Riedelsperger, Salz, t2, w Rup, 36 d Cath

Appendix 2

(Eischberger, Mar, 63 m Joh Mart Greiner)
Eischberger, Rup, Salz, t2, h Mar, 47 pres, gr 57 Mil Dis, dd 62
Eppinger, An Bar I, w Joh, 59 d An Mag
Eppinger, An Bar II, d Fr II, dd 73
Eppinger, An Mag, 1759, d Joh
Eppinger, Fr I, dd 69
Eppinger, Fr II, 73 pres
Eppinger, Joh, h An Bar I, 59 buys lot in Sav, gr 61 Ogeechee, gr
   69, 70
(Eppinger, Mag, wid, 70 m Joh Scheraus)
Ernst, Chna, née Kusmaul, d Jac, w Lud, 77 d Slm, 80 s Dav
Ernst, Jo, 1708, Bav, t6, h Mar, dd 40
Ernst, Joh, s Jo, 41 pres, dd 70
Ernst, (Joh) Lud, 1735, s Jo, h Chna, 55 CB Eb, gr 50, 57 Beth, 64,
   69 Beth, 71, 74
(Ernst, [An] Mar, 1705, Bav, t6, wid Jo, m Scheffler)
Ernst, Sab, Bav, 1733, t6, d Jo
Ernst, Sus, Bav, 1735, t6, d Jo, 41 pres, 52 conf
Eysperger. *See* Eischberger

Famm, Fr, gr 68 St Math
Faul (Fowl), Geo, 1724, Swab, t 15, h Reb, gr 54 Eb, 57, 55 CB Eb,
   dd 68
(Faul, Reb, Swab, wid Geo, 69 m J F Briest)
Felser, Geo, 1686, Salz, t2, dd 36
Fettler, An Urs, née Moser, 61 m Mart
Fettler, Mart, fr Sav, 61 m An Urs Moser
(Fetzer, Ab, Swab, t13, dd in passage)
(Fetzer, An, d Seb, 67 m F Ochs)
(Fetzer, An, 67 m G L Roth)
Fetzer, An Mag, w Jon, 79 spon
Fetzer, An Mar, 1717, wid Staeheli, 64 m Seb Fetzer I, dd 69
Fetzer, ———, t13, wid Ab, buys freedom
Fetzer, Bar, 1720, Swab, w Ulr, t13, 56 s Joh Gotl, 58 s Chrn, dd 64
Fetzer, Chrn, 1740, s Ab, Swab, t13, sv Schrempff, dd 58
Fetzer, Jha, née Mohr, Swab, t13, 65 m Ulr, s Joh Ulr
Fetzer, Jon Gotl, 1756, h An Mag, 74 pres, 79 spon
Fetzer, Seb, Swab, t13, h Urs, gr 58 Mil Dis, 64 m A M Staeheli, dd
   70
Fetzer, (Joh) Ulr, 65 m Jha Mohr, gr 59 Ab, dd 73
Fetzer, Urs, 1719, Swab, t13, w Seb, 58 s Joh, 60 s Joh Chph, dd 63

Finck, (An) Marg, w Paul, 56 d An Marg, 62 d Slm, gr 59 Beth
Finck, Paul, h Marg, gr 55, 57 Beth
Fischer, An Cath, 1728, Swab fr Langenau, 1st w Geo, 56 s And, dd 58
Fischer, An Dor, née Meyer, 1721, wid Rieser, 60 m Geo, 62 s Tob,
    dd 63
Fischer, (Joh) Dav, t13, gr 50
Fischer, Geo, Swab fr Langenau, h An Cath, 60 m A D Rieser, 64
    m Mar Mack, gr 52, land at Hali
Fischer, Mar, née Mack, 64 m Geo, 65 d Mar, 67 s Mat, 69 d An
    Cath
Fischer, Mich, gr 52: 63 CB Hali
Fischer, Nik, gr 52
Fleiss, Balt, 1707, Salz fr Gastein in Salz, t1, dd 34
Flerl (Floerel), An Mar, née Hoepflinger, 1693, Salz, t6, 36 m
    Hans, dd 74
Flerl, Carl, 1705, Salz, t6, bro Hans, by 50 m Mar, gr 56 Eb, dd 64
Flerl, Dor, née Kieffer, 74 m Joh
(Flerl, Han, d Hans, 1733, 54 conf, 58 m T Schweighoffer)
Flerl, Han Elis, née Brandner, 1743, 65 m Joh II, 65 d Jud, 67 d
    Mar, 69 s Joh, dd 73
Flerl, Hans (Joh I), 1712, Salz, t6, bro Carl, 36 m An Mar Hoep-
    flinger, 55 CB Eb, gr 56 Mil Dis, 60, dd 70
Flerl, Joh II, s Hans, 57 CB Eb, 65 m H E Brandner, gr 60 Mil dis,
    74 m Dor Kieffer, 74 pres, 76 capt
(Flerl, Jud, 63 m G Schleich, 64 m Sam Kraus)
Flerl, Mar, née Kroehr, wid Moshammer, wid Gruber, by 50 m
    Carl, 58 spon
Floerel. See Flerl
Folcker, An Mag, 56 m Tho
Folcker, Tho, 56 m An Mag, gr 70, 75
Fowl. See Faul
Francke, Bar, née Kieffer, d Theo I, w Paul, 57 d Soph, 59 s Con,
    62 s Chrn
Francke, (Joh) Paul, fr Pbg, 50 returns from Indian country, m Bar
    Kieffer, gr 50
Francke, Soph. 1757, d Paul, dd 70
Freyermuth, (Joh) Ad, 66 m M E Buehler, 74 pres
Freyermuth, (An) Cath, née Groll, 69 m Pet, 73 s Tob, 75 s Jsa Pet,
    80 s Sal
Freyermuth, Mar Elis, née Buehler, 66 m Ad, 69 s Joh Ad, 70 s Joh
    Ad, 74 s Is, dd 81

Freyermuth, (An) Marg, by 57 gr Beth
Freyermuth, (Joh) Pet, 69 m An Cath Groll, 74 pres
Frick, An Cath, née Strubler, fr Pbg, 55 m Jac
Frick, Jac, fr Pbg, 55 m An Cath Strubler
Frick (Fruick), Paul, gr 58 Eb
Frickinger, Bar, née Greuser, 56 m Con, 61 s Joh Con
Frickinger, (Joh) Con, 56 m Bar Greuser, by 59 gr Beth
Frisch, Lud, h Sus, 78 spon
Frisch, Sus, w Lud, 79 d An Mar
Fritsche (Fritsee), Hr, gr 59 Ab

Gabel (Gebel), Ab, s Joh, gr 53, 63
Gabel, Joh, 55 CB Ab, gr 50 Ab, 59, 60, dd by 63
Gebhart, Elis, 1724, Pal, t8, d Ph I
Gebhart, Eva, 1728, Pal, t8, d Ph I
Gebhart, Hans Geo, 1736, Pal, t8, s Ph I, gr 52
(Gebhart, Mag, 1719, Pal, t8, d Ph I, m Sim Reiter)
Gebhart, Mar Cath, 1721, Pal, t8, d Ph I
Gebhart, Martha, 1695, Pal, t8, w Ph I, dd by 43
Gebhart, Ph I, 1693, Pal, t8, h Martha
Gebhart, Ph II, 1732, Pal, t8, s Ph I
Geiger, Ab, 82 pres
Geiger, Apol, w Ulr, 69 d Rachel
Geiger, Chrn, fr Ogeechee, gr 62 St Math
Geiger, ———, w Chrn, 74 s Cornelius
Geiger, Felix, 82 pres
Geiger, Joh, 82 pres
Geiger, Luc I, h Sib Reg, 55 sur, dd 57
Geiger, Luc II, gr 61
Geiger, Mar, w Tho, 81 spon
(Geiger, Sib Reg, wid Luc I, 61 m J G Niess)
Geiger, Tho, h Mar, 81 spon
Geiger, Ulr, h Apol
(Gerber, An, wid, 55 m J Hueter)
Gerber (Garbet), Casp, 60 m C B Haefner, gr 62
Gerber, Chna Bar, née Haefner, 60 m Casp
Gerber, Paul, gr 52
Glaner, Ben, s Geo, 75 m H M Bach, 74 pres
Glaner (Glamer, Glauer), Geo, 1704, Salz fr Rastadt, t9, h Gert
    Lemmhoffer, 50 m Sib Zant, gr 50 Eb, 56, 61, 55 CB Eb, dd 71

Glaner, Gert, née Lemmhoffer, 1703, Salz fr Rastadt, 1st w Geo, 47 pres, dd 48

Glaner, Han Elis, d Mat, w Joh, 79 s Sal, 81 d Chna

Glaner, Han Marg, née Bach, 75 m Ben, 79 d

Glaner, Joh, s Geo, h Han Elis, 82 pres

Glaner, Sib, Salz, 1st w Geo, 57 s Joh, 59 spon, 60 spon

Glantz, Seb, 1693, Salz, t2, dd 35

Glocker (Klocker), Bern, 1703, Salz fr Kropfsberg im Zillertal, h Elis, t9, dd 42

Glocker, Elis, 1698, Salz fr Kropfsberg im Zillertal, t9, w Bern, dd 42

Glocker, Eva, 1734, Salz, t9, d Bern, 47 conf, dd 50

Glocker, Gert, 1732, Salz, t9, d Bern, 47 conf, 50 m in Go

Glocker, Paul, 1740, Salz, t9, s Bern, dd 41

Glocker, Seb, 1737, Salz, s Bern

Gnann, An, née Gress, Swab, t14, 1st w Geo, ca 45 s Andrew, ca 47 s Mich, 49 s Jacob, 58 d Elis, 60 d Abigail, 62 s Sal

Gnann, An Franziska, née Rottenberger, d Chph, 71 m And, 72 s Chph, 74 d Jha, 75 s Tim, 78 s And, 81 d Slm, 87 d An Cath, 91 s Ben

Gnann, And I, 1745, Swab fr Langenau by Ulm, t14, s Geo, 71 m An Franziska Rottenberger, gr 73, dd 1800

Gnann, And II, 1778, s And I, m Ag Kraemer, 82 pres

Gnann, Chph, 1772, s And I

Gnann, Elis, d Geo (?), 54 conf

Gnann, (Joh) Geo, 1704, Swab fr Langenau by Ulm, t14, bro Jac I, 44 m An Gress, gr 59 Beth, 65 Beth, 74 pres, 83 pres

Gnann, Han, née Metzger, 73 m Jac II, 73 d Elis, 78 d Marg

Gnann, Jac I, 1708, Swab, fr Langenau by Ulm, t14, bro Geo, 58 m wid Mar Marg Depp, gr 52, dd 73

Gnann, Jac II, 1749, s Geo, 73 m Han Metzger, 74 pres, dd 1814

Gnann, Jha, 1774, d And I

Gnann, Joh, 82 pres

Gnann, (Mar) Marg, wid Depp, 58 m Jac I, 60 s Joh, 62 s Jon, 64 s Dav, 66 s Jac, 69 d Dor

Gnann, Mar Mag, wid Weber, 72 m Mich

Gnann, Mich, 1747, s Geo, gr 71, 72 m wid Mar Mag Weber, née Greiner

Gnann, Sal, 1762, s Geo, m Slm Weber

Gnann, Slm, née Weber, 1765, m Sal

Gnann, Tim, 1775, m Cath Leinberger

Goebel, An Bar, w Joh, 59 spon

Goebel, Joh, h An Bar, 59 spon

Grabenstein (Grovenstein), Cath, née Biddenbach, 63 m Justus, 64 s Chrn, 65 s Hr Lud, 66 d Mar, 69 s Joh Just, 70 s Hr Lud, 73 s Chph, dd 79

Grabenstein, (Joh) Justus, 63 m Cath Biddenbach, gr 65 Beth, 74 pres

Graeff, Cath, w soldier fr Frederica, 52 pres

Graeff, ———, h Cath, former soldier fr Frederica, 52 pres

Graniwetter (Cranwetter), (Joh) Casp, 1705, Salz, t9, dd 48

(Graniwetter, [An] Cath, née Stuermer, 1718, Swab fr Noerdlingen, t9, wid Casp, 49 m Casp Walthauer, gr 57 Eb)

Graves. See Greve

Greiner, And, 56 m Bar Hirschmann, gr 52, 61 CB Hali, 68 St George, dd 71

Greiner, Bar, née Hirschmann, 56 m And

Greiner, Carolina Mag, wid Bornemann, 58 m Casp I, 60 s Chrn Ph

Greiner, (Joh) Casp I, 58 m C M Bornemann, gr 52, 61 CB Hali, 62 Briar Creek, 73 spon

Greiner, (Joh) Casp II, s Casp I, fr Hali, gr 52, 72 m Jha Chna Lackner

Greiner, Jac, gr 52

Greiner, Jha Chna, née Lackner, 72 m Casp II, dd 1811

Greiner, Joh Mart I, 63 m Mar Eischberger, gr 52

Greiner, Joh Mart II, gr 68 Hali, 76 capt Hali

Greiner, Mar, née Eischberger, w Joh Mart, 65 s Tim, 66 s Joh Jac, 68 s Joh, 72 d Slm, 75 s Joh Casp

Greiner, Mar Dor, dd 70

(Greiner, Mar Mag, 54 m Mich Weber)

Greiner (Grenier), Pet, gr 68

Gress, Apol, dd 66

(Gress, Elis, 66 m J Oechsele)

Greve (Graves, Groves, etc.), An Cath, née Heinrich, 56 m Sam, 57 d Mar Mag, dd 57

Greve, Geo, gr Beth

Greve, Joh Hr, Swab, t15, gr 52 Briar Creek

Greve, Luisa Marg, 1st w Sam, dd 56

Greve, Marg, née Huber, 58 m Sam, 59 d Elis

Greve, Sam, h Luisa Marg, 56 m An Cath Heinrich, 58 m Marg Huber, gr Beth, dd 66

Grimmiger, And, 1708, Aust, t6, h Sab, 40 m An Mar Bischoff
Grimmiger, An Mar, née Bischoff, Pal, t8, 40 m And
(Grimmiger, Cath, 1735, d And, 41 pres, 52 conf, 58 m Joh
    Schneider)
Grimmiger, Sab, 1710, Aust, t6, 1st w And, dd 36
(Groll, An Cath, 69 m J P Freyermuth)
Groll, An Mar, w Mati, 75 spon
(Groll, Mar Urs, 55 m Ad Paulus)
Groll, Mati, h An Mar, gr 59 Beth
(Gronau, Cath, 1716, Sal, t1, née Kroehr, d Bar Rohrmoser, 34 m
    Is, 46 m H H Lemke)
(Gronau, Fried Mar, d Is, gr 57, 69 m Triebner)
(Gronau, Han Elis, 1738, d Is, gr 57 Eb, 58 m Wertsch)
Gronau, Is Chrn I, 1714, fr Koppenstedt, t1, 34 m Cath Kroehr
Gronau, Is Chrn II, s Is I,
Gross (Grase), Apol, wid Geo, gr 65 Bl Ck
Gross, Elis, d Apol, gr 65 Bl Ck
Gross, Geo, 1716, gr 60 Beth, dd 61
Gross, Mich, Swab fr Leutzhausen by Ulm, t15, gr 52
Grover, Groover. *See* Gruber
Gruber, Elis, née Schwarzwaelder, Pal, 58 m Geo, 60 s Geo, 62 s
    Joh Jac, 64 s Sal, 67 d Elis, 69 s Joh, 72 s Dav, 78 d Slm
Gruber, Geo, 58 m Elis Schwarzwaelder, 74 pres
Gruber, Hans I, 1689, Salz fr Gastein, t1, dd 34
Gruber, Hans II, s Hans I, 41 pres, 55 CB Eb, gr 56 Eb
Gruber, Joh, s Pet I, 54 conf, gr 65; 65 m M M Kalcher
Gruber, (Mar) Mag, née Kalcher, Salz, 65 m Joh, 66 s Joh, 69 s Sal,
    72 s Jo, 78 spon, 78 s William
(Gruber, Mar, née Kroehr, Salz, t1, wid Mosshamer, wid Pet
    Gruber, by 50 m Carl Flerl)
Gruber, Pet I, 1700, Salz fr Gastein, t1, 36 m wid Mosshamer, dd
    40
Gruber, Pet II, s Pet I
Gruber, Wilh, gr 60
Gschwandl, Marg I, née Hofer, 1712, Salz, t1, 1st w Tho, dd 35
Gschwandl, Marg II, 1732, d Tho, dd 61
Gschwandl, Sib, née Schwab, 1698, Salz, wid Resch, 38 m Tho, dd
    58
Gschwandl, Tho I, 1695, Salz, t1, h Marg I, 38 m wid Sib Resch, 55
    CB Eb, gr 57 Mil Dis, dd 61
Gschwandl, Tho II, s Tho

Gugel (Kugel), An Mar, w Joh, 57 s Joh Chph, 58 s Sam, 61 s Joh, 62 d Slm, 64 s Dav, 68 s Jsa

Gugel, Chph, 82 pres

Gugel, (Joh) Chrn, s Joh, 74 pres

(Gugel, Han Elis, 72 m Nik Michel)

Gugel, Joh, Pal, t12, buys freedom, h An Mar, gr 57 Beth, 60, 65, 74 pres, 83 pres

Gugel, Mati, Pal, t12, sv Mati Zettler, 58 owns lot in Sav, 59 sells lot, gr 61 Beth

Gugel, ———, w Mati, 66 s Dan

(Gunter, Cath, Pal, t12, 49 m Mati Seckinger)

Haberer, An Eva, wid Weidmann, 71 m Mich, 74 d An Mar, 79 spons

Haberer, (An) Bar, née Franck, 1701 Swab fr Bopfingen, t9, w Mich, dd 70

Haberer, (Joh) Chph, 1741, Salz, t9, s Mich

Haberer, (Joh) Mich, 1714, Salz fr Werffen, t9, h Bar, 71 m An Eva Weidmann, gr 54, 56 Eb

Haberer, Wal, 1723, Salz fr Werffen, d Mich

Haberfehner, Fran, 1688, Aust, t6, dd 36

Haberfehner, Mag, 1724, Aust, t6, d Fran, dd 40

Haberfehner, Mar I, 1689, Aust, t6, w Fran, dd 36

Haberfehner, Mar II, Aust, t6, d Fran, dd 36

Haberfehner, Sus, 1720, Aust, t6, d Fran, 41 pres

Hack. *See* Heck

(Haefner [Havener], An Mar, d Con, 54 conf, 58 m Jac Haeussler)

(Haefner, Chna Bar, d Con, 60 m C Gerber)

Haefner, Con, Pal, t7, h Pieta Clara, gr 43

Haefner, Joh Geo, 1735, Pal, t7, 48 ar Eb, dd 50

Haefner, Mar Dor, 1733, Pal, t7, d Pieta, 52 conf, dd 63

(Haefner, Pieta Clara, 1711, Pal, t7, 42 fr Vern, wid Con, m Straube, 48 ar Eb)

Haeussler (Heusler), An Mar, née Haefner, Pal, 58 m Jac, 59 d Han Marg, 61 d Chna, 78 d Han

(Haeussler, Bar, wid Lackner, 58 m J M Zischler)

(Haeussler, Chna, 1721, Salz, t9, fr Memmingen, 42 m Zuebli)

Haeussler, (Joh) Jac, 58 m An Mar Haefner, 74 pres

Haeussler, Joh, 79 spon

(Haeussler, Marg, 72 m J N Schubdrein)

Hagemeyer, Euphrosyna, 1722, Swab fr Blaubeyern, t15, d Jul, dd 53

Hagemeyer, Jul, 1682, Swab fr Blaubeyern, t15, gr 52, dd 52
Haid. *See* Heidt
Haisler. *See* Heisler
Hammer, An Ros, 1717, Saxon, t14, w Pet, dd 60
Hammer, Elis, 1743, Saxon, t14, d Pet, dd 63
Hammer, Pet, Saxon fr Chemnitz, t14, h An Ros, gr 59
Hangleiter, Ag, 1765, d Joh I
(Hangleiter, Cath, d Joh I, 73 spon, 74 m J M Kraemer)
(Hangleiter, Han Elis, 1759, d Joh I, 78 m J C Buntz)
Hangleiter, Joh I, h Urs, gr 57 Beth, 65, 66 Turkey Branch, 73
    spon, 74 pres
Hangleiter, Joh II, 1762, s Joh I
Hangleiter, Mar Mag, 1758, w Joh II, 77 s Chrn, 83 spon
Hangleiter, Urs, 1729, w Joh I, 58 d Mar Mag, 59 d Han Elis, 62 s
    Joh, 65 d Ag, 69 d Jha, dd 73
Hansler. *See* Hensler
Hapacher, Ag, w Joh, 58 s Chrn
Hapacher, Joh, h Ag, gr 60
Hapacher, Mar, d Joh, dd 58
Hartstein, Han, w Joac, 56 d Cath
Hartstein, Joac, h Han, gr 61
Hasenlauer, Elis, née Rau, wid Hunold, 57 m Seb, 60 s Jac
Hasenlauer, Seb, Swab fr Langenau, t15, 57 m Elis Rau, dd 64
Hauge, Geo, gr 59 Ab
Haus, Con, fr Pa, dd 75
Heck, An, w Casp, 57 d Marg, 59 d An, 61 d Angelica, 64 d Dor,
    67 s Joh
Heck, An Urs, w Casp, 57 d Marg, dd 57
Heck, Angelica, Swab fr Langenau, 54 conf
Heck (Hack), Casp, Swab fr Langenau an der Brenz, h An, gr 59
    Beth, 62, 65; 83 pres
Heck, Geo, h Mar
Heck, Mar, w Geo, 59 d An
Heck Marg, 79 spon
Heckel, Angelica, d Geo(?), 54 conf
Heckel, An Marg, née Heinrich, 71 m Joh, 72 s Chrn Fr, 74 s Chph
    Fr
Heckel, Geo, Swab fr Holzkirch by Ulm, t15, gr 57 Eb, dd 72
Heckel, Joh, Swab fr Langenau by Ulm, t15, 55 CB Eb, gr 65, 71 m
    (H)an Marg Heinrich, 74 pres, dd 77
Heckel, Tho, gr 52

(Heckel, Urs, 71 m Mich Heinsmann)

Heidt (Hyde), Eleonora, née Kurtz, 1730, Salz, d Mati, 42 ar, w
    Geo, 58 s Joh, 61 s Chrn Is, 65 s Abiel, dd 69

Heidt, (Joh) Geo, Pal, t12, sv Sim Reiter, 55 CB Eb, gr 59 Beth, 54
    m Eleonora Kurtz, 70 m wid Mar Mag Schleich, dd 70

Heidt, Is Chrn, s Geo, dd 75

Heidt, Mar Mag, wid Schleich, 70 m Geo

Heil, Casp, 74 pres

Heinle (Hinely), Bar, 1709, Swab, t13, dd 56

Heinle, Chna, wid Meyer, 69 m Jac I, 72 s Sam, 72 d Chna, dd 72

Heinle, Han Elis, née Thilo, 73 m Jac I, 74 d Slm

Heinle, (Joh) Jac I, Swab, t13, s Joh I, sv Joh Schmidt, 57 CB Eb, gr
    61; 69 m wid Chna Meyer, 73 m Han Elis Thilo, 74 pres

Heinle, Joh I, Swab fr Gaerstetten, t13, sv at mill, dd 51

Heinle, Joh II, Swab, t13, s Joh I, sv Glaner, 54 conf, 55 CB Eb, gr
    59 Go, 61; 60 m Mar Kogler, 68 m wid M B Schneider, 74 pres

Heinle, Mar, 1738, née Kogler, 60 m Joh II, 60 s Joh, 62 s Joh, 65 s
    Dav, dd 68

Heinrich, Cath, 1718, Swab, t8, d Pet

(Heinrich, [An] Cath, 1718, Swab, t8, d Pet, w Sam Greve, dd 57)

Heinrich, Eva (Bar), Swab, 1716, t8, d Pet,

(Heinrich, Han Marg, 1723, Swab, t8, d Pet, 71 m Joh Heckel)

Heinrich, Joh Geo, Swab fr Wuertemberg, t8, s Pet, gr 57 Go

Heinrich, Jul, 1684, Swab, t8, w Pet, dd 38

(Heinrich, [An] Mag, 1719, t8, Swab, d Pet, 42 m Sig Ott)

(Heinrich, [An] Mar, 1715, Swab, t8, d Pet, 39 m P Zittrauer)

Heinrich, Pet, 1690, Swab, t8, dd 39

Heinsmann, Mich, 71 m Urs Heckel

Heinsmann, Urs, née Heckel, 71 m Mich

Heintz, Joh Chrn, 59 m Reg Bar Hirsch

Heintz, Reg Bar, née Hirsch, 1726, 59 m Joh Chrn, 60 d Mar
    Judith, 61 s Joh And, dd 64

Heisler (Haisler), Dav, gr 54

Heisler, Geo, 61 sur Beth

Heisler, Joh, 61 sur Beth

Heissmann, Mich, 74 pres

Held, Condrit, 1686, Pal, t8, dd 40

Held, Elis I, 1685, Pal, t8, w Condrit, dd 39

(Held, Elis II, 1721, Pal, t8, d Condrit, w Gab Maurer)

Held, (Joh) Geo, Pal, sv cowpen, buys 50 acres in Eb for Mich
    Schneider

Held, Mar, wid Kuenlin, Salz, t9, 42 m Mich
Held, (Hans) Mich, 1715, Pal, t8, s Condrit, 42 m wid Kuenlin, 53
 sells lot
Helfenstein, Blandina Mag, w Fr, 56 d Jha Fried, 58 s Dan
Helfenstein, (Mar) Chna, Pal, 1725, d Joh Jac I
Helfenstein, Chrn, Pal, t6, s Joh Jac I, 41 pres
Helfenstein, Dor, Pal, t6, w Joh Jac I
Helfenstein, (Joh) Fr, 1723, Pal, t6, s Joh Jac I, h Blandina Mag, 41
 pres, gr 46, 55 CB Ab, gr 56 Ab
(Helfenstein, [Mar] Fried, 1721, Pal, t6, d Joh Jac I, w Thilo)
Helfenstein, Jeremias, 1727, Pal, t6, s Joh Jac I, gr 52
Helfenstein, (Joh) Jac I, 1679, Pal, t6, dd 36
Helfenstein, (Joh) Jac II, 1727, Pal, t6, s Joh Jac I, gr 52, 59, 72
Helfenstein, Joh, 1733, Pal, t6, s Joh Jac I, gr 59, 70
Helme, Mar Mag, w Nik, 78 s Dav
Helme, Nik, Swab fr Albeck by Ulm, t13, sv Mart Lackner I, h Mar
 Mag, gr 74
Hensler (Hansler), Jac I, gr 52
Hensler, (Joh) Jac II, s Jac I, gr 52, 61
Herb, Fr, gr 62 Ogeechee
Herrnberger, An Justina, née Unselt, Pal fr Pbg, 38 m Fran, 40
 dep for Pa
Herrnberger, Fran Sigmund, fr Hungary, 1698, t6, 38 m A J Un-
 selt, 40 dep for Pa
Herse. See Hirsch
Hertzog, Geo, Swab, t13, dd 51
Hertzog, Mart, 1698, Salz fr Pinzgau, t1
Hessler, Chrn, Salz, t2, dd 66
Hessler, Elis, Salz, 1710, w Chrn, 50 pres, dd 67
Hierl, Mar, 1711, Salz fr Lichtenstein-Saalfeld, t1
Hinely. See Heinle
Hirsch, (Joh) Mich, 1709, Swab, t15, h Reg Bar, gr 53 Eb, 54 sur,
 57 Mil Dis, dd 59
Hirsch, Reg Bar I, w Joh Mich
(Hirsch, Reg Bar II, d Joh Mich, 59 m Joh Chph Heintz)
(Hirschmann, Bar, 55 m And Greiner)
Hirschmann (Hersham), (Joh) Casp I, gr 52 Hali, 64 m Ros Kue-
 bler
Hirschmann, (Joh) Casp II, gr 52 Hali, after 75 m Soph
Hirschmann, Elis, 1775, d Joh Casp I
Hirschmann, Ros, née Kuebler, 64 m Casp, 75 d Elis, 75 spon

Hirschmann, Soph, after 75 m Casp II, 79 d Slm
(Hoepflinger, An Mar, Salz, 1715, t6, w Hans Flerl)
(Hofer, An, Salz fr Gastein, 1708, t1, 34 m Schweiger, dd 35)
(Hofer, Marg, 1st w Tho Gschwandel)
Holtzendorff, Elis, née Ehrenhardt, 74 m Joh
Holtzendorff, Joh, 74 m Elis Ehrenhardt
Holtzendorff, Wilh, 83 justice of the peace of Effingham County
(Holtzer, Cath, Aust, 1724, t6, d Sus, m Pet Arnsdorff, dd 51)
Holtzer, Sus, Aust, 1689, t6, wid, dd 36
Huber, An, Swab, 1742, t13, sv J G Meyer
(Huber, An Bar, 67 m Joh Seckinger)
Huber (Hover), Con, gr 57 Ogeechee
Huber, Hans, Salz, 1723, s Lor, dd 35
Huber, Helena, Swab, t13, sv L Krause, 50 twins
Huber, Jac, Swab, t13, Beth, dd 56
Huber, Lor, Salz fr Gastein, 1680, t1, dd 34
Huber, Mag, Salz, 1720, d Lor, dd 35
(Huber, Marg, Salz, 1728, d Lor, 58 m S Greve, dd 75)
Huber, Mar, Salz, 1725, d Lor, dd 35
Huber, Mar Mag, Salz, 1682, née Maendelleithner, w Lor, dd 34
Huber, Sara, Swab, t13, sv J Cornberger
(Huber [Hover], Sus, 77 m Joh Merkel)
Hueter, An, née Gerber, 55 m Jac
Hueter, Jac, 55 m wid An Gerber
(Humbart, Sus, 57 m Joh Lohrmann)
Hunold, Elis, née Rau, w Joh, gr 57 Beth
Hunold, Joh, h Elis, gr before 56, dd 66
Hyde. *See* Heidt

Ihle (Illy), Ag, Pal, t11, w Jac I
Ihle, And, 1732, Pal, t11, s Jac I
Ihle, Cath, w Joh, 81 spon
Ihle, (An) Eva, Pal, t11, w Jac I, 57 s Joh Jac, 58 s Joh, 59 s Jon, 60
   s Sam
Ihle, Han, w Jac II (?), 81 d Mar
Ihle, Jac I, Pal, t11, sv Wm Stephens, h Ag, h Eva, gr 54, 59 Go, 70;
   76 2nd Lt
Ihle, Jac II, Pal, t11, s Jac I, 78 m Jane Border
Ihle, Jane, née Border, 78 m Jac II
Ihle, Joh, Pal, h Cath, 81 spon
Ihle, Mich, Pal, t11, s Jac I, gr 53

Ihle, Sam, 1760, s Jac I
Ihle, ———, w Sam, 80 d Mar
Ihle, Wilh, 1735, Pal, t11, s Jac I,
(Ihler, An Marg, Pal wid fr Pbg, 38 m J M Rieser)
Ihler, ———, child of above

Jackocho, Ab Fr, 78 m Jenny Kain
Jackocho, Jenny, 78 m Ab Fr
Jaeckli, An Reg, née Birckholtzer, 64 m Jac, 80 s John Jac
Jaeckli (Yakeley), (Joh) Jac, 1739, Pal, t11, apprentice to Bohr-
   mann, gr 50 St Math, 60 Go, 64 m A R Birckholtzer, gr 69, 82
   pres
Jansen, Marg, wid Leinberger, 64 m Pet
Jansen, Pet, 64 m wid Marg Leinberger
Juninger, Ab, Swab, t13, sv at store in Sav

(Kaemmel, Mar, wid, 56 m Jac Tussing)
Kaesemeyer, Cath, 1702, Pal, t7, w Mart
Kaesemeyer, Clemens, 1736, Pal, t7, s Mart, 41 pres
Kaesemeyer, Dor, d Mart, 41 pres
Kaesemeyer, (Joh) Mart, 1693, Pal, t7, h Cath, gr Eb by 57
(Kalcher, Han Marg, d Rup, Salz, 68 m J G Rentz)
(Kalcher, Mar, 1739, d Rup, 54 conf, 58 m Mart Rheinlaender)
(Kalcher, Mar Mag, 1741, d Rup, 65 m J Gruber)
(Kalcher, Marg, née Gunther, Salz, t2, w Rup, 39 d Mar, 41 d Mar
   Mag, m Chph Kraemer I)
Kalcher, Rup, Salz, t2, h Marg, dd 52
Kalcher, Urs, 1735, d Rup, 52 conf
Kaup, Bar, w Jac
Kaup, Jac, Pal, h Bar, t12, sv to mill
Keebler. *See* Kuebler
Keefer. *See* Kieffer
Kember, An Mar, 1754, dd 71
Kessler, Ad, 70 m Han Kieffer
Kessler, Han, née Kieffer, 70 m Ad
Kiebler. *See* Kuebler
Kieffer, An Dor, w Geo, 59 s Dan
Kieffer, An Elis, née Depp, Pal, 40 m Jac I
Kieffer, An Mar, née Winnagler, w Fr, 57 d Mar
Kieffer, An Marg, 1692, Pal fr Pbg, w Theo I

Kieffer, Chna, 1758, 73 spon, dd 81
Kieffer, Dor, née Reiter, 67 m Jac II, 68 s Sal, 73 s Joel, 78 d Lydia
(Kieffer, Dor, 74 m Joh Flerl)
(Kieffer, Elis Cath, d Theo I, 40 m Mati Zettler)
(Kieffer, Elis Mar, d Theo, w Nik Kronberger)
(Kieffer, Elis [Marg], 1731, d Theo I, 67 m Sal Zant)
Kieffer, Emanuel, 74 pres, 82 pres
Kieffer, (Jac) Fr, 56 m An Mar Winnagler
Kieffer, (Sib) Fried, née Unselt, Pal, w Theo II
Kieffer, Geo, ca 1726, s Theo I, dd 59
Kieffer, ———, w Geo, 57 d Han
(Kieffer, Han, d Geo, 70 m A Kessler)
Kieffer, Han Marg, née Schubdrein, Pal, 73 m Is
Kieffer, (Joh) Is, s Theo II, 73 m H M Schubdrein, 74 pres
Kieffer, (Joh) Jac I, 1716, s Theo I, 40 m A E Depp, dd 47
Kieffer, (Joh) Jac II, s Jac I, 67 m Dor Reiter, 68 sur, dd by 83
Kieffer, Mar, Salz, wid Meyer, d Mati Bacher, 42 m Theo II, 57 s
    Is, 59 s Emanuel
(Kieffer, Marg, 1718, Pal, d Theo I, 38 m Tho Bichler)
Kieffer, Theo I, Pal, 1683, fr Pbg
Kieffer, (Joh) Theo II, Pal, 1719, s Theo I, 42 m wid Mar Meyer,
    née Bacher, gr 56, 60, 68
Kieffer, Urs, Pal, 1700, dd 69
Kikar, German soldier, 37 sick
Klammer. See Glaner
Klein, (Mar) Chna, née Oechsele, 55 m Joh, 59 s Joh Ad, 61 s Dav,
    63 s Jon, 65 d Han, 70 s Dav
Klein, Joh, ca 1737, 55 m Chna Oechsele, gr 59 Go, 69, dd 77
Klock, Bar, née Schaeffer, 55 m Casp
Klock, Casp, fr Pbg, 55 m Bar Schaeffer
Klosmann (Closeman), Fr, gr 68 Hali
Koecher, Apol, née Nissler, 1697, Swab fr Michelsheim, t9, w Geo,
    dd 51
Koecher, (Joh) Geo I, 1706, Salz, t9, schoolmaster on plantations,
    gr 50
Koecher, (Joh), Geo II, 1732, Salz, t9, s Geo, 47 conf
Koecher, Mar Helena, 1697, Salz, t9, dd 51
Koegler, Bar, née Rossbacher, Salz, t2, wid A Riedelsperger, 37 m
    Geo Kogler, 39 d Marg, 59 s Joh, dd 72 (Can this be one
    person?)
(Koegler, Elis, d Geo, 69 m J C Wertsch)

Koegler, Geo, 1708, Salz fr Rastadt, t2, 37 m Bar, wid Riedel-
sperger, 55 CB Eb, gr 56, dd 66
Koegler, Joh, s Geo, 74 pres
(Koegler, Mar, 1739, d Geo, 60 m Joh Heinle)
Kohleisen, Mar, née Wechselberger, 1692, Salz fr Zell im Zillerthal,
t9, w Pet, dd 42
Kohleisen, Pet, 1701, Salz fr Zell im Zillerthal, t9, h Mar, gr 50, 56
Mil Dis, 55 CB Eb, dd 56
Kohler, Bar, Pal, t12, sv L Krause
Koller, Engel, Swiss, kinswoman of Kruesy
Koller, Mar An, d Engel, 41 pres
Kornberger. *See* Cornberger
Kraemer, Cath, née Hangleitner, 74 m Chph II, 74 s Joh Chph, 81
s Chph III
Kraemer (Krihmer), (Joh) Chph I, 1689, Pal, t8, h Clara, Marg, dd
by 47
Kraemer, (Joh) Chph II, 1726, Pal, t8, s Chph I, 47 conf, 52 m Jha
Marg, née Mueller, wid Brueckner, 55 CB Eb, gr 57 Eb, 59 Eb,
61 Ab, 68; 74 m Cath Hangleitner, 76 1st Lt, dd 77
Kraemer, Clara, 1695, Pal, t8, w Chph I
Kraemer, Jha Marg, née Mueller, 1724, Salz, t9, w Chph II, 69
spon, dd 73
Kraemer, Marg, wid Kalcher, Salz, t2, m Chph I
Kraemer, Rup
Kraeuter (Kreuter, Kriuter), Joh, Swab, t14, barber, 55 CB Eb
(Kraeuter, Wal, wid, 67 m C Oechsele)
(Kraft, An Bar, née Brant, wid Dav, 53 m Rabenhorst, dd 79)
Kraft, Dav, Swab fr Ravensburg, t14, h An Bar, gr 52 Mil Dis, dd
52
Krause, Bar, née Einecker, 1704, Salz, t6, 36 m Leon
Krause, Elis, d Leon
Krause, Jac, h Sus
Krause, Jud, née Flerl, 64 m Sam, 65 d Slm, 77 spon
Krause, Leon, 1715, Salz, t6, 36 m Bar Einecker, 55 CB Eb, gr 56
Mil Dis, dd 62
Krause, Marg, d Leon
Krause, Sam, 64 m Jud Flerl, gr 64; 68 CB St Math, 77 spon, 83
justice of the peace for Effingham County
Krause, Sus, w Jac
Krause, Tho (Stueckhauptmann), t15, gr 52
(Kroeder [Kreder], Apol, 1709, Salz, t9, 42 m Paul Mueller)

Kroeder (Kreder), Cath, 1715

(Kroehr, Cath, 1716, Salz, t1, d Bar Rohrmoser, 34 m Gronau, 46
    m H H Lemke)

(Kroehr, Gert, 1717, Salz fr Grossarl, t1, d Bar Rohrmoser, 35 m
    Boltzius)

(Kroehr, Mar, 1705, Salz, t1, sis Bar Rohrmoser, 36 m Pet Gruber,
    by 50 m Carl Flerl)

Kronberger, Elis Mar, née Kieffer, w Nik, 57 s Joh Chph, 74 spon

Kronberger, Jac, gr 59 Eb, 68, 69; registrar of probates

(Kronberger, Jha, 69 m Fr Roesberg)

Kronberger, Lucia, 69 spon

Kronberger, Nik, 1717, fr Pbg, h Elis Mar, gr 50, 57, 59, 60, dd 75

Kruesy, Adrian, 1729, s Hans, 41 pres, 47 conf, dd 51

Kruesy, Hans, Swiss fr Pbg, dd ca 50

(Kuebler [Keebler], An Cath, d Jac, 58 m Luc Moser)

Kuebler, Cath, w Jac, 56 s Geo Jac, dd by 64

Kuebler, Elis, née Reiter, w Jac, 78 s Jeremias

Kuebler, Han, fr Go, 74 spon

Kuebler, (Joh) Jac, Swab, t12, h Cath, River Ness, 55 CB Go, gr 57
    Ab, gr 57 Go, 64 m Elis Reiter, 76 capt

(Kuebler, Ros, 64 m J C Hirschmann)

Kuenlin, Con, 1699, Salz fr Degenstein by Lindau, t9, h Mar, dd 41

Kuenlin, Joh, 1739, Salz fr Degenstein by Lindau, t9, s Con

(Kuenlin, Mar, née Hoesslinger, 1707, Salz fr Goldeck, t9, wid Con,
    42 m Mich Held)

Kugel. *See* Gugel

Kuhn, Balt, Pal, t12, runs away to Congarees

Kurtz, An, Salz, w Mati, ar 42, dd 48

Kurtz, Eleonora, Salz, d Mati, 47 conf, 54 m Geo Heidt

Kurtz, Gert, 1732, Salz, d Mati, 47 conf, dd 51

Kurtz, Mati, Salz, ar 42, h An, dd 43

(Kusmaul, An Ros, 70 m Mat Weinkauf)

Kusmaul, Jac, Pal, t11, h Sevila, 55 CB Eb, gr 59 Ab

Kusmaul, Sevila, Pal, t11, w Jac

Kustobader, Kunigunde, 1684, Pal, t8

Lackner, Cath Bar, née Ulmer, 1719, Salz fr Pappenheim, t9, w
    Mart II, 56 d Dor

Lackner, Elis, 52 m Mart Lackner I, dd 52

Lackner, Elis, Salz, sis Mart, t8a, dd 39

Lackner, Fr, gr 65, dd 71
Lackner, (Joh) Fr, gr 65 St Math, 74 m Jha Schubdrein
Lackner, Gert, 1707, t8a, sis Mart, dd 39
Lackner, Han, 1740, d Mart, 41 pres
Lackner, (Chrn) Is, 75 spon
(Lackner, Jha Chna, 72 m J C Greiner)
Lackner, Jha Marg, 74 m (Joh) Fr Lackner, 75 s Joh Fr, 78 spon
Lackner, Marg, née Egger, 1709, Salz, t8a, 39 m Ulich, 39 m Mart
    I, 40 d Han, dd 52
Lackner, Mart I, 1707, Aust, t6, 39 m wid Ulich, gr 57, 59 Go, dd
    58
Lackner, Mart II, 1712, Salz fr St Veit, t9, h Cath Bar
Lackner, Tob, 1694, Salz fr Gastein, t1, dd 34
Lamprecht, And, s Geo, gr 64 Ab
Lamprecht, An Mar, t12, w Geo
Lamprecht (Joh) Geo, Pal, t12, h An Mar, sv Rup Steiner, herds-
    man, gr 52, 54 drowns
Landfelder, Ag, 1732, Salz, t2, d Veit, 41 pres
Landfelder, Marg, Salz, t2, wid Schoppacher, 34 m Veit, dd 35
Landfelder, Urs, née Wassermann, Salz, t8a, 38 m Veit, dd 68
Landfelder, Veit, 1717, Salz, t2, 35 m wid Schoppacher, 38 m Urs
    Wassermann, 52 m Urs Eckhart, gr 57 Eb, dd 68
Lang, (Gotl?), gr 52
Lang, An Mar, 61 spon
Lang, Dr Chrn, h Mar Mag
Lang, Geo, gr 52
Lang, Jac, 1747, dd 72
Lang, Joh I, gr 52
Lang, Joh II, gr 52
Lang, Mar Mag, w Chrn, 79 s Chrn
Lastinger, (An) Bar, w Joh, 68 d Han, 76 s Joh Geo, 78 s And, d
    Elis, 80 d Mar
Lastinger, Joh, h Bar, gr 69
Lechner, Bar, 1719, w Mart I, dd 42
Lechner, Cath Bar, w Mart II, 56 d Dor
Lechner, Elis, 1731, Salz fr Goldeck, t9, d Veit
Lechner, Mag, 1693, Salz fr Goldeck, t9, w Veit, dd by 42
Lechner, Mar, 2nd w Veit, 57 d Mar Elis, 58 d Dor
Lechner, Mart I, 1710, Salz, t9, gr 50, 55 CB Ab, dd 66
Lechner, Mart II, h Cath Bar, gr 50

Lechner, Rup, Salz fr Goldeck, 1722, t9, s Veit
Lechner (Lackner), Veit, 1713, Salz fr Goldeck, t9, h Mag, after 42
    m Mar, gr 50 Eb, 57, 61, 55 CB Ab, 74 pres
Leihoffer, An, 36 m Rup Zittrauer
Leinberger, Apol, née Daumer, 64 m Is, 65 d Han Marg, 69 d Slm,
    74 s Chrn & s Sam, 77 s Joh & d Cath, 80 s Dav (Posthumus)
Leinberger, Cath, 1777, d Is, 99 m Tim Gnann
Leinberger (Leimberger), Chrn, Salz fr Loigam, 1710, t1, 40 m
    Marg Staud, wid Bach, gr 50, 57 Mil dis, 59, dd 63
Leinberger, (Chrn) Is, s Chrn, 64 m A Daumer, 74 pres, dd 80
(Leinberger, [Mar] Marg, née Staud, fr Kirckel in Zweibruecken,
    1718, Pal, t7, wid Gab Bach, w Chrn, 64 m P Jansen, gr 65 Eb)
Leinebacher, Geo Ad, 1736, Pal, t11, bro Salma, dd 48
Leinebacher, Salma, bro Ad, 1735, Pal, t11
Leitner, (Cath) Dor, wid Arnsdorff, w Jo, dd 64
Leitner, Jo, 1712, Aust, t6, h Dor, gr 64 Go, dd 67
Leitner, Veit, s Jo, gr 71
Lemke, Cath, née Kroehr, 1717, Salz, t1, wid Gronau, 46 m H Hr,
    dd 76
Lemke, Jha Chna, d H Hr, 74 spon
Lemke, Rev Hermann Hr, fr Fischbeck in Schaumburg, 1720, t11,
    gr 51, 55, 56, 61, 67; 55 CB Eb, dd 68
(Lemke, Slm, d H Hr, 77 m Dan Weidmann)
Lemke, Tim, 1752, s H Hr, 74 pres, dd 76
Lemmenhoffer, Mar, née Halbenthaler, Salz, t2, w Veit, 36 s, dd 50
Lemmenhoffer, Mar, d Veit, 41 pres
Lemmenhoffer, Paul, 1716, Salz, t2, dd 37
Lemmenhoffer, Veit, Salz, t2, h Mar, dd by 49
Lewenberger, Chrn, 1706, Pal, t8, h Marg, sv Ortmann, dep for
    Vern, gr 43 Mil Dis
Lewenberger, Marg, 1703, Pal, t8, w Chrn
Linger, Nite. *See* Neidlinger
Lohrmann, Joh, Swab fr Ulm, t15, 59 m Sus Humbart, 77 spon
Lohrmann, Sus, née Humbart, 59 m Joh, 79 s Jac

Mack (Mock), An Bar, wid Mayerhoffer, 55 m Wolfgang
Mack, Bart, 1730, 55 m Mar Stund(?), gr 59 Beth, dd 64
(Mack, Chna, 68 m M Weinkauf)
Mack, Jac, gr 61, 74 pres
Mack, Jonas, 55 CB Go
Mack, Mar, née Weinkauf, 65 m Tho

(Mack, Mar, w Bart, 58 d Mar Bar, 60 s Mich, 61 s Paul, 63 d Mar
& s Tho, 64 m G Fischer)
Mack, Mich, 74 pres, 83 pres
Mack, Tho, gr 59 Beth, 65 m Mar Weinkauf
Mack, Wolfgang, Swab fr Langenau by Ulm, t15, 55 m An Mar
Mayerhoffer, gr 65 Beth, dd 75
Madreiter, Han, w Hans
Madreiter, Hans, 1696, Aust, t2, dd 35
Mann, Luc, capt (German?)
Martin, Clement (German?), gr 60 Ab
Martin, Dan, gr 48
Mauer, Maur. *See* Maurer
Maurer, An, née Eigel, 59 m Gab, 60 d Han, 62 d Cath Marg, 65 s
Mich
Maurer, An, wid Mueller, w Joh II, 78 s Sal
Maurer, Bar, 1712, Salz, t6, single
Maurer, (An) Cath, née Meyer, wid Ossenecker, 36 m Hans, 38 d
Elis, dd 42
Maurer, Elis I, née Held, w Gab, dd 53
Maurer, Elis II, w Jac, gr 59 Eb
(Maurer, Elis III, d Gab, 41 pres, 54 conf, gr 59; 68 m J P Mueller,
dd 68)
Maurer, Gab, Salz, t2, h Elis I, h Mar II, gr 57 Mil Dis, 59 m An
Eigel, dd 66
Maurer, (Joh) Geo I, s Joh I, Salz, t9, 74 pres, dd 75
Maurer, (Joh) Geo II, 75 m Mar Sib Saecht
Maurer, Han Marg, wid, dd 75
Maurer, Jac, h Elis II, gr 58 Eb, 59
Maurer, Joh I (Hans), 1715, Salz fr Rastadt, t9, h Mar Wemmer, h
An Cath, 55 CB Eb, gr 57 Mil Dis, 67, 69
Maurer, Joh II, Salz, t9, s Joh I, 41 pres, 67 m M M Zant, gr 67, 70
Eb, 77 m An Mueller
Maurer, Mar I, née Wemmer, 1715, Salz fr St Johannis, t9, w Joh I,
dd by 42
Maurer, Mar II, 2nd w Gab, 58 s Is, 59 s Joh, dd 59
Maurer, Mar III, w Jac, 58 s Is
Maurer, Mar Mag, née Zant, 67 m Joh II, 69 d Cath, 73 s Joh, 75 s
Sal, 78 s Sal, dd 75
Maurer, Mar Mag, 63 m G Schleich, 70 m Joh Geo Heidt
(Maurer, Marg Sib, née Saecht, 75 m Geo II)
Mauts, Joh Geo, gr 52

Maxen, D (Dr?), fr Go, 78 spon
Maxen, ———, wife of above, 78 spon
Mayer. *See* Meyer
Mengeldorff, Ab, fr Pbg, 77 spon
Mengersdorff, Chna, w Jac, 77 s Joh, 80 s Geo
(Mengersdorf, Eva Mar, fr Pbg, 65 m J N Strobart)
Mengersdorff, Geo, 1704, fr Pbg, 78 spon
Mengersdorff, Jac, h Chna
(Mengersdorff, Mar Elis, fr Pbg, 65 m J Mart Burgemeister)
Merkel, Joh, fr Go, 77 m Sus Huber (Hover)
Merkel, Sus, née Huber, 77 m Joh
(Metzger [Mescher], Han, 73 m Jac Gnann)
Metzger, Jac I, Pal fr Pbg, dd 50
Metzger, (Joh) Jac II, h Marg, h Slm, gr 57 Beth, 60, 68, 74, dd 81
Metzger, (Joh) Jac III, 83 pres
Metzger, Jo, 70 spon
Metzger, ———, w Jo, 70 spon
Metzger, Marg, née Schwarzwaelder, w Jac II, 58 d Sara, 60 d
    Cath, 62 d Lucia, 65 s Dav, 83 pres
Metzger, Ph, gr 50
Metzger, Phillippa, gr 57 Beth
Metzger, Sam, 74 pres
Metzger, Slm, w Jac II, 81 spon
Meyer, An, 1715, Salz, t6
Meyer, Bar, née Zorn, 50 m Joh Lud, 56 s Chrn, 59 d Marg, 61 d
    Jha, 63 d Mar
(Meyer, Chna, née Remshard, 66 m Joh, 68 m Jac Heinle)
Meyer, Elis, gr 61
Meyer, Elis, née Mueller, 1701, Swab fr Memmingen, t9, 1st w Joh
    Lud, dd 49
Meyer, (Joh) Geo, 1720, t9, Swab fr Memmingen, bro Joh Lud, ca
    42 m Mag Roner, gr 50, 52, dd 67
Meyer, Hr, Pal, t7, sv Trustees' sawmill, h Mar, gr 52, ca 63 m Mar
    Franziska
Meyer, (Joh) Jac, Pal fr Pbg, 55 CB Beth, gr 50, 57 Beth, 60 Beth,
    65, 67, 69; 71 m (An) Jul Schmidt
Meyer, Joh, gr 52, 66 m Chna Remshard, dd 57
Meyer, (An) Jul, wid Schmidt, 71 m Jac, 79 spon
Meyer, (Hr Joh) Lud, 1715, t9, Swab fr Memmingen, h Elis, 50 m
    Bar Zorn, 48 justice of the peace, gr 49 Parker's Mill, 51, 56 Ab,
    57, 59, 55 CB Eb, dd 63 (?)

Meyer, Mag I, née Roner, Salz, t9, w Geo

Meyer, Mag II, Swiss, 35 ar Sav, 41 ar Eb, mo of Urs

(Meyer, Mar, 1718, Salz, t9, d Mati Bacher, 42 m Theo Kieffer II)

Meyer, Mar, w Hr, 53 d Mar, 55 ss Joh & Hr, 58 d Slm, 59 d Jul, 63
d Sara

Meyer, Mar Cath, 1720, dd 70

Meyer, Mar Franziska, 2nd w Hr, 64 d Elis, 66 s Dav

Meyer, Mati, Salz, t9, gr 59 Beth, 74 pres

Meyer, Urs, d Mag II, 49 m Swiss, plantation by mill

Meyers. *See* Meyer

Michel, Han Elis, née Gugel, 72 m Nik

Michel, Joh, h Mar, gr 65, 79 spon, 83 pres

Michel, Mar, w Joh, 59 d Mar Bar, 79 spon

Michel, Nik, gr 71; 72 m Han Elis Gugel, 74 pres

Michler, Cath, Swab fr Nerensteten by Ulm, t13, sv Mart Lackner
II

Michler, Joh, gr 59 Beth, 83 pres

Michler, Jost, Pal, t12, sv Jo Leitner, 49

Michler, Nik, gr 71 Beth

Mick. *See* Mueck

Millen, Stephan, gr 58, 60, 61, 67, 69

Millen, ———, w Stephan, 58 s Gotl

Miller. *See* Mueller

Mittersteiner, Mat, 1693, Salz, t1, dd 34

Mock. *See* Mack

(Mohr, An Mar, w Jac I, 59 m Joh Scheraus)

(Mohr, Cath, d Jac I, m And Seckinger II)

Mohr, Elis, wid Walliser, 58 m Jac II

Mohr, Jac I, 1700, Swab, t12, sv Chrn Riedelsperger, h An Mar, gr
52 Eb, 59 Beth, dd ca 64

Mohr, Jac II, fr Pbg, 48 pres, 55 CB Go, 58 m Elis Walliser, gr 59
Go

(Mohr, Jha, 65 m J U Fetzer)

Mohr, Joh, gr 50

Mohr, Rachel, dd 73

Moser, An Cath, wid Kuebler, 1711, 58 m Luc, dd 58

(Moser, An Urs, 61 m Fettler)

Moser, Jac

Moser, ———, w Jac

Moser, Luc, 58 m wid An Cath Kuebler, gr 52 Hali

Mosshamer, Joh, 1699, Salz, t1, h Mar, dd 35

(Mosshamer, Mar, née Rohrmoser, 1705, Salz, t1, w Joh, 36 m Pet
  Gruber, m by 58 Carl Flerl)
Mueck (Mick), An Mar, Pal, t11, w Jonas
Mueck, Cath, w Joh Casp, d Cath, 80 spon, 81 spon
Mueck, Fr, gr 70
Mueck, Joh Casp, h Cath, 80 spon, 81 spon
Mueck, Jonas, Pal, t11, h An Mar, gr 58 Go, 59 Go, 61, 58 spon
Mueck, Mati, gr 71, 81 spon
Mueck, ———, w Mati, 81 spon
Mueckenfuss, Mich, gr 71
Muehler, Joh, 83 pres
(Mueller, An, née Seckinger, 69 m J P Mueller II, 77 m Joh
  Maurer)
(Mueller, An Mar, née Kraemer, 41 m Paul)
(Mueller, An Marg, 64 m J Remshardt)
Mueller, Apol, 2nd w (Joh) Paul, dd 67
Mueller, (An) Chna, t6, w Fr Wilh, 51 pres
Mueller, Elis, née Maurer, 68 m (Joh) Paul I, 69 s Fr Wilh, 72 s Joh
  Paul
Mueller, (Ag) Elis, 1726, Pal, t6, d Fr Wilh
Mueller, Fr Wilh, Pal, t6, h Chna, dd by 51
Mueller, (Joh) Geo, m 56 wid Ros Schubdrein, gr 59 Go, 68 CB
  St Math
Mueller, Joh, Pal, t8, gr 52 Eb
Mueller, Malachi, Pal, t11, h Marg, gr Go before 57
(Mueller, [An] Marg, 1724, Pal, t6, d Fr Wilh, gr 59 Go, 64 m Joh
  Remshardt, dd by 73)
Mueller, Marg, t11, w Malachi
Mueller, (An) Mar Mag, 1733, Pal, t6, d Fr Wilh,
Mueller, (Joh) Paul I, 1721, Pal, t6, s Fr Wilh, h An Mar Kraemer,
  42 m Apol Kreder, 55 CB Eb (Powell Millar), gr 57, 58, 59 Mil
  Dis, 60, 68; 68 m Elis Maurer III, dd 72
Mueller, (Joh) Paul II, 1745, s Joh Paul I, 69 m An Seckinger, gr
  71, dd 72
Mueller, Ros, wid Schubdrein, 56 m Geo, 57 d An Mar
Mueller, (Joh) Sim, 1719, Pal, t6, s Fr Wilh, dd 37
Muggitzer, Hans Mich, Salz, t2, dep ca 37

Neibling (Nuebling), Alexander, Swab, t14, gr 52 Briar Ck
Neibling, Bart, Swab fr Langenau by Ulm, t14, 71 m Mar Ochs
Neibling, (An) Mar, née Ochs, 71 m Bart

Neidlinger, (Joh) Gotl, 55 CB Eb, 74 pres, 83 justice of the peace of
Effingham County
Neidlinger, Mar Mag, 2nd w Ulr II, 73 spon
Neidlinger, Mati, Swab, t12
Neidlinger, Sib, 76 pres
Neidlinger, (Joh) Ulr I, Swab, t13, dd 51
Neidlinger, ———, 1685, w Ulr I, dd 51
Neidlinger, (Joh) Ulr II, Swab, t13, s Ulr I, h Wal, 55 CB, gr 54, 59,
h Mar Mag, 74 pres
Neidlinger, Wal, w Ulr II, 58 s Sam, 61 s Dav, 70 d Jha, dd 70
Nessler, Dor, w Joh Ad, 79 spon, 79 d Elis
Nessler, Joh Ad, h Dor, 79 spon, 3rd Lt Hali
Nett, Elis (Mag), 1702, Pal, t8, w Fr
Nett, Fr (Lud), 1707, Pal, t8, h Elis
Niess, Cath. 60 m (Joh) Geo, 60 s (Joh) Geo, dd 61
Niess, Chna Elis, née Schmidt, 67 m Leon, 70 d Jha Fried, 79 Goth
Is
Niess, (Joh) Geo, Swab, t15, gr 53 Beth, 55 CB Beth, 55 m Mar
Oechsele, 60 m Cath, 61 m Sib Reg Geiger, dd 72
Niess, (Joh) Leon, gr 52, 64; 67 m C E Schmidt, gr 68
Niess, Mar, née Oechsele, 1732, 55 m Geo, 58 d Reb, dd 60
Niess, Marg, 1707, wid, dd 73
Niess, (Joh) Mart, Swab, t15, gr 52
Niess, Sib Reg, wid Geiger, 61 m Geo

Ochs, An, née Fetzer, 67 m Fr, 68 d An, 69 s (Joh) Fr, 70 s Dav
(Ochs, An Mar, 71 m Bart Neibling)
Ochs, (Joh) Fr, 1700, 67 m An Fetzer, gr 69, dd 69
Odem, Ab I, gr 64 St Math
Odem, Ab II, gr 67 St Math
Oechsele (Oechselin, Exley), Angelica, w Chrn I, 57 s Chrn, 59 s
Joh, dd 66
(Oechsele, Bar, Swab, t14, 50 m Mart Soldner)
Oechsele, (Joh) Chph, Swab, t14, s Melchior, gr 65 Beth, 74 pres
Oechsele, Chrn I, Swab, t14, s Melchior, h Angelica, 67 m wid Wal
Kraeuter, gr 59 Beth
Oechsele, Elis, née Gress, 66 m Joh, 69 d Mar, 76 spon
Oechsele, Joh, Swab, t14, s Mich, 66 m Elis Gress, gr 67 Beth, 74
pres, 76 spon
(Oechsele, Mar, Swab, t14, d Melchior, 55 m J G Niess)
(Oechsele, Mar Chna, Swab, t14, d Melchior, 55 m J Klein)

Oechsele, Melchior, gr 52

Oechsele, (Joh) Mich, Swab, t14, gr Beth by 57, dd by 67

Oechsele, Wal, wid Kraeuter, 67 m Chrn I, 70 d Marg, 73 d (name not known)

Ortmann, Chrph, German schoolmaster, t1, 41 pres, ca 42 dep for Vern

Ortmann, Jul, t1, w Chrph, pres 41, ca 42 dep for Vern

(Ossenecker [Ossenegger], An Cath, née Meyer, wid Tho, 36 m Hans Maurer)

Ossenecker, Tho, 1711, Salz, t6, 36 m An Cath Meyer, dd 36

(Ott, Agn, 73 m Jo Schubdrein)

Ott, (Joh) Gotl, s Sig, 74 pres

Ott, (An) Mag, née Heinrich, 43 m Sig, 57 s Nath

Ott, (Carl) Sig, Salz, t2, 42 m An Mag Heinrich, gr 57 Mil Dis, gr 59, 74 pres

Ott, ———, 1st w Sig, fr Sav, dd 42

Ott, Nath, s Sig, 83 pres

Paulinger, (Joh) Geo, gr 59 Beth

Paulitsch, An Mag, w Ph, 58 d An Mag, 64 s Joh Geo

Paulitsch, (Joh) Mart, 54 m Urs Schwinkhofer, gr 57 Beth, 74 pres

Paulitsch, (Joh) Ph, h An Mag, gr 74 Beth, 74 pres

Paulitsch, Urs, née Schwinkhofer, 54 m Mart, 57 d Sulamith, 59 d Han Elis, 61 d Gratiosa, 63 s Jon, 65 s Gideon

Paulus, (Joh) Ad I, Swab, t15, gr 52 Beth, 74 pres

Paulus, (Joh) Ad II, Swab, t15, s Ad I, gr 52, 55 m (Mar) Urs Groll, gr 74, dd 74

(Paulus, An, 1741, Swab, t15, d Ad, 70 m Mat Biddenbach, dd 78)

Paulus, An Urs, w Ad I?, dd 81

Paulus, (Mar) Urs, wid Groll, 55 m Ad II, 58 s Joh Ad

Pflueger (Fleger), Bar, née Rau, 57 m Joh I, 59 d An Mar, 62 s Joh, 64 s Is, 66 s Dav, 69 s Jon, dd 77

Pflueger, Joh I, Swab fr Langenau by Ulm, t15, gr 52; 57 m Bar Rau, gr 60 Beth

Pflueger, Joh II, 1761, dd 77

(Piedler, Cath 1711, Salz, t1, w Step Riedelsperger)

Piltz (Beltz), An

Piltz, And, 1705, Salz fr Rastadt, t9, h Sib, dd 42

(Piltz, Sib, 1714, Salz fr Rastadt, t9, w And, after 42 m Bart Zant)

Piltz, Sig, Swab, t15, gr 54, 61 Beth

Pletter, Elis I, née Wasserman, Salz, t8a, 39 m Joh

Pletter, Elis II, d Joh, 41 pres
Pletter, Joh, 1705, Aust, t6, 39 m Elis Wasserman, gr 57 Mil Dis
Polhill, An, wid, gr 67, name possibly not German
Pollinger. *See* Bollinger
Portz, Jac, Pal, t11, h Mag, 55 CB Go, gr 57, 60
Portz, Mag, Pal, t11, w Jac
Portz, (Geo) Ph, Pal, t11, gr 50 Go, 57 Ab, 58 Ab, 60; 56 CB Go
Preisier, Chrn, 73 m Jha Dopp
Preisier, Jha, née Dopp, w Chrn
Preysing, Chrn I, gr 52
Preysing, Chrn II, gr 52
(Pricker, Elis, Swab fr Langenau, 52 m Mart Lackner I)

Rabenhorst, Rev. Chrn, fr Poggenkoepp in Hinterpommern, 1728,
    t15, 52 m wid An Bar Kraft, gr 56, 57, 59, 61, 63, 65, 71; 55 CB
    Eb, dd 76
Rabenhorst, An Mar, née Brant, wid Kraft, t14, 52 m Chrn, dd 79
Rahn, (An) Bar, née Paulitsch, w Con, 58 s Obadiah, 60 d Lydia, 62
    s Jon, 64 d Mar, 67 d An Marg, 69 s Jo, 72 s Jac
Rahn, Casp, gr 52
Rahn, Con, Swab fr Ulm, t13, h An Bar, gr 57 Beth, 60, 67, 74
    pres, dd by 83
Rahn, Jon, s Con, 83 pres
Rahn, Mar, dd 69
Rahn, Mati, 76 1st Lt
(Rau, An Cath, 1697, m Joh Geo Zieger), dd 59
(Rau, Bar, 57 m Hans Pflueger)
Rau, Geo, Swab, t15, s An Cath, dd 53
Rauner, Leon, Swab fr Hirnstein by Ulm, 1706, t1, 35 m wid Mar
    Mag fr Pbg, dd 40
Rauner, Mar, 1732, d Mar Mag, 41 pres
(Rauner, Mar Mag, wid fr Pbg, 35 m Leon, 41 m Schartner)
Rauner, Mati, 1725, s Leon, 41 pres
Regnier (Reinier, Ranier, Renniger), Joh Francis, Swiss, former
    Moravian, ar 35, dep 38, gr 70 Go, dd by 77
Regnier, ———, wife Joh Francis, dd 77
Rehm, Fr, 82 pres Ogeechee
Reiser, Reser. *See* Rieser
Reiter, Carl, gr 62 Go
(Reiter, Dor, 67 m J J Kieffer II)
(Reiter, Elis, 70 m C E Zittrauer)

(Reiter, Gert, née Schoppacher, wid S Steiner, wid Pet Reiter, m B Bacher)

Reiter, Han, d Sim, 68 spon

(Reiter, Jha, 70 m Ernst Zittrauer)

Reiter, Joh, Pal, t7, 55 CB Eb, gr 54, 57 Mil dis, 61, 68

Reiter, Mag, née Gebhart, wid Sim Steiner, 41 m Pet Reiter, dd 41

Reiter, (Mar) Mag, 1718, d Sim, dd 70

Reiter, Mar, Salz fr St Ulrich in Tyrol, 1707, dd 34

Reiter, Pet, 1715, Aust, t6, h Gert, 41 m Mag, gr 57

Reiter, Sim, fr Gastein in Salz, 1707, t1, 55 CB Eb, gr 57 Mil Dis, 59

Remshard, An Marg, née Mueller, 64 m Joh, 65 s Dan, 67 d Cath, 68 d Jud, 73 s Chrn & d Chna, dd 73

(Remshard, Chna, 66 m Joh Meyer)

Remshard, Chna Elis, née Schubdrein, 73 m Joh, 78 d Elis

Remshard, Dan, Swab fr Langenau, t14, h Marg, gr 59 Mil Dis, dd 67

Remshard, Joh, s Dan, gr 60, 68 St George; 64 m A M Mueller, 73 m Chna Schubdrein, 74 pres, dd by 83

Remshard, Marg, w Dan, 57 d Chna, 68 gr, 73 s Chrn & d Chna

Rentz, Bar, née Unselt, 54 m Joh, 56 s Joh, 61 s Gotl, 61 d Jha Chna, 64 d Mar Fried, 70 d Cath Mar

Rentz, (Joh) Geo, t12, sv Mat Burgsteiner, 68 m Han Mar Kalcher, dd 70

Rentz, Han Mar, née Kalcher, 68 m Geo, dd 70

Rentz, Joh, 54 m Bar Unselt, gr 59, 72, 74

Resch, And, Salz, t2, 34 m Sib Schwab, 35 lost in woods

(Resch, Sib, née Schwab, wid And, 38 m Tho Gschwandl)

Rester (Resta), (Geo) Fr, Pal fr Durlach, 55 m M M Mengersdorff, 67 CB St Math; 76 1st Lt

Rester, Mar Marg, née Mengersdorff, 55 m Fr, 65 s Fr

Reuschgott, Sim, 1711, Salz, tr1, dd 35

Reuter. *See* Reiter

Rheinauer, An Bar, w Leon, 56 s Ab

Rheinauer, Leon, h Bar

Rheinlaender, Chrn, s Fr, pres 41

Rheinlaender, Fr, Pal, 34 ar Eb, h Mar An I, dep for New York, dd by 50

Rheinlaender, Frid Cath, née Brueckner, 63 m Mart

Rheinlaender, Mar, 1739, née Kalcher, 58 m Mart, dd 60

Rheinlaender, Mar An I, w Fr

Rheinlaender, Mar An II, d Fr, 41 pres

Rheinlaender, (Joh) Mart, 1735, s Fr, 52 conf, 55 CB Eb, 58 m Mar Kalcher, 63 m F C Brueckner, gr 50 Beth, 70, dd 76

Richard (Reichert, Ritschard?), Iscariot, Pal, t11, s Tho, bro Wilh, ran away to Congarees

Richard, Lor, 1736, Pal, t11, sv wid Graniwetter, 49 ran away to Congarees

Richard, Wilh, Pal, t11, s Tho, bro Iscariot, ran away to Congarees

Riedelsperger, Ad, 1701, Salz, t2, h Bar, dd 36

Riedelsperger, An, w Rup, 38 s Joh

(Riedelsperger, Bar, Salz, t2, wid Ad, 37 m Geo Kogler)

Riedelsperger, Cath, née Valentin, 36 m Step, dep 38

Riedelsperger, Chrn I, Salz fr Lichtenstein-Salfeld, t2, dd 50

Riedelsperger, Chrn II, Salz fr Lichtenstein-Salfeld, 1715, t2, s Chrn I, 41 m Mar Schweighoffer, gr 51, 54, 55 CB Eb, 56 gr Go, 57, dd 60

Riedelsperger, Mar, née Schweighoffer, 1702, Salz, t1, w Chrn II, 56 s Sam Leberecht

(Riedelsperger, Mar, 60 m John Wilson)

Riedelsperger, Nik, 1688, Salz, t2, dd 36

Riedelsperger, Rup, Salz, t2, h An

Riedelsperger, Step, Salz fr Lichtenstein-Salfeld, t2, h Cath Piedler, 36 m Cath Valentin, dep 38

Rieser, Ad, gr 70

(Rieser, An Dor, née Meyer, 54 m Geo, 60 m G Fischer)

Rieser, An Mar I, 1709, Salz, t6, wid Steiger, w Mich I, dd 37

Rieser, An Mar II, née Winnagler, 56 m Jac Fr, 57 d Mar

(Rieser, Apol, w Mich II, 60 d Cath, 62 d Mar, 65 s Dav, 78 m Mat Biddenbach)

Rieser, Balt, Salz fr Gastein, 1724, t2, s Bart, 52 m Mar Bacher, wid Bichler, 55 CB Eb, gr 59 Beth, 65, 74 pres

Rieser, Bart, Salz fr Gastein, t2, h Mar Zugeisen, dd 48

Rieser, Ben, h Cath, 74 pres

Rieser, Cath, w Ben, 79 d Mar

Rieser, Dor, d Is, w Nath, 78 spon, 79 d Chna

(Rieser, Dor, gr 70; 75 m S Zant)

Rieser, (Joh) Geo, 1726, Salz, t2, s Bart, 54 m An Dor Meyer, 55 CB Bl Ck, gr 58 Bl Ck, 59 Go, dd 60

Rieser, Gotl, 1735, Salz, t6, s Mich I

Rieser, Han (Mag), née Schubdrein, w Is, 78 d Elis

Rieser, (Joh) Is, 74 m Han Schubdrein, 79 spon, 82 pres

Appendix 2

Rieser, Jac Fr, 56 m An Mar Winnagler
Rieser, Mag, née Biberger, 1702, Salz fr Saalfeld, t9, w Sim, dd 42
Rieser, Mar, née Zugeisen, 1712, Salz, t2, w Bart, dd 37
Rieser, Mar, w Balt, 58 s Joh Goth, 60 s Mich, 64 d Cath
Rieser, (Joh) Mich I, 1704, Salz, t6, h An Mar, 38 m wid Ihler, 48 dep
Rieser, Mich II, 1721, Salz, t2, s Bart, h Apol, 48 pres, 55 CB Eb, gr 56, 61 sur Mil Dis, dd 75
Rieser, Nath, h Dor, 78 spon
Rieser, Sib Reg, Salz, t2, w Geo, 63 d Elis
Rieser, Sim, 1685, Salz fr Kropfsberg, t9, h Mag
Ring, Chph, gr 66 Ogeechee
Rittenberger, Joh, 74 spon
Roesberg, Fr, fr Sav, 69 m Jha Cronberger, gr 73, 75 Beth
Roesberg, Jha, née Cronberger, 69 m Fr
Rohrmoser, Bar, Salz fr Salfeld, 1697, t1, mo of Chna & Gert Kroehr, dd 35
(Rohrmoser, Mar, sis Bar, w Moshamer)
(Roner, Mag, 1712, Salz fr Bischofen, t9, w Joh Geo Meyer)
Rosch, Ab, h Han
Rosch, An Mar, fr Pbg, 54 conf
Rosch, Han, w Ab, 70 s Gideon
Roth, An, née Fetzer, 67 m Geo Lud
Roth (Rott), Geo Bart, Bav fr Wuerzburg, 1688, t1, dep 35, dd 35
Roth, Geo Lud, 67 m An Fetzer
Roth, ———, 1st w Geo Lud, 66 s Joh Chrn
Roth, Mar Bar, née Oswald, Bav fr Wuerzburg, 1701, t1 Geo Bart, dep 36
(Rottenberger, An Franziska, 1750, d Step, 71 m And Gnann)
Rottenberger, Cath, née Piedler, Salz, t2, w Step, 50 d An Franziska
Rottenberger, Chph, h Elis, 55 CB Eb, gr 56, 69 Beth
Rottenberger, Chrn, s Step, gr 50, 56 Beth, 60 Eb, 69; 74 pres
Rottenberger, Dav, 1741, s Step
Rottenberger, Elis, w Chph, 51 pres, 59 d Elis
Rottenberger, Joh, s Chrn, 74 pres, 78 spon
Rottenberger, Step, Salz fr Lichtenstein-Salfeld, 1711, t2, h Cath
Rottenberger, Sus, d Step, dd 48

(Saecht, Mar Sib, 75 m J G Maurer)
Salffer, (Joh) Ad, gr 52
Salffer, Leon, gr 52

Salffer, Mati, gr 52

(Sanftleben Elis, sis Geo, Silesian, t8a, 40 m Mich Schneider)

Sanftleben, Geo, Silesian, t2, 40 m Mag Arnsdorff, dd 49

Sanftleben, Mag, née Arnsdorff, 40 m Geo, 41 s

Sauler, ———, fr Ogeechee, 72 pres

Sauler, ———, w of above, 72 s Jac

Schade, Cath, 58 spon

(Schaeffer, Bar, fr Pbg, 55 m Casp Klock)

Schartner, Jac, Salz, t2, 41 m wid Mar Mag Rauner

Schartner, Mar Mag, wid Rauner, 41 m Jac

Scheel, Chrn Fr, Pal fr Weyerbach, dd 69

Scheffer, Joh Fr, Pal, t12, ran away to Congarees

Scheffler, An Mar, 1705, wid Ernst, 42 m Joh I

Scheffler, Cath, 1697, Salz, t9, née Kroener, w Joh, dd 42

Scheffler, Fr Carl, s Joh

Scheffler, Joh I, 1686, Salz, t9, h Cath

Scheffler, Joh II, 1737, Salz, t9, s Joh I

Scheides, Ph, 79 spon

Scheraus, An Mar, née Mohr, 59 m Joh II, 69 d Sim, 70 s Is, 72 s
  Joh, 74 d An Mar

Scheraus, (Joh) Geo, Swab fr Ulm, t13, gr 56 Go, 58, 59

Scheraus, Joh I, 1686, Salz, t9, h Mar Helena, gr 50, 55 CB Bl Ck,
  dd 67

Scheraus, Joh II, 1706, Swab fr Bermeringen by Ulm, t9, s Joh I,
  59 m An Mar Mohr, gr 57 Go

Scheraus, Joh III, 1735, s Joh II, Swab fr Bermeringen by Ulm,
  Joh II, t9, gr 60, 70 m wid Mag Epinger, 74 pres

Scheraus (Mar) Mag, wid Epinger, 70 m Joh III, 72 d Marg, 75 d
  Han, 77 d Mag, 79 d Dor, 80 d Cath

Scheraus, Mar Fried, 79 illegitimate d Slm by Mart Dasher

Scheraus, Mar Helena, née Gott, 1697, Swab fr Ulm, t9, w Joh I

Scherer, Mich, dd 66

Schick, Fr, 82 pres

Schick (Sheek), Joh, gr 60

Schiedmann, Mart Hr

Schiedmann, ———, w Mart Hr, 73 s Geo, 75 d Elis

Schiele (Schuele, Sheley), An, w Joh, 60 s Joh Geo, 73 spon

Schiele, Joh, h An, gr 59 Beth, 65 Beth

Schiele, Joh Geo, s Joh, dd by 83

(Schiermeister, Amalia, sv Boltzius, 52 pres, 54 m Jo Alther, 55
  widowed)

Appendix 2

Schleich(er), Geo, ca 1713, Swab, t13, sv Rup Eischberger, 63 m M M Maurer, 56 CB Eb, dd 69

(Schleich, Mar Mag, née Maurer, 63 m Geo, 64 s Dav, 70 m J G Heidt)

Schmidt, Bar, 1738, d Hans, 41 pres

Schmidt, Cath, née Zehetner, 1705, Aust, t6, w Hans

(Schmidt, Chna Elis, 67 m Joh Fr Ochs)

Schmidt, Han Elis, w Is, 79 spon

Schmidt, Hans (=Joh I), 1708, Aust, t6, h Cath, gr 57, 59, dd 67

Schmidt, Is, h Han Elis

Schmidt, (Joh) Jac, 1733, Aust, t6, s Hans, dd 36

Schmidt, Jac, 74 pres

Schmidt, Joh II, s Hans, gr 74

(Schmidt, wid An Jul, 71 m Jac Meyer)

Schmidt, Sam, 1742, dd 60

Schneider, An, 1708, Pal, t8, 1st w Mich, dd 39

Schneider, And, Swab, t15, gr 52 Bl Ck, gr 59 Go, 71 sur

Schneider, (An) Bar, née Schneider, sis Mar Cath, Pal, t12, sv P Zittrauer, 58 m Geo, 59 s Sam, 61 d Reb, 62 s Joh, 64 s Chrn, 65 d Han, 66 d Slm, dd 57

Schneider, Bar, fr Trimbach, conf 54

Schneider, Cath, née Grimmiger, d And, 1735, Aust, t6, 58 m Joh, 59 s Sam, 61 s Jon, 64 s Nath, 66 s Joh, 70 d Mar Cath

Schneider, (Mar) Cath, Swab, t12, sv Mart Lackner

Schneider, Elis, Silesian, 1698, née Sanftleben, sis Geo, 40 m Mich, dd 60

Schneider, (Joh) Geo, 1726, Pal, t8, s Mich, 47 conf, 58 m An Bar, 54 sells lot, gr 57, 59, dd 67

Schneider, Hr, gr 69

Schneider, ———, 1st w Geo, dd 57

Schneider, Joh, 1732, Pal, t8, s Mich, 58 m Cath Grimmiger, gr 59 Mil Dis

Schneider, Joh Gotl, s Geo, 74 pres

Schneider, Mar Bar, w Geo, 60 d Mar Cath

Schneider, Mar Cath, t12, sis Bar, sv Mart Lackner

Schneider, (Hans) Mich, 1698, Pal, t8, h An, 40 m E Sanftleben, gr 57, dd 57

Schoppacher, Ag, Salz, t2, d Rup

(Schoppacher, Mar I, Salz, t2, née Wasserman, wid Rup, 35 m Veit Landfelder)

Schoppacher, Mar II, Salz, t2, d Rup, dd 35

Schoppacher, Marg, Salz, t2, d Rup, dd 35

Schoppacher, Rup, 1686, Salz, t2, h Mar, dd 35

Schoppacher, Sara, d Rup, 41 pres

Schrempff, Bar, née Brickl, t9, 42 m Rup, dd 42

Schrempff, Chna Elis, ca 72 m Fr, 73 s Sal, 77 s Wilh, 78 d Chna Elis

Schrempff, (Joh) Fr, s Rup, gr 59 Beth, 69; 70 m Sarah Dixon, ca 72 m Chna Elis, gr 74

Schrempff, Rup, 1722, Salz, t9, 42 m Bar, 43 m Kieffer (?), gr 50 Beth, dd 53

Schrempff, Sal, s Rup, gr 68, dd 80

Schrempff, Sarah, née Dixon, 70 m Fr

Schrind, ———, fr Pa

Schrind, ———, w of above, 74 d Han Elis

Schroeder, Sam, millwright fr Danzig, 50 pres

Schroeder (Schroter, Schruder), Tho, gr 71

Schroter, An, Swab fr Langenau by Ulm, t14

Schubdrein, Agn, née Ott, 73 m Jo, 79 spon

Schubdrein, An Mar, née Zuericher, 58 m Nik, 59 ss Joh Gotl & Sam, 62 s Sam, 64 d Jud, 66 d Slm, 68 s Is, 69 d Chna, dd 72

(Schubdrein, Chna, 1757, d Dan, 73 m J Remshardt)

Schubdrein, Dan, Pal, t12, h Mag, sv Zouberbuhler, 55 CB Eb, gr 57 Beth, 59, dd 68

(Schubdrein, Han Marg, 73 m Is Kieffer)

(Schubdrein, Jha Marg, 74 m Fr Lackner)

Schubdrein, Jo I, Pal, t12, h Mar Brandner, sv Zouberbuhler, gr 57 Beth, 59, 61, 62, 68 St Math, 71; 73 m Agn Ott, gr 78, dd 80

Schubdrein, Jo II, killed by 83

Schubdrein, Jo III, gr 84

Schubdrein, Mag, w Dan, 57 d Chna, 60 d Han Elis, 62 s Chrn, 65 d Mar Mag

Schubdrein, Mar, née Brandner, w Jo, 56 d Mar, 58 s Jo, 60 d Mar, 63 s Dav, 65 s Jo, 70 s Mati, dd 73

Schubdrein, ———, ca 1682, Pal, h Marg, dd 52

Schubdrein, Marg I, Pal, 1685, dd 64

Schubdrein, Marg II, née Haeussler, 72 m Nik, 73 d Cath, 75 d Cath, 79 d Han

Schubdrein, (Joh) Nik, 58 m An Mar Zuericher, gr 57 Beth, 61, 62, 72 m Marg Haeussler, 83 pres

Schubdrein, (Joh) Pet, Pal fr Nassau-Saarbrueckenn, t12, 50 dep for Germany, 51 returns t14

Schubdrein, Ros, mo Pet, 52 pres
Schubdrein, Sal, s Pet
Schubdrein, ———, sis Jo, 53 drowns
Schuele. *See* Schiele
Schumann, Mart, h Tobita, 73 spon
Schumann, Tobita, w Mart, 73 spon
(Schwab, Sib, Salz, t2, 34 m Resch)
Schwartzwaelder, An Mar, 1695, Pal, t7, w Joh, dd 42
(Schwartzwaelder, Elis, d Joh, 58 m Geo Gruber)
Schwartzwaelder, Hans Mich, 1735, Pal, t7, s Joh
Schwartzwaelder, Joh, 1693, Pal, t7, sv at Trustees' mill, h An Mar,
    43 moves fr Old to New Eb, dd by 54
Schwartzwaelder, Mar Elis (Mariaket), d Joh, 54 conf
Schwartzwaelder, Marg, 1726, Pal, t7, d Joh
Schweiger, An, née Hofer, 1709, Salz, 1st w Geo, dd 35
Schweiger, An Marg, 70 spon
Schweiger, (Mar) Cath, 1739, d Geo, dd 39
Schweiger, Eva Reg, née Unselt, fr Pbg, 1713, 2nd w Geo, 41 s, 58 s
    Fr Gotl, dd 60
Schweiger, Geo, Salz fr Gastein, 1714, t1, 34 m An Hofer, 35 m
    Eva Reg Unselt, 61 m Marg Zittrauer, 55 CB Eb, gr 57 Mil Dis,
    58, 67, 74 pres
Schweiger, Gratiosa, 77 spon
Schweiger, (An) Marg, wid Zittrauer, 61 m Geo, 77 spon
Schweighoffer, Han, née Flerl, 1740, 58 m Tho, 58 s Abiel, 60 s
    Benajah, 61 s Tho, 62 d Slm, 64 s Elisha, 66 s Obadjah, 69 d Elis,
    dd 69
(Schweighoffer, Mar, 1726, Salz, t2, d Paul, w Chrn Riedelsperger)
Schweighoffer, Marg, Salz, ca 1692, t2, née Pindlinger, w Paul, 49
    pres
Schweighoffer, Paul, Salz fr Mietosil, 1692, t2, h Marg, dd 36
Schweighoffer, Tho, 1728, Salz, t2, s Paul, 55 CB Eb, 58 m Han
    Flerl, gr 58 Mil Dis, 59, 60, 67, dd 72
Schweighoffer, Urs, 1728, Salz, t2, d Paul
Schweikert, Chrn, 1711, t1, sv Baron von Reck, dd 35
Schweitzer, Mich, sv Jas Haselfoot, gr 51, 59
Schwinkhoffer, Benajah, dd 65
Schwinkhoffer, Marg, 1683, dd 66
Seckinger, Ag, wid Ziegler, 56 m And I, 78 d Chna, 79 spon
(Seckinger, An, Pal, 1747, d Mati, 69 m J P Mueller II, 77 m Joh
    Maurer)

Seckinger, An Bar, née Huber, 67 m Joh Geo
Seckinger, An Cath, née Gunter, Pal, t12, 41 m Mati, 58 s Jon, 60 d
  Lucia
Seckinger, And I, 1722, Pal, t12, bro Mati, sv Boltzius, h Cath
  Mohr, 56 m wid Ag Ziegler, gr 52, 72, 79 spon
Seckinger, And II, t12, h Cath II
Seckinger, Cath I, née Gunter, 49 m Mati
Seckinger, Cath II, née Mohr, w And II, 78 d Christiana
Seckinger, Han Elis, dd 78
Seckinger, Joh Geo, 1744, s Mati, 67 m An Bar Huber
Seckinger, Jon, s Mati
Seckinger, Lucia I, 1727, Pal, t12, sis And I and Mati, sv Boltzius
Seckinger, Lucia II, 1760, d Mati
Seckinger, Mati, 1717, Pal, t12, bro And I, sv Boltzius, 49 m Cath
  Gunter, gr 59, dd 61
Siegfried, An Bar, gr 63 Ab
Siegfried, Geo, gr 55 Whitmarsh Island
Slesing, Joh, 52 pres
Soldner, An, Swab, t13, dd 51
Soldner, Bar, née Oechsele, Swab, t13, 50 m Mart
Soldner, Mart, Swab, t13, gr by 57 Beth, 50 m Bar Oechsele
Spielbiegler, Joh, Salz, t6, dep 40
Spielbiegler, Ros, 1685, Salz, t6, mo Joh, dep 40, dd 40
Stab, Joh, 55 CB Go, gr 59 Bear Creek, 66
Staeheli (Stehlen, Staley), (Ben) Fr, 1734, Pal, t11, s Joh, 54 conf,
  59 gr
Staeheli, Gotl, 1729, Pal, t11, s Joh, gr 52 Eb, 57 Go, 59 Bear
  Creek, 66
Staeheli, Jac Rudolf, Pal, 1746, Go, dd 69
Staeheli, Joh I, Swab fr Wuerttemberg, t11, 55 CB Go, gr 57 Go,
  59, 60
Staeheli, Joh II, s Joh I, Swab fr Wuerttemberg, t11, gr 57 Go
Staeheli, Mag, d Joh
Staeheli, Ph Jac, 1733, Pal, t11, s Joh
Staley. *See* Staeheli
(Staud, Mar Marg, 1718, Pal fr Saarbruecken, t7, 40 m Gab Bach)
Steinbacher, Bar, 1719, Salz fr Rastadt, t9
Steiner, An Marg, née Zimmerebner, w Dav, 64 d Mar Mag, 66 s
  Dav, 74 d Cath, 77 d Elis
Steiner, Chph, sur 67
Steiner, Chrn I, 1705, Salz fr Gastein, t2, dd 35

Steiner, Chrn II, 60 m Dor Farr, 56 CB Eb, gr Mil Dis, 57, 69, 76 3rd Lt

Steiner, Dav, s Chrn I, 41 pres, 63 m Marg Zimmerebner, 57 CB Eb, gr 60 Mil Dis, 65, 68, 74 pres, dd 80

Steiner, Dor, née Farr, 60 m Chrn II, 62 d Han, 64 d Mar, 79 s Sam

(Steiner, Gert, Salz, t2, née Schoppacher, wid Sim, w Pet Reiter)

Steiner, Joh, 61 CB Eb, 74 pres

(Steiner, Mag, wid Simon, 41 m Pet Reiter)

Steiner, Mar, née Winter, Salz, t2, 1st w Rup, 37 s, dd 49

Steiner, (An) Marg, née Zimmerebner, 63 m Dav, 64 d Mar Mag, 69 d Sylvia

Steiner, Rup, Salz fr Radstatt, 1707, t2, h Mar, 52 m Urs, dd 52

Steiner, Sara, d Sim, 41 pres

Steiner, Sim, Salz fr Werffen, 1691, t2, h Gert, m Mag, dd 40

Steiner, Urs, née Ecker, 52 m Rup

Stiedler, Dav, 1768, s Pet

Stiedler, Pet

Stiedler, ———, w Pet, 68 s Dav

Stierlin (Stierle), Gregorius, Swiss fr Birmensdorff by Zurich, 59 m Mar Ros Hammer

Stierlin, Mar Ros, née Hammer, 59 m Gregorius, 55 d An Mar

Stirk (Stuerck), Ben, gr 67 Ab, 71

Stirk, Han, gr 71

Stirk, Joh, gr 71 Briar Creek, magistrate for St Math

Stirk, Sam, 79 chosen delegate to Continental Congress, 83 attorney general

Stocher, ———, w Tho, 43 pres

Straube, Ad, 1701, Pal, t8, 48 ar at Eb fr Vern with six children, h Pieta, 55 CB Eb Mil Dis, dd 57

Straube, Pieta Clara, wid Haefner, w Ad, gr 49 pres, 57 Mil Dis, dd 62

Striegel, Geo, gr 67 St George, 68 Hali

Stroebel, Joh Chph, 79 spon

Strohacker, Elis, 70 spon

Strohacker, Rud, gr 68, 71; 68 CB St Math, gr 73

Strohbart, Ab, 1777, s Nik

Strohbart, An I, Swiss, w Joh, Pbg, 77 d An

Strohbart, An II, 1777, d Joh

Strohbart, Eva Mar, née Mengersdorff, 65 m Joh II

Strohbart, Geo, 71 sur, dd by 73

Strohbart, Jac, fr Pbg, h Mar Cath, h Jud Jourdaine, 77 spon
Strohbart, Joh, h An I
Strohbart, Joh (Nik), fr Pbg, s Jac, h Mar An, 65 m Eva Mar
  Mengersdorff
Strohbart, Jud, née Jourdaine, w Jac, 77 spon
Strohbart, Mar An, w Nik
Strohbart, Mar Cath, w Jac, 65 d Marg
Strohbart, Sus, 69 m John Jones

Taescher. *See* Dasher
Tanner, Jac, gr 42
Tanner, Joh, s Lud, gr 68 Hali, 72, 74
Tanner, Lud, gr 72, 74
Theiss (Dice), Jac, 1709, Pal, t7, sv Trustees' mill, h Mar Marg, gr
  52
Theiss, Mar Marg, 1711, Pal, t7, w Jac, sv Trustees' mill
Thilo, (Chrn) Ernst, t6, gr 60 Eb, 39 m Fried Helfenstein, dd 65
Thilo, Fried, née Helfenstein, 39 m Ernst, dd 57
(Thilo, Han Elis, d Ernst, 73 m J J Heinle)
Torth, Isaac
Torth, ———, w Isaac, 73 s Isaac & d Mar
Tretler, Dan, 76 3rd Lt
Treutlen, (Joh) Ad, 1733, Pal, t11, fr Vern, 47 conf, m Marg Du-
  puis, 78 m wid An Unselt, 55 CB Eb, gr 60, 64, 67 Beth, 69, 70;
  77 elected governor, dd 81
Treutlen, An, wid Unselt, 78 m Ad
Treutlen, Elis, d Ad, 78 m Wm Kennedy
Treutlen, Fr, Pal, t11, bro Ad, h Marg, gr 57 Go, 58
Treutlen, Marg, née Dupuis, w Ad, 57 d Chna Elis, 58 s Jon, 60 d
  Elis, 62 d Dor, 64 d Mar, 66 d Han, 70 s Joh Ad, dd 77
Treutlen, Marg, w Fr, 58 d Elis
Treutlen, Rachel, d Ad, 74 pres
Triebner, Chrn Fr, 1740, fr Poesneck in Thuringia, ar 69; 69 m
  Fried Mar Gronau, 82 dep
Triebner, Fried Mar, née Gronau, d Is Chrn, 69 m Chrn Fr, 70 s
  Chph Aug Gotlob, 75 s Chph Is, 77 s Tim Traugott
Tussing (Dussign), Jac, gr 54 Eb, 55 CB Eb, 56 M wid Mar Kaem-
  mel, gr 60 Beth, 76 capt
Tussing, Mar, wid Kaemmel, 56 m Jac, 57 s Joh Jac, 59 d An Marg,
  61 s Joh Paul, 63 s Jo

Uhland, Elis Bar, d Geo, granddaughter Joh Ring, 54 lot in Sav
Uhland, Geo, tailor in Sav, gr 43, 54; 54 lot in Sav
Ulich, Joh Casp I, 1711, t8a, 39 m Marg Egger, dd 39
Ulich, Joh Casp II, s Joh Casp I
Ulich, Marg, née Egger, t8a, w Joh Casp
Ulmann, Con Ph, 1738, Pal, t11, apprentice to Brachfeld
(Unselt, An, Pal fr Pbg, wid Dav II, 78 m Ad Treutlen)
(Unselt, An Justina, Pal fr Pbg, 38 m Frantz Herrnberger)
(Unselt, Bar, Pal fr Pbg, 54 m Joh Rentz)
Unselt, Dav I, fr Bernstadt by Ulm, 1692, Swab, t14, gr 53 Beth, dd
    62
Unselt, Dav II, s Dav I, Swab fr Bernstat by Ulm, h An, gr 65, 68,
    dd 71
(Unselt, Eva Reg, Pal fr Pbg, 35 m Geo Schweiger)
(Unselt, [Sib] Fried, m Henry Bishop)
Unselt, Geo, 78 spon
Unselt, Han, gr 61
Unsolt (Unselt?), Urs, fr Giegen by Ulm, 54 conf

(Valentin, Cath, Salz, 36 m Step Riedelsperger, dep 38)
Vigera, Joh, 1701, t9
Volmar, Mich, Pal, t6, fled to Charleston

Waldpurger, Jac, gr 52
(Walliser, Elis, wid Mich, 58 m Jac Maurer)
Walliser, Mich, Swab, t14, gr 54, dd 57
Walthaur, Ag, w Joh Casp, 64 s Geo, 66 spon, 69 s Wm Ewen
Walthaur, Agn, née Ziegler, 58 m Jac Casp II, 59 d Marg, 60 d
    Lydia, 67 d Han, 74 spon
Walthaur, (Marg) Bar, Pal, t11, 41 pres
Walthaur, Bar, 1724, Pal, t8
Walthaur, (An) Cath, née Stuermer, wid Graniwetter, 49 m Joh
    Casp I
Walthaur, Chph Con, Pal, t11, gr 57
Walthaur, Han, 1767, d Casp
Walthaur, (Geo) Jac, Pal, t11, gr 57 Go, 70, 74 pres
Walthaur, Joh Casp I, 1694, Pal, t11, 49 m Cath, wid Graniwetter,
    gr 51; 55 CB Go, dd 66
Walthaur, Joh Casp II, 1731, Pal, t11, s Joh Casp I, 55 CB Ab, 58
    m Agn Ziegler, gr, 76 magistrate St Math
Walthaur, (Geo) Mich, 1732, Pal, t11, s Joh Casp I

(Wassermann, Elis, Salz, t8a, 39 m Pletter)
(Wassermann, Urs, Salz, t2, 38 m Veit Landfelder)
Weber, (Mar) Mag, née Greiner, 54 m Mich, 58 d Mar Mag & d
    Chna Elis, 61 Mag Dor, 65 d Slm, 72 m Mich Gnann)
Weber, (Geo) Mich, Pal, t12, sv Joh Flerl, 54 m Mag Greiner, gr 57,
    59, dd 67
Weber, (Joh) Mich, gr 57 Ab, 59
(Weber, Slm, 1765, d Geo Mich, m Sal Gnann)
(Weidmann, An Eva, w Lud, 57 s Tobias, 58 d Carolina Cath, 63 s
    Mat, 65 s Jededjah, 67 s Sal, 71 m J M Haberer)
Weidmann, Dan, 74 pres, 77 m Slm
Weidmann, (Joh) Lud, 1726, h An Eva, gr 57 Beth, 59, 68, dd 69
Weidmann, Slm, 77 m Dan, 78 d Jha Slm
Weinkauf, An Ros, née Kussmaul, 70 m Mat, 81 s Mat
Weinkauf, Chna, née Mack, 1744, 68 m Mat, 69 d Marg, dd 69
(Weinkauf, Mar, 65 m Tho Mack)
Weinkauf, Mat, 68 m Chna Mack, 70 m An Ros Kussmaul
Weinkauf, Mich, Swab, t14, gr 54 Eb, 59 Beth, 61, 62, 65
Weinkauf, ———, w Mich, 52 pres
Wertsch (Han) Elis, née Gronau, 1738, 58 m Joh Casp, 59 s Chrn
    Is, 61 s Benaja, 63 d Cath, dd 69
Wertsch, Elis, née Kogler, 69 m Joh Casp
Wertsch, Joh Casp, Pal, t12, sv Carl Flerl, 58 m Elis Gronau, 69 m
    Elis Kogler, gr 56, 59 Beth, 60, 64, 65, 71, 73; 65 CB Eb, dd 79
West. See Wuest
Wiesenbacher (Wyssenbakher), Chph, t11, 60 sur Go, 47 drowns
Wiesenbacher, Jac, Pal, t11, h Marg
Wiesenbacher, Marg, Pal, t11, w Jac
Winckler, An Bar, w Nik, 65 d Marg
Winckler, An Mar, w Lud, 66 d An Marg
Winckler, Elis, fr Pbg, 77 m Joh Vernieur
Winckler (Hans) Geo, Swab fr Niederstotzingen by Ulm, t14, gr 54
    Go, 59 Ab, 71; 77 m wid Mar Rieser
Winckler, Lud, 1724, fr Pbg, h An Mar
Winckler, Mar, wid Rieser, 77 m Geo
Winckler, Nik, 1716, fr Pbg, h An Bar
(Winnagler, An, Mar, fr SC, 56 m Jac Fr Rieser)
Wuest, An Dor, 1738, Pal, t11, d Mati
Wuest, Cath, Pal, t11, mo of Mati
Wuest, Mag, née Ratz, t11, w Mati, 59 d Chna, 83 pres
Wuest, Mati, Pal, t11, h Mag, 55 CB Go, gr 57 Go, dd by 83

Yakely. *See* Jaeckli

Zant, Bart, Swiss, t2, h Sib, dd 45
Zant, Dor, née Rieser, 75 m Sal
Zant, Elis, 1747, née Kieffer, 67 m Sal, 69 s Benaja, 72 s Jsa, dd 73
(Zant, Mar Mag, d Bart, 67 m J Maurer)
Zant, Sal, s Bart, gr 56 Eb, 67; 67 m Elis Kieffer, 75 m Dor Rieser, dd by 78
Zant, Sib, née Bacher, wid Piltz, w Bart, 49 pres, 50 m Geo Glaner
Zant, Slm, 1746, w Sal
Zettler, Dan, s Mati, h Han, gr 70
Zettler, Elis Cath, née Kieffer, 1723, 40 m Mati, 59 d Esther, 61 s Nath, 63 d Ros, dd 68
Zettler, Elis Cath, 65 m L Leen
Zettler, Han, w Dan, 72 s Chrn
Zettler, Mati, Salz, t2, 40 m Elis Cath Kieffer, gr 50, 51, 55 CB Eb, dd 69
Zettler, Nath, s Mati, gr 70
(Zettler, Slm, 65 m Luc Ziegler)
(Ziegler, Ag, 56 m And Seckinger)
(Ziegler, Agn, née Hermann, Swab fr Giegen, wid by 54, 3 children, 58 m Joh Casp Walthaur)
Ziegler, (An) Cath, née Rau, 56 m Geo, 57 d Han Elis, 60 d Han Elis, 62 s Immanuel, 63 d Mar, 67 d Cath, 69 s Dav, 79 d Lydia
Ziegler (Joh) Geo, Pal, t12, sv Gschwandl, 56 m An Cath Rau, gr 58 Beth, 60, 67, 74 pres, 83 pres
Ziegler, Jac, gr 52
Ziegler (Siegler), Luc, gr 65, 72; 65 m Slm Zettler, 83 pres
Ziegler, Lucia, gr 52
Ziegler, (Joh) Mich, Swab fr Giengen an der Fils by Ulm, t14, gr 52, 60
Ziegler, Slm, née Zettler, 65 m Luc, 66 d Lydia, 68 d Agn,
Zimmerebner, August
(Zimmerebner, [An] Marg, d Rup, 63 m Dav Steiner)
Zimmerebner, Marg, née Berenberger, Salz, t8a, 40 m Rup
Zimmerebner, Rup, Salz, t2, 40 m Marg Berenberger, 55 CB Eb, gr 56 Mil Dis
Zipperer, An Mar, w Chrn, 57 s Chrn Jon, 59 s Jon
Zipperer, Chrn (Jon), fr Bernstadt, gr 59 Eb, 70; h An Mar, 68 CB St Math, 78 m Gratiosa Zittrauer, dd 81

Zipperer, Elis, née Kuebler, w Joh, 80 spon
Zipperer, Gratiosa, née Zittrauer, 1757, 78 m Chrn, 79 s Joh Chrn
Zipperer, Joh, h Elis, 80 spon
Zipperer, Pet, Swab, fr Bernstadt, s Chrn, t14, gr 61 Go, 68 CB St
    Math
Zischler, Bar, née Haeussler, wid Lackner, 58 m Joh Mich, 61 s
    Sam
Zischler, Joh Mich, 58 m wid Bar Lackner, née Haeussler
Zittrauer, An, née Leihoffer, 36 m Ruprecht, 41 s, 47 in SC
Zittrauer, An Mag, née Heinrich, m Paulus, 49 s Ernst Chrn
Zittrauer, Apol, née Kieffer, w Paul, 57 d Gratiosa
Zittrauer, Cath, née Brandwein, 61 m Geo, 62 s Tim, 66 s Joh Gotl,
    68 d Mar Marg, 74 d Mar Marg
Zittrauer, (Ernst) Chrn, 1749, s Paulus, 70 m Han Reiter
Zittrauer, (Joh) Geo, gr 59, 61 m Cath Brandwein, 74 pres
(Zittrauer, Gratiosa, 1757, d Paulus, 78 m Chrn Zipperer)
Zittrauer, Gratiosa, 1778, d Ernst
Zittrauer, Han, née Reiter, 70 m Chrn Ernst
Zittrauer, Jac, 41 pres
Zittrauer, Joh, 41 pres
Zittrauer, (An) Marg, née Heinrich, 39 m Paulus, 41 child, 49 s
    Ernst Chrn, 57 d Gratiosa, 61 m Geo Schweiger
Zittrauer, Paulus, 1714, Salz, t2, 39 m (An) Marg Heinrich, 55 CB
    Eb, gr 56 Mil Dis, dd 58
Zittrauer, Rup I, Salz, t2, 36 m An Leihoffer, 47 in SC, 74 pres, dd
    48 in Charleston
Zittrauer, Rup II, 74 pres
Zoller, (Joh) Balt, Pal, t12, h Ros, sv at mill, ran away to Congarees
Zoller, Mati, 55 CB Eb
Zoller, Ros, Pal, t12, w Joh Balt
(Zorn [Zoning], Bar, Pal, d Marg, t11, 50 m Lud Meyer)
Zorn, Marg, Pal, t11, sv Gronau, dd by 48
Zuebli, Ambrosius, Swiss, bro Jac, 37 ar fr Pbg
Zuebli, Christiana, née Haeussler, m either Ambrosius or Jac
Zuebli, (Joh) Jac, bro Ambrosius, 37 ar fr Pbg
(Zuericher, An Mar, 58 m Nik Schubdrein)
Zwiffler, (Joh) And, t1, dep 37, dd 49
Zwiffler, An Reg, 1692, w And, ar 35, dd 36

❧ Bibliography ❧

Primary Manuscript Sources

1. British Public Record Office, Colonial Office Papers, Class 5, vols. 636–712. See no. 5 below.

2. Franckesche Stiftungen—Missionsarchiv Abtheilung 5A, Universitäts- und Landesbibliothek Sachsen-Anhalt, Halle, DDR.

3. Phillips Collection, Egmont Papers, University of Georgia Libraries. Most valuable is *A List of Persons Who Went from Europe to Georgia on Their Own Account, or at the Trustees' Charge, or Who Joyned the Colony or Were Born in It, Distinguishing Such as Had Grants There or Were Only Inmates* (serial no. 14220). See nos. 33 and 34 below.

4. Records of the Register of Records and Secretary: Marks and Brands, 1755–1778, 1785–93, Department of Archives and History, Atlanta.

Primary Published Sources

5. *The Colonial Records of the State of Georgia,* ed. Allen D. Chandler, vols. 1–19, 21–26, Atlanta, 1904–13. Vols. 20, 27–39 in typescript at Georgia Department of Archives are now being published by Kenneth Coleman et al., Athens, Ga. The following have appeared; vol. 20 (1982); vol. 27 (1978); vol. 28, pt. 1 (1975); vol. 28, pt. 2 (1979).

6. *The Revolutionary Records of the State of Georgia,* ed. Allen D. Candler, 3 vols., Atlanta, 1908.

7. *Ausführliche Nachrichten von den Saltzburgischen Emigranten, die sich in America Niedergelassen haben. . . ,*ed. Samuel Urlsperger, Halle, 1735ff. See nos. 9, 21–31 below.

8. *Americanisches Ackerwerck Gottes,* ed. Samuel Urlsperger and later J. A. Urlsperger, Halle, 1754ff. Continuation of no. 7 above.

9. *Detailed Reports on the Salzburger Emigrants Who Settled in America,* trans. and ed. George F. Jones et al., 7 vols., Athens, Ga., 1968ff. Translation of no. 7 above.

10. *Henry Newman's Salzburger Letterbooks,* ed. George F. Jones, Athens, Ga., 1966.

11. *Entry Claims for Georgia Landholders, 1733–1755,* ed. Pat Bryant, Atlanta, 1975.

12. *English Crown Grants in St. Matthews Parish in Georgia, 1733–1775,* ed. Pat Bryant, Atlanta, 1974.

13. *Abstracts of Colonial Wills of the State of Georgia, 1733–1777,* ed. Mary Givens Bryan, Atlanta, 1962.

14. *Abstracts of Georgia Colonial Conveyance Book C-1, 1750–1761,* comp. Frances Howell Beckemeyer, Atlanta, 1975.

15. *Abstract of Georgia Colonial Book J, 1755–1762,* comp. George Fuller Walker, Atlanta, 1978.

16. *The Journal of William Stephens, 1741–1745,* ed. E. Merton Coulter, Athens, Ga., vol. 1, 1958; vol. 2, 1959.

17. *The Journal of the Earl of Egmont, 1732–1738,* ed. Robert G. McPherson, Athens, Ga., 1962.

18. Patrick Tailfer et al., *A True and Historical Narrative of the Colony of Georgia,* ed. Clarence L. Ver Steeg, Athens, Ga., 1960.

19. *The Journals of Henry Melchior Muhlenberg,* ed. Theodore G. Tappert and John W. Dobertson, Philadelphia, 1942–48. (First visit, vol. 1, 60–64.)

20. Ibid., vol. 2, 595–686.

21. "Henry Muhlenberg's Georgia Correspondence," ed. Andrew W. Lewis. *Georgia Historical Quarterly* 49 (1965): 424–54.

22. "Johann Martin Boltzius Answers a Questionnaire on Carolina and Georgia," ed. Klaus G. Loewald et al. *William and Mary Quarterly,* 3d ser., 14 (1957): 218–61.

23. "August, 1748, in Georgia, from the Diary of John Martin Boltzius," and "September, 1748, in Georgia, from the Diary of John Martin Boltzius," trans. and ed. Lothar L. Tresp. *Georgia Historical Quarterly* 47 (1963): 204–16, 320–32.

24. "Baron von Reck's Travel Journal 1734," trans. and ed. George F. Jones. *The Bulletin of the Society for the History of the Germans in Maryland* 33 (1963): 83–90.

25. "Commissary von Reck's Report on Georgia," trans. and ed. George F. Jones. *Georgia Historical Quarterly* 47 (1963): 94–110.

Bibliography

26. "John Martin Boltzius Reports on Georgia 1739," trans. and ed. George F. Jones. *Georgia Historical Quarterly* 47 (1963): 216–19.

27. "Von Reck's Second Report from Georgia," *William and Mary Quarterly*, 3d ser., 22 (1965): 319–33.

28. "Pastor Boltzius' Letter of June 1737 to a Friend in Berlin," trans. and ed. George F. Jones. *Georgia Review* 19 (1965): 457–61.

29. "Journal of a Trip from Georgia to South Carolina in 1734, by John Martin Boltzius," trans. and ed. George F. Jones. *Lutheran Quarterly* 19 (1967): 168–74.

30. "The Secret Diary of Pastor Johann Martin Boltzius," trans. and ed. George F. Jones. *Georgia Historical Quarterly* 53 (1969): 78–110.

31. "Two 'Salzburger' Letters from George Whitefield and Theobald Kieffer II," ed. George F. Jones. *Georgia Historical Quarterly* 62 (1978): 50–57.

32. *Von Reck's Voyage*, ed. Kristian Hvidt, Savannah, 1980. (Excellent drawings of flora, fauna, Indians, and settlement of the Salzburgers.)

33. "John Martin Boltzius' Trip to Charleston, October 1742," trans. and ed. George F. Jones. *South Carolina Historical Magazine* 82 (1981): 87–110.

34. "The Fourth Transport of Georgia Salzburgers," trans. and ed. George F. Jones and Don Savelle. *Concordia Historical Institute Quarterly* 56 (1983).

35. *Ebenezer Record Book*, trans. A. G. Voigt, ed. C. A. Linn, Savannah, GA., 1929.

Secondary Sources

36. *A List of the Early Settlers of Georgia*, ed. E. Merton Coulter and Albert B. Saye, Athens, Ga., 1949. (Alphabetized version of Egmont's list, no. 3 above.)

37. "German-speaking Settlers in Georgia, 1733–1741 (Based on the Earl of Egmont's list)," ed. George F. Jones. *The Report: A Journal of German-American History* 38 (1982): 35–51.

38. *Georgia Salzburger and Allied Families*, comp. Pearl Rahn Gnann, Savannah, 1956; revised by Mrs. Charles LeBey, Vidalia, Ga., 1970.

39. *A Compilation of the Original Lists of Protestant Immigrants to South Carolina, 1763–1773*, ed. Janie Revill, 1874. Reprint, Columbia, S.C., 1939.

Bibliography

40. *Die Salzburger Emigration in Bildern,* ed. Angelika Marsch, Weisshorn Bayern, 1979. (Contemporary illustrations of Salzburger expulsion.)

41. *The Clamorous Malcontents,* ed. Trevor R. Reese, Savannah, 1973. (Criticisms and defenses of the colony of Georgia.)

42. *The Most Delightful Country of the Universe,* ed. Trevor R. Reese, Savannah, 1972. (Promotional material about Georgia.)

43. *Lists of Swiss Emigrants to the American Colonies,* ed. Albert B. Faust and Gaius M. Brumbaugh, Baltimore, 1976.

Studies

44. Brantley, R. L. "The Salzburgers in Georgia." *Georgia Historical Quarterly* 14 (1930): 214–22.

45. Coleman, Kenneth. *Colonial Georgia; A History.* New York, 1976.

46. Crane, Verner W. "A Lost Utopia of the First American Frontier." *Sewanee Review* 27 (1919): 48–61.

47. De Vorsey, Louis, Jr., ed. *De Brahm's Report of the General Survey in the Southern District of North America.* Columbia, S.C., 1971.

48. Florey, Gerhard. *Bischöfe, Ketzer, Emigration.* Graz, 1967.

49. Fries, Adelaide. *The Moravians in Georgia, 1735–1740.* Winston-Salem, N.C., 1967.

50. Hacker, Werner. "Auswanderer aus dem Territorium der Reichstadt Ulm," *Ulm und Oberschwaben. Zeitschrift für Geschichte und Kunst* 42/43 (1978): 161–257.

51. Hofer, J. M. "The Georgia Salzburgers." *Georgia Historical Quarterly,* 18 (1934): 99–117. (Based on no. 5 above; best account up to its time.)

52. Jones, George F. "In Memoriam: John Martin Boltzius, 1703–1765, Patriarch of the Georgia Lutherans." *Lutheran Quarterly* 17 (1965): 151–66.

53. ———. "Georgia's Second Language." *The Georgia Review* 21 (1967): 87–100.

54. ———. "John Adam Treutlen." Forthcoming in *Forty Years of Diversity: Essays on Colonial Georgia.* Edited by Harvey H. Jackson and Phinizy Spalding. Athens, Ga., 1984.

55. ———. "Sergeant Johann Wilhelm Jasper." *Georgia Historical Quarterly* 65 (1981): 7–15.

56. Knox, Mellon, Jr. "Christian Priber's Cherokee 'Kingdom of Paradise.' " *Georgia Historical Quarterly* 57 (1973): 319–31.

Bibliography

57. Krön, Peter et al. *Reformation Emigration: Protestanten in Salzburg.* Salzburg, 1981.

58. Newton, Hester W. "The Industrial and Social Influence of the Salzburgers in Colonial Georgia." *Georgia Historical Quarterly* 18 (1934): 335–53. (Based mainly on no. 7 above but also on outdated secondary sources.)

59. Ortner, Franz. *Reformation, Katholische Reform und Gegenreformation in Salzburg.* Salzburg, 1981.

60. Pennington, Edgar Legare. "The Reverend Bartholomew Zouberbuhler." *Georgia Historical Quarterly* 18 (1934): 354–63.

61. Prinzinger, A. "Die Ansiedlung der Salzburger im Staate Georgia." *Mitteilungen der Gesellschaft für Salzburger Landeskunde* 22 (1882): 1–36.

62. Rubincam, Milton. "Historical Background of the Salzburger Emigration to Georgia." *Georgia Historical Quarterly* 35 (1951): 99–115.

63. Smith, John A. M. "Purrysburgh." *South Carolina Historical and Genealogical Magazine* 10 (1909): 189–219.

64. Spalding, Phinizy. *Oglethorpe in America.* Chicago, 1977.

65. Tresp, Lothar L. "Early Negro Baptisms in Colonial Georgia by the Salzburgers at Ebenezer." *America-Austriaca* 2 (1973): 159–70.

66. Tresp, Lothar L. "The Salzburger Orphanage at Ebenezer in Colonial Georgia." *America-Austriaca* 3 (1974): 190–234.

67. Winde, Hermann. *Die Frühgeschichte der Lutherischen Kirche in Georgia.* Unpublished dissertation. Martin-Luther-Universität, Halle-Wittenberg, 1960.

Index

Index

Index

Index

Index

Index

Index

Index

Index

Index

Index